D0712976

The Psychology of Risk

Mastering Market Uncertainty

ARI KIEV

John Wiley & Sons, Inc.

Published by John Wiley & Sons, Inc., New York.
Published simultaneously in Canada.

This publication is designed to provide accurate and authoritative information in regard to
the subject matter covered. It is sold with the understanding that the publisher is not
engaged in rendering professional services. If professional advice or other expert assistance
is required, the services of a competent professional person should be sought.

Library of Congress Cataloging-in-Publication Data:

Kiev, Ari.
    The psychology of risk : mastering market uncertainty / Ari Kiev.
      p. cm.
    ISBN 0-471-40387-3
  1. Investments—Psychological aspects.   2. Portfolio
management.   3. Risk management.   I. Title.
HG4529.5 .K54 2001
332.6'01'9—dc21   20001007197

Printed in the United States of America.

10 9 8 7 6 5 4 3 2 1

For Phyllis,
with all my love

PREFACE

Since 1990, I have been helping Wall Street traders master psychological obstacles to trading success and develop strategies for winning that would sustain them in the face of the uncertainty and unpredictability of the markets. My first book on this subject, *Trading to Win: The Psychology of Mastering the Markets* (Wiley, 1998), presented a step-by-step goal-oriented program for building the mental and emotional stamina not only to win but to win on an unprecedented level. A second book, *Trading in the Zone: Maximizing Performance with Focus and Discipline* (Wiley, 2001), examined specific techniques for achieving and sustaining peak performance levels by entering into the zone—a focused state of concentration and goal-directedness.

The present book provides further explorations into the psychology of trading to win, focusing in particular on the appetite for risk taking, on ways of modulating and managing risk, and dealing with some of the pathological patterns of risk taking that often incapacitate traders. What is it that allows some traders to assume risk with considerable impunity and translate their analyses into action, whereas others with equally good understanding of the companies they are analyzing and the stocks they are trading are inhibited from trading as effectively as they can?

A willingness to take risks, set goals, persevere, and not be influenced by the opinions of others is critical for success. What distinguishes the best traders is their willingness to acknowledge their feelings, to ask for help, and to keep monitoring and adjusting their performance in light of specific trading objectives. Traders who "trade not to lose" don't take enough risk or trade recklessly and emotionally when in drawdown and jeopardize their capital. Trading success requires you to manage your risk objectively to be able to cut losing trades and stay longer in winners. To do all of these things well requires an appetite for risk and risk management and the ability to handle such distinct tendencies as perfectionism, decision paralysis, hoarding, and impulsiveness.

I explore these and other psychological obstacles to trading success in this book. I also examine a variety of psychological techniques or principles that may help you to trade independently of your emotional responses to the stress of trading. To convey a sense of the kind of communication that transpires in my coaching sessions, I have included a few dialogues with traders. Traders who have reviewed them have found them useful in exploring some of their own trades. My hope is that the examples and recommended solutions I describe will give you a glimpse into the trading world from my perspective and enhance your ability to take risk and master market uncertainty.

You will notice that I have deliberately avoided naming specific companies traded because I have been more interested in illuminating useful trading strategies than in specifics about particular companies. Finally, as in my previous books, I have disguised the identities of traders because my purpose is more to draw out generic principles that might be applicable to other traders than to talk about their own unique personal experiences.

It is my hope that, as with my previous two books, you will profit from your reading and periodic perusal of the concepts in this book, and that it will provide you with a new and stimulating perspective that will enhance your trading success.

ARI KIEV

New York, New York
March 2002

ACKNOWLEDGMENTS

As with my previous books on trading, *Trading to Win* and *Trading in the Zone*, many people have helped me to develop the concepts explored in this book.

First and foremost, I want to thank the various firms with whom I have consulted over the past several years. They have provided me with the chance to help traders develop their potential and produce amazing results despite the difficult markets we have experienced during this time.

I am most grateful to the various traders who have shared their perspectives with me and taught me so much about risk taking in all its dimensions. I also want to thank the traders who read and commented on portions of the manuscript and helped me to clarify some of the concepts that I have explored in this book.

I especially want to thank Tricia Brown, who has helped me to organize thousands of pages of transcripts and notes into a workmanlike manuscript, integrating a mass of trading material with the psychological and philosophical premises that I believe undergird the task of taking risk. I also want to thank Grace Lichtenstein, who was so helpful in reviewing the book in its final stages.

In addition, I want to thank my editor Pamela van Giessen for being a committed listener who has helped keep me on track, especially during the final stages of preparation of this manuscript.

Last, but not least, I want to thank my wife, Phyllis, for her support and encouragement throughout all stages of this project, from inception to completion. Her practical coaching helped me to stay on task during the entire course of this project.   A.K.

CONTENTS

Contents

Contents

PART FOUR
THE PRACTICE OF RISK TAKING

INTRODUCTION

Psychologically, most of us prefer comfort and safety to risk taking. That might sound reasonable and even normal. But it can be detrimental, especially to traders. Conditioned from early childhood to survive, our lives are governed by various adaptive life principles that structure the world and make it predictable while they keep us locked into habitual routines, even at the cost of our creativity and vitality. These adaptive mental mechanisms structure the world for us but also explain why many of us are afraid to initiate the essential first steps needed to take creative risks related to a larger vision of our lives. In trading, this condition often shows up in a tendency for traders to rely on what the markets will give them and a reluctance to commit proactively to specific profit targets.

A variety of recent behavioral economic studies have shown that most people are willing to accept risks in order to avoid losses but have a built-in tendency to avoid risks when seeking gain. My own observations after 40 years of psychiatric practice is that it is hard for most people to summon the nerve to take risks and to live their lives in the creative realm of possibility where there are no guarantees or certainties and where you can become only what you are willing to commit yourself to becoming. Although the willingness to take risks and manage them is the quintessential activity of trading, traders often suffer the same lack of courage.

Most traders are willing to accept risk in order to avoid a loss (e.g., holding on to losing positions) and are more cautious when dealing with potential gains (e.g., reluctant to add to winning positions). In other words, a trader would be more willing to take a greater risk in an effort not to lose $500 than he would to gain $500.

Given this propensity, you might understand why a trader would stay in a losing position in hopes that the tide will turn. Known as Weber's Law, this and many other principles of human behavior highlight the importance of understanding the psychological underpinnings of risk taking.

Put another way, many people prefer to make decisions related to a certain gain (as in holding on to losing positions) over decisions that might lead to something better but have the element of a gamble (as in getting bigger or adding to winning positions). Whereas most of us tend to avoid the adrenaline-producing rush of risk taking, as a trader you cannot avoid it. The very essence of trading involves risk taking, and how you manage your risk is what defines the line between success and failure.

In an effort to contain our fears, we establish certain perspectives early in life that stabilize the world for us but that eventually constrain us and distort our view of reality. As a result, most of us don't create our lives independently of the life principles developed in the past. As shown throughout this book, the same holds for traders—many of whom must learn to function independently of their own constraining influences in order to survive and to succeed in the face of the unpredictable and random swings of the marketplace.

Taking risks, from my point of view, means being willing to create a vision from which to trade to increase your capacity to interact with reality without being limited by your fears or your past perspectives. This means looking at reality without the constraints of prior rationalizations or self-justifications. When you view reality this way, you begin to tap the hidden potential that enables you to become more fully engaged in your life.

In the trading arena, being fully engaged means making realistic assessments of the market and being willing to face the truth about your positions (your gains as well as your losses) without being caught in the throes of rationalization and denial that are so readily triggered by events.

Introduction

By giving up beliefs and defenses from the past and being in the world in a more open and vulnerable way, you can expand your appreciation of reality and discover a dimension of the world heretofore unknown to you—largely because most of the time you have been operating out of limited notions about the way you are, as if that were a permanently fixed way of being in the world. These kinds of notions are expressed by various traders throughout the chapters in this book.

Risk taking means the willingness to act outside the vicious circle of concept-dominated experiences without a guarantee of success or approval. It means being willing to live life as the risk it is and not in terms of the limiting notions of your own self doubts.

To live at risk is to engage in activity spontaneously and naturally. The psychology of risk taking means being willing to commit yourself to living from a future vision without any certainty. It is a willingness to commit to your vision and create goals related to the vision, irrespective of the frightening inner voices that predict failure or ridicule. In the trading arena, it involves a willingness to commit to a specific financial objective, to work backward to develop a strategy consistent with that objective, and to focus in the present moment on the implementation of this strategy without obsessive concern with reaching the goal.

Risk taking does not mean exposing yourself to danger. It does mean acting beyond the vicious circle of what you already know—where past concepts color your perspective and experience. It does mean making decisions with incomplete information and before you have checked everything out with the experts. Risk taking means letting go of past habits and values that lock you into fixed ways of relating to the world so as to trade with a new concept of what is possible.

Nowhere do these principles of pushing the envelope and stepping out of the box apply more than in the field of trading, where the trader must consciously seek to develop ways for mastering the natural inclination to avoid risk. The risk taking aspect of trading is about taking deliberate action in the face of the uncertainty, unpredictability, and undetermined odds of the market. It requires that you stay with your hypotheses and discipline in a way that produces consistent results. It means trading on the basis of an accurate assessment of such catalysts as earnings, analyst upgrades, and company announcements, getting more aggressive with your winners, and getting out of high-risk ideas when you lack an analytical edge.

You can control your risk by understanding patterns in the markets, the sector, and the companies you are trading, your past experience, your own habitual distortions of perspective based on the nature of the market, and your characteristic ways of handling stress. Reviewing your past performance is the first step for defining recurring, underlying patterns of behavior that may be contributing to trading success or failure and that you may want to consciously continue, modify, or eliminate.

Statistical studies of risk management have consistently demonstrated that most trading profits come from a small percentage of trades, approximately 3–10 percent, irrespective of the instrument being traded. These statistics point to the importance of maximizing profitability when the opportunity presents itself, which in itself is contrary to the natural impulse to hold on to losers and get out of winners. Furthermore, the most successful traders make more in their winning positions than they lose in their losing positions, thus enabling some to be right in their stock selection as little as 40 percent of the time and still be profitable. This fact also points to the importance of being able, counterintuitively, to cut losses and maximize winning positions by getting bigger or holding longer.

The best traders recognize that small changes make all the difference and that the critical steps to success often occur in the last percentage of time, the last minutes of the game, or near the goal. The best traders are able to hang in there to the end and wait for the miracles to happen in the *final* moments of events. The best traders see marginal opportunities and are a little bit more efficient on the best trades than the ordinary trader and less sloppy on most trades. They have learned that a small percent makes the biggest difference, which is why they can have a 40–50 percent stock selection success and yet do wondrous things in managing their risk once the opportunities for maximizing performance begin to appear.

What differentiates the winners from the losers is invariably their capacity to stay on target and maintain an appropriate level of risk in the face of the stress responses and emotional reactivity triggered by the uncertainty of trading. Successful risk taking requires a willingness to commit to a specific result (as opposed to trading in terms of what the market will give you). Then it requires that you do what it takes in terms of sizing the position, measuring the probabilities of the upside reward against the downside risk, as well as getting out when things go against you and adding when they are going in your favor. Establishing a target empowers the best traders to keep asking powerful questions about what more they need to do to produce the results or what may have dropped out of their trading approach when their results decline.

The master trader is focused on being profitable. He is always challenging himself with questions such as:

- What more do I need to know?
- What additional work can I do?
- What can I learn from my own emotional reactivity to the markets?
- How long should I hold a position?
- How fast should I get out?
- What kind of loss limit is tolerable?

The master trader invariably gets out of a losing position unless he is absolutely certain from his fundamental analysis that the rumors that are forcing the price down are unfounded, which gives him the confidence to hold despite negative price action. *Hope* (that a stock will turn around) does not play a part in his calculation. Rather he prefers to take his loss and buy the stock back when it returns and starts moving in a more positive direction.

Traders who are less successful may be inclined to take on too much risk by swinging for the fences or take on too little risk by using insufficient capital to produce specific results. They also are more likely to be distracted by their own self-doubts and inhibitions that invariably appear when they have begun to move toward their objectives. Less successful traders are also reluctant to commit to a specific result for fear that they will be disappointed or humiliated if they don't produce the result. The fact is they are much less likely to achieve a specific result if they don't commit to it and use it as a blueprint for defining what they must do in the here and now to reach the result that they want.

For example, lack of a specific target was a chronic problem for one trader I know who invariably made $20,000 at the start of the trading day but whose gambling impulse to triple his winnings usually led him to lose everything he had made in less well thought-out trades. This type of high-risk behavior—taking shots at hitting home runs—only left him flailing about with unsuccessful trades. Such behavior is particularly problematic in drawdown situations and often leads to even deeper drawdowns and eventual withdrawal from the markets when capital is depleted.

Another trader was so motivated by his fear of losing that he would get out of his positions when they went a half point against him. His losses were minimal, but he was equally reluctant to hold positions long enough when they were working. Therefore, he failed to benefit from the full range of the move. He was also reluctant to use all of his allocated capital and rarely, if ever, made significant amounts of profit.

Digging deeper into the motives behind such behaviors can be extremely interesting and may unearth attitudes learned early such as feelings of unworthiness or not deserving to succeed. Some child-hood experiences may have led to life principles of excessive self-criticism, which are manifested in feelings of guilt about achieving the outsized financial rewards often associated with trading success.

The psychology of successful risk taking means taking a proactive rather than passive approach to the market and continually examining what you are doing that may be interfering with the trading process, whether you are stubbornly holding on to losing positions because of ego or not wanting to admit you are wrong, or trading in a contrarian way because of some unconscious need to be creative and to go against the tide. It means being more conscious of your own responses to the market and how those responses influence your decision-making process.

Ultimately, this book is an effort to encourage you to develop a greater sense of responsibility for your results, to learn to function in the gap between where you are and where you are committed to being. This learning may mean redeploying assets in terms of your greatest strengths. It may mean learning how to handle yourself when you are choking or experiencing panic. Or it may mean learning how to ride out fear and anxiety by timing such experiences and keeping a log of emotional responses so that you build objectivity and some mastery over difficult feelings.

What gives you the conviction to put more at risk and how you delineate the premise of the trade are two critical components to successful trading. To succeed at trading, you must probe the reasoning behind why you are trading the size you are trading. In order to maximize your risk-taking ability you must be able to get bigger, and to do this you need to determine exactly what is getting in the way of your current risk taking.

There is something in a trader's basic makeup that leads each one to receive and translate fundamental data differently and then to implement trades differently as well. Each trader needs to consider:

- What can I do to change my self-limiting habits and attitudes that are leading to repeated failures or insufficient success?
- If a habit or attitude or life principle can't be changed, what new approaches to trading can I adopt that could transform my trading and empower me to realize my goals?
- What can I do to trade in a more risk-controlled way?

Failure in this business is behavioral and intellectual, and most traders need to keep learning more about the behavior of trading, the behavior of taking risk, the behavior necessary to be comfortable taking risk. When working with a trader, I always ask:

- What is the trader experiencing at the moment she is assessing the trade?
- What does she see?
- How does she see reality and take action in the face of uncertainty?

Less experienced traders often get out of winning trades too soon and then regret missing a trade. Other traders take on too much risk because they are action junkies. These are some of the kinds of patterns that I have sought to identify, explain, and help traders modify. Consider:

- How do you deal with ambivalence, uncertainty, and indecision?
- How do you avoid being trapped by overanalysis, regrets over previous losses, and other *things* that preoccupy you and keep you from trading in the present moment?
- What steps do you need to take to make sure you get past your inhibitions and your perfectionism and can take the trade based on the tradability of the idea?

This book has been written to explore these issues and many more. I seek to explain some of the most common behavioral components of trading from a psychological perspective. I do this by ex-

Introduction

amining certain principles of successful trading and the reasons why various traders have difficulty in applying these principles, and I outline solutions for individuals with these various behavioral problems.

Quite understandably, many traders are often reluctant to consider how they are creating problems in their trading and how much of their difficulty stems from the grip of their own past programming. They continue to act in a self-protective way, designed to preserve their image and to avoid certain kinds of frightening experiences. In acting this way, they fail to see how much they are managing their emotions because of a need to *appear* in control and how this behavior generates more stress and keeps them from actually trading successfully.

In reality, if you are not achieving your trading objectives, it is not due to circumstances or bad luck, but because you are creating the very reality that you consciously or subconsciously expect. You may even work harder and harder without producing a new result and be convinced that you are doing the right thing and that the lack of results is due to circumstances. If you explore these issues, you will soon discover that a commitment to a meaningful and concrete trading objective is missing. Learning to increase your risk, and therefore your profit potential, is a matter of consciously deciding what must be done. To achieve different, higher objectives, you have to shift the focus of your thoughts and begin to commit to new and more specific objectives.

Expect reluctance. It is inherent in the process of commitment and is the source of the creative tension between where you are and where you can be. Expect reluctance. You may be reluctant to read this book. You may be reluctant to take the recommended actions. You may be reluctant to accept responsibility for your trading career.

But you can awaken the sleeping giant within you and unleash your hidden potential. You can radically alter your trading experiences and learn to take risk in a better and more successful way. Take the first step. Turn this page, and begin learning about the psychology of risk.

PART ONE

THE ESSENTIALS OF RISK TAKING

CHAPTER ONE

DEFINING RISK

There must be some benefit to risk. Otherwise, why would anyone ever take it? The answer, of course, is that handy saying: "No gain without pain." To put it another way, there is no reward without risk.

Conventional definitions of risk focus on "the possibility of loss or injury" or "a dangerous element or factor." They emphasize the fact that when we take risk, we "expose ourselves to hazard or danger." In this book, I prefer expanding the notion of risk and putting at its center the elements of uncertainty and unpredictability, since they are particularly applicable to trading.

Ron S. Dembo and Andrew Freeman proposed this kind of broader definition in their book *Seeing Tomorrow: Rewriting the Rules of Risk* (Wiley, 1998). Noting that risk results from the uncertainty we face in the future, they characterized risk as "a measure of the potential changes in value that will be experienced in a portfolio as a result of differences in the environment between now and some future point in time" (p. 35). When you calculate the risk of a trade, you are weighing its chances of going up so much versus its chances of going down so much in a particular market.

To my way of thinking, this designation is useful because it considers the amount of risk you are willing to assume against the potentiality of reward in the face of the uncertainty and volatility of the marketplace.

The willingness to take a chance with a certain amount of your capital to produce a certain result is the essential ingredient of trading. Moreover, how much uncertainty you can handle and how well you manage your risk ultimately determines how successful you are.

And one of the best ways of doing this well, in particular handling the uncertainty and randomness of the marketplace, is to commit to a future-oriented goal and then develop a strategy consistent with it. In addition, you need to do all that it takes to stay in line with your strategy and goal. When you follow this plan, you put yourself in a position to reduce the elements of uncertainty and to make the risk more manageable.

In order to profit, it is necessary to put something at risk. If you put nothing at risk, you cannot make any profit. If you put too much at risk in a thoughtless manner (without the necessary infrastructure, data flow, understanding of the fundamentals of the stocks you are buying, and the character of the market at a particular time), you put yourself in jeopardy.

Your objective: finding the right amount of risk to take to realize the specified goals you set for yourself. If you take too little risk, you may not reach your objectives; if you take too much risk, you may lose your capital and forfeit opportunities to trade in the future. To assume the right amount of risk requires:

- Considerable practice.
- Work at understanding the fundamentals of the companies you are trading.
- Having some awareness and control over your own psychological contribution to the process.

If a trader is too risk averse then she will not play big enough or hold long enough to realize the profits she needs to reach her target.

Defining Risk

If she is too risk prone, she may risk too much and be unable to cycle out of the psychologically and self-perpetuating vicious circle that often ends up in deep drawdown. Similarly, as a trader increases the size of his portfolio and raises his trading objectives, he needs to consider ways of increasing the amount of risk that he is willing to take or that he *must* take to reach new targets. Here too he will come face-to-face with the obstacles, inhibitions, and fears that keep him from expanding his own trading style.

With concentrated effort you can learn to tolerate the uncertainty and to ride out the discomfort of drawdowns so as to reach a greater level of success. Over time, you can learn to trade in what I call "the zone"—not some magical place of positive thinking but a mind-set of total action, focusing on the present moment, without concern for your emotions or past mistakes. Being in the zone allows you to take appropriate risk, to balance your risk, to size your risk, and to tolerate the uncertainty of the risk. Being in the zone means you can tolerate the pain better.

Risk taking means acting outside the vicious circle that fear creates. It means being willing to make your trades based on a goal that you have previously set and following an action plan that you have already outlined, irrespective of any limiting notions or subconscious self-doubts and life principles. Therefore, to manage your risk is to engage in your trading in a spontaneously and naturally open and honest way.

According to Andrew, a successful bond trader, "The psychology of risk is the psychology of confidence. Trader confidence means knowing what to do in all situations. Good markets make geniuses. Certain things are more clear-cut in the market, and the confidence that people have, the trader's edge, away from the distributions of return, is the confidence that they are going to do it so that they might as well do it bigger. That is the key. If you can get people to make money steadily, then you only have to turn up the gas a little bit and

15

play bigger. Step one is to develop a methodology that makes some money. Put on the trade that has the highest chance of making some money, and if you do that trade consistently, then you will have the most even distribution of returns. The smoother it is, because leverage isn't an issue, the greater the return."

Given the uncertainty and randomness in the market, the problem you as a trader must contend with is how to capitalize on your ability to control risk to maximize profitability. To do this, each trader assumes only a certain amount of risk in his portfolio, depending of course on his tolerance for risk and the quality of his techniques for managing volatility such as hedging, using options, and running longer- and shorter-term accounts. Problems occur when the propensity for risk is mismatched with the amount of risk that is taken.

As Anthony, a relatively new telecommunications trader noted: "Anything other than cash is risk. Risk is how much you are willing to lose on any single bet. This has to do with your tolerance—your tolerance for uncertainty. You don't want to make any one single bet so volatile that loss in the position could blow you out of the game. That is the reason to diversify and minimize the risk with any number of noncorrelated trades, to keep making money, and to stay in the game through difficult periods."

The question is how to get to the point where you can choose your risk, not out of fear, but by creating a powerful framework of opportunity and excitement in which to carry on your trading.

In effect, if you can get in touch with the core of your being, you may be able to shape your trading without any preconceptions whatsoever. That's really the key—how you can be in the market at this moment and from this moment on and in the next moment without any preconceptions, without any notions that you already know what's going to happen.

Considering a
New Approach

The traditional approach to managing risk has generally been a long-term valuation-based approach wherein an individual would buy stocks at a low price and hold them for an extended period of time, hoping to sell them at a higher price. Such a strategy meant that the stock would be held throughout the many fluctuations that occurred over the course of time in the hope of obtaining ideally a 40 or 50 percent return on the investment as the stock eventually increased in value. While this longer-term buy-and-hold value approach to investing has been coming back into vogue in the past year or two, my own experience over the past decade has been more involved with traders using a shorter-term trading approach to trading companies that were growing earnings and attracting the attention of momentum buyers who were helping to push stock prices higher.

The shorter-term trading approach is focused around understanding the impact and relevance of news events that could impact the price of a stock in the short term. This approach lends itself to the discipline of setting daily or weekly targets or run rates and trying to manage risk by reducing the amount of loss and increasing the amount of profits in trades. By focusing on short-term events and setting daily targets, traders can manage their risk by capturing the intraday volatility of securities and reducing the long-term risk of the portfolio.

In the short-term approach, the objective is to minimize risk and maximize profitability by taking profits during the high point of the intraday volatility over the period of one to three days. If this pattern is followed, whereby the stock is sold near the high point of the intraday volatility and then bought back on pullbacks at cheaper prices, it is possible for a given stock to produce earnings of as much as 200 percent over the course of a year—in contrast to the smaller percentage accrued if the stock were bought and held over time (in line with the traditional value-oriented fundamentalist approach to stock selection and management).

The traders with whom I have been working have often been very successful because of their willingness to take on big risk in a controlled manner. Year in and year out those traders have been able to maintain their high returns and not regress to the mean, as would be predicted by the efficient market hypothesis and which so often happens to traders who have had outsized performances.

According to Anthony: "You are trying to minimize the impact of the variables that contribute to the randomness. You are trying to reduce the randomness. You know the stock will move up and down. So, you set a target. You look for data points that will create some movement. That is different than being a long-term fundamental player where you assess the value of the company, or as the fundamentals change, you adjust your target. You understand the company and believe that the business model works, but you don't know where the stock will go."

The short-term strategy allows for greater profitability by reducing the trader's dependency on the uncertainties of the market. The trader makes decisions on the basis of fewer data points than the fundamental analyst might rely upon. She is also more interested in how other traders are likely to perceive the incremental analysis available than might be the case for the fundamental analyst who is only interested in the basic facts about a company, not as much in how a company might be trading in response to the perceptions of the marketplace. The investor is basing her decisions on the basic realities about a company. The trader wants to understand the reality, but she is also concerned with how the world is perceiving the stock and the company. By focusing on incremental data points and their impact on short-term movements of stocks, the trader is able to control her risk in a proactive way. She trades in and out of a stock in response to more short-term movements in the market and thereby increases the chance of achieving her goal.

A long-term investor is looking for a good company and wants the value to increase over time. He is willing to expose himself to risk over a longer time period to capture longer-term effects. The trader, by contrast, is more performance oriented and is looking for shorter-term results. He drives his capital in a different way whereby he is maximizing opportunities at all times and minimizing his risk.

The success of this short-term, catalyst-driven approach to trading equities (which puts value on understanding events that will influence the movement of stock prices over the short term) stands in stark contrast to the random walk theory of the market, which suggests that success in the market is related to random events. This randomness certainly doesn't explain repetitive outsized performance year in and year out. In fact, in a short-term, hedged trading account, it is possible to capture the intraday swings (volatility) of the market while keeping the swings in the daily P&L (profit and loss results) relatively low. By hedging the portfolio with long and short positions, the short-term trader is able to eliminate systemic market risk. He reduces company-specific risk by improving the quality of analysis on which he trades.

The power of this model for controlling risk and maximizing daily opportunities was brought home to me recently when I spoke to Jim, a value-oriented portfolio manager who was integrating the short-term, catalyst-driven, goal-oriented approach to trading with his longer-term buy-and-hold approach. Jim was particularly impressed with the concept of goal setting, which, to my way of thinking, provides the focal point and structure for taking appropriate risk while minimizing randomness.

"Find the ideas that are hot for the day," he said. "Drill down in terms of information and make a decision as to how you are going to trade them for the day or the next several days. Go for the goal—the actionable, event-driven story that we will pursue daily in order to obtain a daily profit. The goal is to find a good entry point, feel it out, play it out, not to chase the stock. Execute it well. What is new to me as a long-term, fundamentally driven, value-type portfolio manager, is to have this as an everyday requirement and to cut through the hyperbole to the essence of a story and to the essence of a short-term trade."

According to Jim, the daily, goal-oriented approach is to be differentiated from analytically oriented, longer-term trades. Most people don't think in short-term, goal-oriented terms. Fundamentalists are playing stories over an extended time line of three months to six months to a year. With that approach, according to Jim, "there is a lot of wasted time and less productivity than looking at the curve of volatility in stocks on a daily basis, which is actionable daily."

What is the metaconcept here?

"The productivity created by this strategy is greater than any other strategy," said Jim. "You are not wasting time, and you are focusing on inflection points in stocks that have news and events that make for great productivity and offset any deficiency in knowledge about the stocks that you may have. You are also trading when the volatility is the greatest and the opportunities for profit maximization are the greatest."

The strategy has extraordinary power in the hands of a master trader, but it also provides a greater capacity for handling risk in a manageable and rational way for ordinary traders. By focusing on what it will take to realize their targets, traders are forced to consider all the ways available for managing the risk of their trades. They set goals based on the probability of events and the profit opportunities that might derive from them, and they look for trades where risk is low and reward is high. If a catalyst (such as an earnings announcement, a brokerage house upgrade, a company conference, or road show) is immediate and clear, for example, a trader might take a good size position. If the catalyst is clear but doesn't have too much relevance to the stock, he will take a smaller size position. These catalysts are always weighed in the context of the value of a stock, anticipated earnings numbers, where it is trading relative to its recent range, and whether the near-term fundamentals in terms of earnings and profitability are clear. Also significant are such things as the state of the market, how other companies in the same sector are doing, whether a stock is lagging, and how the technicals appear.

Jim continued, "Everyday I am looking at a stock with volatility so that every day has the potential for productivity. The requirement to be productive on a daily basis forces me to look for these opportunities and increases the chances that positive results will be realized. People who use less information but in a focused way can be more productive than those with a lot of information whose emphasis is on knowledge and not on results. Ten percent of information and good intellect enables you to make subpar decisions but on productive days offsets being right more of the time on longer things with wasted days. Why don't most traders see this? Because it is counter to the fundamental discipline that everyone is accustomed to using. Setting goals efficiently forces you to capture the essence of the trading opportunities at a minimum of risk. The daily goal forces you to change your strategy. It encapsulates all that you need to maximize profitability."

Daily targets require you to manage your risk on a day-to-day basis. They force traders to take more responsibility for the way in which they are handling their trading, which in turn forces them to examine their own personal attitudes and habits that may be interfering with maximizing profit and minimizing risk. I discuss more about goal setting in Chapter Two.

This book examines factors that pertain to the trader's style of risk taking: the kinds of trades he is most attracted to, the type of data he is likely to gather to increase his confidence, and the kinds of attitudes and habits of mind likely to play a part in his assumption of risk. All of these factors become critical for understanding how a given trader approaches risk taking and how he can improve his ability to take on greater risk in a risk-controlled way.

To study risk, you need to consider the following:

- Your ability to set a target and then take on the appropriate amount of risk in a measured way to be able to reach the target.
- How you are trading and methods for expanding your performance.
- The kinds of chart patterns that attract you and what kind of analytical edge you are developing.
- Your confidence about producing results and your willingness to do the work.

I consider each of these in more detail throughout the book.

The key to risk taking that I want to hammer home in this book is having a vision of trading success and then trading in terms of specific, concrete goals related to the vision. To accomplish this you have to understand the trading implications and probabilities of events in the context of the fundamentals about a company, the market, and the macroeconomic trends. The master trader uses as much data and analysis as possible in making his assessments. Unlike a portfolio manager, he is taking concentrated risk because he is minimizing his time exposure in that stock. He is not buying a stock to hold for a year. He is buying one stock to hold for a day or several days. Moreover because of his focus on shorter time periods he is able to focus on situations that have a high probability of working and where the risk/reward is to his benefit, because with shorter holding periods he has less variability with which to contend. This is critical to the process of risk taking because it brings to the fore a variety of trading problems such as are seen in traders who are reluctant to use sufficient capital to reach their objective or those who are so driven to take risk that they do so in a foolhardy way or put themselves at greater peril by not managing their risk appropriately. While the risk manager is concerned with measuring performance in terms of degree of volatility, standard deviation, rate of return, and the like, my focus in this book is on the personality features and attitudes that are at the center of the efforts I have been making over the years to help traders enhance and maximize their performances.

Understanding the Psychology

One of the most useful insights into a trader's performance is to examine a trade that he defines as typical of his trading style and then to consider a number of critical questions about how he handled the trade. In this way he can see what psychological factors may have been influencing him.

I asked Anthony about his trading in several different ways:

- Do you think you trade a particular part of the swing in a stock?
- What part of the chart do you like?
- If one were to chart your trades, where in the cycle of the chart are you most likely to be buying it or selling it?
- Are there any regularities or patterns to your trade selections?

He answered as follows:

"I put the most wood to work when the stock is down and get out when it is higher. The problem is that those that I sell at the high point of the chart often go higher because they are in an uptrend. That is counter to the argument that you should buy more as stock prices rise. The general environment keeps changing, and you have to factor that into your trades. That is a typical value player thing to do. The lower they go, the more you buy, if the fundamentals are good. If you like them at 20, you like them at 15, and you like them at 10, as long as nothing has changed in the story.

"I try to go with the chart if it is going down. I am trying to short it or buy it very slowly, realizing that those trends last. Whatever big mutual fund is creating that trend by selling it, everyone will pile on it. It will go lower. You have to respect the trend.

The challenge for me is to do this with a bigger portfolio, hedged, with a lot of names and on a bigger scale. I don't play only one part of the curve. It depends on the market and on the stock. If I hate a stock, and it goes up, I will short more. If I love a stock and it is coming in, I'll buy more, again keeping up with the news flow. Some people always buy a chart regardless. I think you have to know what the stock is doing, although I must resist the temptation to be biased by focusing only on the positive information."

From Anthony's answers, I can glean many hints to his trading personality and help him tweak his strategy to take more effective risk. For example, Anthony needs to balance his long positions with some short positions so that he is hedged and therefore has protected his portfolio, especially if he is trading highly volatile stocks that respond dramatically to market movements and don't necessarily act in conformance with fundamental data.

When performing an exercise such as this, I ask traders to consider a specific trade and then to answer a number of questions about that trade, in particular how they were feeling as they entered the trade and how their feelings influenced their assessment of the risk factors associated with the trade. These questions are useful in illuminating their willingness to take on more risk in the face of increased analysis about a stock so as to increase the chance of profitability. They also suggest to me which traders won't take on risk and would rather cut and run, taking their profit as fast as they can rather than expanding the size of their positions or increasing the length of their holding period by way of increasing profitability. So after asking about how they were feeling as they entered a trade, I also ask them:

- Where in the stock's trajectory did you enter the trade and where did you exit the trade?

- How much were you influenced by emotional factors such as panic and fear of loss?
- Did you take a contrarian viewpoint and buy the stock in anticipation of an inflection point or did you buy it at the bottom of an extended base just as the stock was entering a breakout based on a good understanding of the fundamentals?
- Did you stay with the trade for an extended period of time, or did you get out quickly after making one or two points of profit (because of anxiety)?
- Did you add to your position and ride it up through an extended trend upward as is typical of the long-term, trend-following trader, or were you scared out by a fear of losing?
- If the stock dipped below your original purchase price, did you stick to your fundamental understanding of the company and buy more of the stock, or did you get out of your position to keep your losses down?
- If the price of a stock moved up, did you take a contrarian position and start to short the stock in anticipation of the stock hitting a top and turning downward?

As you can see, these kinds of questions are useful in opening up the dialogue about the emotional and psychological underpinnings of risk-taking decisions and help pave the way for greater understanding of a variety of attitudes that influence trading success. These questions are also useful in illuminating regularities in trading styles. When a trader can identify these patterns, she can begin to see the cutting edge—that boundary or limiting pattern in her approach that needs to be improved upon, expanded, or curtailed so that she can increase her ability to take on more risk and thereby further increase the chance for profitability. These questions also suggest a relationship between the feeling states of the traders and the ways in which they approach the movement of a stock.

Case Study on Various Ways of Increasing Risk

Each person needs to adjust his game so that he is more flexible, more adaptable to the markets, and better able to make profits. There is not one way to make profits. Each person needs to expand his game in terms of the way he is already playing. My kind of psychological input is designed to modify behavior and increase the individual's capacity to handle risk more soundly.

For some traders the issue is holding their positions for longer periods of time. For others, the issue is increasing the size of their positions. For others it is a question of expanding their knowledge base and getting help from analysts. And for still others it may be increasing the number of positions that they hold or trading more volatile stocks with a greater beta (volatility) weight to increase their risk and potential for profit.

It is not always necessary to increase the size of positions. The increased volatility of the marketplaces often increases the risk in a trader's portfolio and the possibility of making greater amounts of money. In volatile markets, traders need to be careful that they don't get too big too fast and increase the possibility of having big losses that may psychologically throw them off.

A beginner like Chris too easily gets scared that the price will go down and gets out of his trades too fast and makes too small a profit. He needs to be able to get bigger and hold longer. To do this he may first want to learn to take some profits and then when there is a dip in prices buy some more and hold the stock longer during an uptrend.

Robin, who had previously been a long-term value player, needs to learn to cut losses in his losing positions even when he believes in the stock, because his long-term orientation tends to interfere with his ability to keep his losses down. As he learns to cut his losses and get back in when things are working his way, he can begin to devote more energy to finding opportunities, not putting out fires.

I asked another trader, Reggie, how he thought he could expand his trading. He answered: "I evaluate my trades every night. I focus on what happened, where we lost money, where I could have made more money, and what I need to do to improve. I always ask myself what opportunities did I miss, but most importantly I always keep doing what is working. Don't mess with what is working."

Reggie is aware of the importance of a thought process behind his trades, to be as clear as possible why he is getting into a position. If you are not clear about the reasons to enter a position, you are going to redefine yourself while you are in the trade, and this can lead to confusion and getting off the target. Obviously, preparation is critical. The trader sets a goal, commits to the result, and decides on how many trades he needs to do to produce the result. He measures the risk of each trade and determines the appropriate size of positions to take. He decides the most beneficial risk/reward entry and exit points—all within the context of a specified goal that motivates the process and its management. The goal and the preparation also give him a template for adjusting to each day's events as they unfold so that he can maximize his flexibility and not simply react willy-nilly to the screen.

These are just a few examples of how I work with traders to learn more about their own trading styles. By answering questions and exploring specific trades, they delve into their own thought processes and reveal the hidden kinks that are holding them back.

Identifying the Problems

Taking risk and mastering market uncertainty requires a willingness to go to the cutting edge, learn new skills, and follow your discipline in the face of difficulties. It requires a willingness to be coached, to accept support from others, to ask questions, to get beyond the need to appear to be in control. The best traders are humble, open, resilient, and willing to keep working on themselves so that they can remain objective in their trading and keep learning additional skills for handling risk.

In addition, taking risk and mastering market uncertainty requires that a trader not be too distractible, argumentative, or opinionated. A trader must be willing to measure risk by assessing the upside and downside of a trade and to step out of the comfort zone of familiar trading size and take on new behavior patterns, ride them out, and master the anxiety associated with developing them. He must develop the ability to get smaller in the face of drawdowns while following the same discipline. He must learn not to become so ego-involved in holding on to a failing trade that he risks greater disaster, and he must have the ability to add resources to his approach so as to increase his knowledge, skill, and capacity to execute.

I asked Gil how these criteria related to his own risk management approach. His answer: "I am trading a $10 million pad versus a $50 million pad. If I can grow, I believe I can do 5 times as much with $50 million as with $10 million. Some traders conversely may think of how much they can lose with the larger amount of money. That is why they are not using all of their capital when they are trading because they are dominated by a need not to lose."

The critical question (addressed throughout this book) is how can a trader expand his risk tolerance, for example, by going from taking 10,000 shares to buying 30,000 shares. The trader does this by recognizing the need to maintain or improve his rate of return and by increasing his overall profitability. This is easier said than done and must be approached in terms of each person's resistance and habitual patterns. If, for example, a trader likes to buy the stock when it is low and take his profit as it moves up a few points on the curve, he may need to learn to hold the positions longer to maximize the amount of profit he can take from a trade. Or he may need to learn to trade in terms of his daily goals and be willing to get out of part or all of his positions to realize his target for the day. Or he may need to change his view about the virtues of being a contrarian and his inclination to short a stock as it rises, expecting that eventually it will reach an inflection point and reverse and give him an opportunity to cover his position (buy back the stock at a lower price than the top).

In the coming chapters, I help you to identify problems that might be increasing your risk profile—whether it is losing too much, not being balanced enough, not being big enough, not using enough capital, or not having enough volatility in your portfolio. I then explore underlying issues that might be generating these problems in your trading—restraints such as particular personality types, debilitating life principles (such as impulsiveness, perfectionism, etc.) and other stopping points. And finally, I consider various steps that you can take to overcome the inner obstacles that are holding you back.

Case Study on Overcoming Constraining Influences

Following is a discussion I had with Martin, to help him gain control over his impulse to pick tops and bottoms—a high-risk trading style with a lot of losses that erode his profitability. This dialogue gets at the essence of this book because we are digging deeply into the constraining influences that must be modified so that the trader becomes nimble and better able to handle risk.

Martin: My goal in 2000 has been to get bigger and smarter, learn more about the companies, and be in front of everyone else. We have the data. We speak to companies and analysts. This part is working well. I am getting into trouble with my market calls. I am too rigid about my opinion on the market. I stay with my bullish view on something even though it is going down. I'll have a market view that we should see capitulation here because there is tax loss selling in the United Kingdom in April, stuff I have no control over. I lost a lot of money making a market call.

Kiev: Is there a pattern to your market call? Do you typically get long when you see the market going down and do you get short when the market is going up?

M: We were long for the turn in cyclicals when they were coming in (going down) and analysts were cutting earnings forecasts and everyone hated them. If you did that in tech, you would go out of business. And now you can't do it in cyclicals either. If the market is going up, just go with it. That's not what we are doing.

K: Is it costing you a lot of money to trade against the trend?

M: Trading the market has lost us a lot of money. If we took out all of our market call bets this year (2000), we would be having an awesome year. We should listen to companies. It is easier to trade these microideas rather than guess market direction.

K: Any idea why you are such a contrarian?

M: I find contrarian trading to have more beta in it, to be sexier, and a lot more stimulating.

K: Is it hard to resist making these trades? Do you feel like you are missing something?

M: I think so. I don't like paying up for something or shorting something way down. I like to get in early to avoid paying up. I like to get stocks at cheap prices.

K: Are you drawn to a particular place in the charts of stocks?

M: Picking tops and bottoms. We always anticipate the inflection point. DRAM prices are going down like tumbleweed:* The costs are going down. They can't afford to make their interest payments. The Korean companies are selling lower and lower. When this is happening, we are buying some of these companies figuring that the lower they go, the cheaper they are priced. When the price gets to a certain level, fewer people will make these

---

*DRAM is an acronym for dynamic RAM (random access memory) or semiconductor memory chips. Every time you start your computer's operating system, launch a program, or open a file, the relevant program code or data is loaded into RAM. Therefore, DRAM pricing is one indicator of end-user demand for computers (spot prices can be tracked easily so one can assess strength or weakness of demand).

chips and fewer people will buy them. Eventually you get to this huge in-flection point or bottom because of supply. Then you need the demand. We will look for the capitulation down there and hope for the huge turn. We buy more and more of it all the way down and then get out as soon as it turns.

K: What compels you to get in so early, before the turn?

M: Probably the satisfaction of being the first one into the trade. I want to be the hero. I picked it up from trading cyclicals—papers, chemicals. Yes-terday on this DRAM call, I was buying a Korean electronic company, scal-ing all the way down. All I had to do was wait for a couple of data points like that and then load up on two or three stocks in the sector. I would have missed the first 10 percent, but then I could have jumped in. Trying to be the first one in, I scaled in as it was going down and ended up losing a bit of money.

K: When do you lose money on those trades?

M: Sometimes the inflection point doesn't happen. The stuff falls 10–30 percent. So, after losing $10 million to $20 million you have to stop your-self out somewhere. Usually at the bottom. We lose money because we get in too early and then can't afford to stay in.

K: What is it that you have to do to manage your risk better?

M: Not be afraid to pay up. Take one company I wanted to buy. It went from 90 euros to 40 euros and then back up to 50 euros. When it goes back up to 50 euros I won't pay up for it. I should buy it at 50. If the story is good and you have a reason to do it, who cares where it came from? Who cares what the chart says?

K: If you know you don't like to pay up for things and are waiting for the sales, that might point to some regular pattern or habit in your trading. Are you tight with money?

M: I hate spending money. I hate paying up for things. It's a waste. I am such a contrarian. I love buying stuff when people are selling. I love know-ing that I am buying from a significant amount of sellers.

K: It seems to me that you are doing the hard part of the trade but not the easy part. You don't mind buying against the crowd if you know something. You are saying: 'We are ahead of the street on the dropping DRAM prices.

So let's start buying it now while it is at 30 and everyone is selling. Then when it gets to 10 and turns around we'll sell it at 12.' Unfortunately you keep taking risk against the possibility of a reversal, which oftentimes doesn't happen. You are governed by the need to save money, not to pay up; to get it cheap, so cheap you are losing money on the trade as the price keeps dropping, waiting for the turn. Is there anything you can do to make these trades more profitable than they have been?

M: I don't want to buy with other buyers. I want to buy with sellers.

K: That's a view of the world that may be hurting you. To be more profitable you have to put your intellect in the service of profitability, even if that doesn't make you unique. You see it going down and say, 'This is a chance to buy it because it will turn or sell it because it will top out and turn.' This gets the juices going and allows you to be different, and it gets in the way of maximum profitability.

M: It makes sense.

K: You are looking for the bargain so much that it is unproductive. Is this personality thing worth the huge losses you have had with this strategy?

M: I'm trying to give up the market call.

K: What you really have to change is your view of the world as it relates to trading. You have to be more flexible.

M: More of a chameleon.

K: Not so stubborn. The market is telling you the truth. The market is reality. You are bringing your own reality—wanting to be different, wanting to be first, wanting to beat the consensus. You have to do it some other way. You have to know about the companies so that you know when the turn will happen so that you can get in after the turn.

M: I have to do it.

K: How are you going to recognize it?

M: I have to start small. I also have to learn patience.

K: You have to catch yourself every time until you have control over the impulse.

M: I need to learn to get in when there are other buyers when I am buying and other sellers when I am selling to sum it up.

I have selected this example because it demonstrates, rather clearly, the nature of my dialogue with traders in an effort to explore how their beliefs and attitudes influence their risk-taking behavior and the kind of self-examination necessary to get them to see what they must do to increase their ability to handle risk in a rational way.

The dialogue with Martin illustrates the significance of reviewing a consistent trading pattern with a trader, especially one that most characterizes the way he typically trades, exploring with him the strengths and weaknesses of this style, the cost to him in terms of profitability, and the danger of continuing to pursue such a strategy.

The next step is exploring how this style relates to some basic personality propensities that are part of a larger metaconcept of life. Martin, for example, takes pride in being a contrarian. Being different counts more for him than profitability. Until he recognizes this basic life principle and makes the conscious decision to pursue a profitability target, he is not likely to change his risk-taking strategy. The real risk for him, therefore, is to let go of the familiar and comfortable contrarian habits and embrace action essential for trading success.

The key to this book and what differentiates it from all the other trading books "out there" is that essentially this book examines a variety of trading styles and systematically explores ways in which traders can begin to change their approach. Unless traders harness their underlying habits and viewpoints, they will not become master traders who manage their risk effectively.

Practical Steps

As a way of understanding what it will take to improve your risk profile, enabling you to take more risk where appropriate and reduce your risk where you are taking inappropriate risk, it is useful to determine your trading styles. To do this, consider the preceding dialogue with Martin and try to imagine how you would have answered the same questions about your own trading style.

More specifically think of a recent trade that you made and look at the chart of that stock over a period of time, say the six months prior to getting into the trade. Answer the following questions in relation to that trade:

- Where did you get into the trade?
- Where did you add?
- Where did you get out, if you got out?
- Was there anything about your trading style that was reflected in the way in which you traded that stock?
- Did you buy it at the bottom and scale into it more as it moved upward? Or did you buy it at the bottom and get out fast as it was going up?
- Conversely, did you see it as an opportunity to start shorting the stock prior to an anticipated inflection point, and did you get out after the inflection point as the stock was going down?
- What does your approach to the trade tell you about your general style of trading?
- Looking at the same chart, can you see how others might have traded the stock?
- Do you know other traders who would have traded it differently?
- What are some of the alternatives that you might have taken, or what steps do you need to take to expand your trading style and your assumption of risk?
- What are the barriers or obstacles to taking these steps?
- What have you experienced in the past in relationship to similar trades that is a sticking point for you—something you have trouble doing because it creates too much anxiety or uncertainty?

- Do you have difficulty increasing the size of your positions, even when you know the fundamentals and the stocks are moving in your direction?

The value of this kind of consideration is that it sheds light on the variety of ways in which you approach opportunities for taking risk. Consider these kinds of questions, and you come face-to-face with the steps needed to become a better, more skilled, and more flexible trader.

CHAPTER TWO

UNDERSTANDING THE APPROACH

Whether you know it or not, you, as a professional trader, have your own personal trading style. And once you decipher it, you can start tailoring it to manage your risks more successfully.

For the past 10 years, I have been helping traders to determine their own unique methodology for making decisions and how to maximize their performance through such techniques as goal setting, performance review, and close examination of their psychological stopping points.

Whether their trading methods are beneficial or limiting, conscious or unconscious, there is definitely a psychology behind each trader's risk-taking methods. This psychology includes, among other things, what behavioral economists call *mental accounting*, a tendency to overvalue what is owned over what is yet to be owned. It often leads traders to overvalue trades they are holding such that they may not get out of losing trades quickly enough. Conversely, traders often underestimate the value of stocks they have yet to buy, leading them to stubbornly refuse to pay up for stocks growing in value, thereby increasing the possibility that they may lose out on potentially winning trades.

Focusing more on losses than gains and more on risks that avoid losses rather than those that lock in sure profits are choices based on the *perception* of outcome as a gain or loss, even if the actual outcome is the same.

In effect the way traders "code" gains and losses often leads to poor trading decisions. Feeling more strongly about the pain that comes with a loss than the pleasure that comes from an equal gain, traders often add to or hold on to losing positions, hoping the tide will turn, at the same time as they are reluctant to add to winning positions to maximize their profitability.

By understanding the way you handle choices, you can begin to judge how much your own decisions are not totally rational but rather a direct result of a combination of your feelings, instincts, and reactions.

Once you understand your approach, you are in a better position to commit to a conscious and successful proactive strategy. Once you understand how you are wired as a human being, you can shape a more counterintuitive approach that takes into consideration the conscious and unconscious attitudes that influence your trading. From this perspective you can begin to handle the challenge of risk taking and supersede those automatic patterns of behavior that currently govern your trading.

The key to this proactive approach to trading is a willingness to commit to an expanded vision of trading success and then to trade in terms of specific and concrete goals related to it. Here I explore the process of commitment and how it serves as the empowering model for risk taking, which I have been imparting to traders over the past 10 years.

Making the Commitment

Commitment is the willingness to risk yourself by promising a result without guarantee of the outcome. In effect, promising to achieve something sets in motion a way of being in the world where you act in terms of your vision and thereby create the possibility of making things happen. Commitment taps enormous energy and creates extraordinary possibilities for realizing your vision by putting you at risk without any certainty.

Usually we are accustomed to thinking only in terms of reasonable, certain, and achievable goals. Therefore we continually search the past to determine whether our goals are achievable and in doing this live in a realm of prediction and certitude. Our experiences are repetitive because we are generally relying on proven formulas and recipes as we approach the future. Then, we either fault ourselves when we don't achieve the sought-after objective or find ourselves frustrated when we achieve the goal and it doesn't bring the satisfaction expected.

Ralph Waldo Emerson writes of some dimension of yourself that flows effortlessly and without friction. It arises when you can step into the realm of uncertainty beyond what you know and commit to the fullest expression of your hidden potential by acknowledging your own vulnerability and being willing to surrender to the unknown so that the extraordinary can happen.

Commitment is an example of what Joe Greenstein, a circus strong man in the early years of the twentieth century, believed was necessary to overcome what he called "impossibility thinking." He believed in a Life Force that we all have but fail to activate because we are constantly thinking, "I can't do that. I'll hurt myself."

According to Greenstein, the little voice in you—that instinct for preservation—does not give us an accurate picture of our capabilities. We all have mental and physical abilities beyond our own estimation, but to realize them the mind must be deconditioned from impossibility thinking. Only after this deconditioning does it become possible to do what you will.

Greenstein believed you could do almost anything if you applied your mind and body to the task with enough diligence. The critical step to take is to overcome the instinct for self-preservation, which inhibits action. To do this, he believed, it is only necessary to become totally focused on the event at hand, with no reservations and fears of anything untoward happening. In traders, this instinct shows up in the form of such things as mental accounting and loss aversion.

Nothing could more vividly illustrate the importance of belief in a favorable outcome without reservations or fear than the large number of people who were able to run sub-four-minute miles *after* Roger Bannister broke the magic four-minute mile barrier on May 6, 1954. Until that time, the four-minute mile, according to Bannister, had become "rather like an Everest—a barrier that seemed to defy all attempts to break it—an awesome reminder that man's striving might be in vain." (Roger Bannister, *The Four Minute Mile*, The Lyons Press, 1955, p. 188).

Once the obstacle had been conquered, that belief immediately changed. The notion of possibility was dramatically extended, and breaking the four-minute mile was no longer a vain, exaggerated dream but an attainable goal that could be reached by any runner who was capable of overcoming the pain, adversity, and anxiety involved in reaching it. Once the barrier had been broken by Bannister, the event itself suddenly became relatively easy. By the end of 1978, as many as 274 runners had broken through the "magic, impenetrable barrier."

Commitment is the point beyond decision where you don't ask yourself, "Can I do it?" but declare instead "I will do it." With this phrase you live in the realm of commitment, where you put yourself at risk by taking the stand that you will do it simply because you have decided to do it. It is based on your creative vision of the future, not on your past history or your self-concept. Commitment requires living in the action immediately before you. You cannot dwell on your yesterdays nor can you project yourself into an unattainable future that looks so imposing and unreachable that you are left with feelings of inadequacy. Rather, commitment is the action in front of you today.

Understanding the Approach

"Most people won't do what is necessary, not because of lack of ambition but because of fear that if they go all out and do it, they will lose," said one trader. "That is the lack of conviction. Without conviction it doesn't matter what you do. I use the word conviction in the sense of setting a goal and reverse-engineering it. It is a trader's conviction that says, 'I know it will happen. Now I have to be patient. I know what I have to do to make it happen.' "

Thomas Aquinas said faith was the highest form of knowledge. First you do a lot of hard work. You do your homework, study for years, go through many business cycles. Then the final step is a leap of faith. You feel that you are right. This is conviction. Nothing is worse than saying that you have conviction and then acting in the opposite manner.

When you commit to a daily target, you are promising not to give in to circumstances, obstacles, or breakdowns but to see them as aspects of the path you are on. Commitment enables you to be fearless in the face of obstacles so that you can turn obstacles into opportunities. When you commit to a larger context or vision for yourself, you become the cause rather than the effect of your life. Your single-mindedness gives you direction and a greater capacity to persist against the odds. It lets you abandon dependency on your image. It helps to energize you and those around you in the face of failure.

Making this move toward a different risk outlook is, in essence, like diving into the water, jumping out of an airplane, or riding the rapids. Having jumped, the situation itself—the experience of the water or free-falling through the air and parachuting to earth—becomes the new context that defines the quality of your experience. Basically, once in the air you must manage your fall, the opening of the parachute, and your landing. These tasks require intense concentration, which are your priorities while you are falling. The water creates the context after diving or when riding the rapids, and what happens next results from the peculiar nature of that environment.

Generally, while these experiences are short-lived, they are valuable in focusing attention or concentrating the senses and in giving you a powerful sense of being very present, in the "now" of your life. The important issue (most clearly seen in skydiving) is that you must pay attention to the context. The context governs your responses and influences your actions.

Having made the commitment to jump, you have no alternative but to manage your flight through the air. Your thoughts and opinions, what you are feeling, your past history, and so forth have little to do with handling the experience. How you respond to the event itself, after jumping, is the critical issue.

The same principle applies to trading. The crucial element is what appears in response to the contexts you create by committing to a particular objective. You have to go beyond the comforts of the planning stages and take action. You have to move beyond reasons why it won't work.

After you jump out of the plane or enter the water, the action starts. Your task is to act consistently with your declaration and trade in the gap between where you are and where you wish to be. The discrepancy or gap between present reality and your future vision is the source of structural or creative tension that can help identify what is missing from your present risk-taking activity and point to what you must do to realize your vision. Committing to a specific result instead of "resigning" to things as they are is a powerful way of dealing with reality, because it invites you to take risks.

Case Study on Committing to a Goal

The fact is, you have to put yourself at risk psychologically by making a commitment to assume more capital risk and produce specific results. By doing this you put yourself in a place in which you are not accustomed to being. This commitment is like jumping out of the plane. It is partially an intellectual process. But more importantly, it is an action process from which you can immediately get feedback as to how things are going.

"The goal provides a different perspective psychologically to investing," explained one trader. "Investing has always been based on the market. But when you trade in terms of a goal, it doesn't matter what the market gives you. Now you are trading in terms of a more powerful question—what can you take out of the market that is consistent with your objectives? What kind of result do you want?"

Determine a number, and from that number you can figure out what you need to do to produce the result. You are more likely to find a way to realize the result if you decide upon it than if you leave it up to the fates.

A beautiful example of the out-of-the-box thinking implicit in what I mean by commitment was presented by Marcus, a currency trader with whom I worked. Marcus was telling me about how his amateur hockey team had failed to win in the first game of a playoff series.

Marcus: We had the season playoff on Sunday night and only five skaters showed up. We played well for the first period. By the middle of the second period everyone was losing focus because we were so tired. Normally we have 10 skaters and are able to take breaks and substitute for each other so that we can play the full game.

Kiev: Was the team committed to winning?

M: The guys who showed up were committed to winning.

K: If the objective was to win, and you would have won if everyone showed up, then even the guys who showed up weren't committed to doing what it would have taken to ensure success. They should have made sure that everyone showed up. One of the ways you win is that everyone shows up.

M: We didn't lose a game all season when everyone showed up.

K: It doesn't sound like the guys who showed up were fully committed to winning.

M: The guys who showed up or the guys who didn't show up?

K: We know about the guys who didn't show up. But I'm saying that even the guys who showed up didn't do all that it took to make sure that you won.

If everybody showed up, you would have won. You didn't commit to making sure that everyone showed up. There are no excuses that couldn't have been surmounted. There is no guarantee that you are going to win, but you are cutting into your chances of winning by not showing up. If you were playing the game like your life depended on it, you would have gotten on the phone to make sure that everyone showed up.

M: We weren't committed to winning, not like that.

K: There is only one way.

M: Everyone wanted to win during the game.

K: But they were not playing the game full out.

M: It doesn't surprise me.

K: That's the human condition. If you want to make it happen, you have to go beyond the ordinary and make that extra bit of effort to account for unexpected events, inertia, and conflicting obligations. I am sure everyone could have found a way to make it to the game. It might have taken some pressure, encouragement, hand-holding, baby-sitters, etcetera.

M: It relates to everything.

K: You had a winning season. Then you slipped up at the last minute. It would be interesting to explore it with those guys. If you want a winning season next year everyone has to show up, even during a storm. Someone was making sure the other team was there. It is a decision to do it and then doing what it takes to make it happen. Wayne Gretzky is not the strongest guy, not the fastest guy. The extra bit of practice and effort translates into trading as well.

Setting a Target

Risk taking, in this book, is being examined in the context of the goal-oriented, short-term, catalyst-driven model of trading first presented in *Trading to Win* and developed further in the sequel *Trading in the Zone.* This model centers around the concept of setting daily targets. It is an approach that encourages traders to take more responsibility for the way in which they handle their trading. This approach in turn forces them to examine those personal attitudes and habits that may be interfering with maximizing profit and minimizing risk. Finally, it encourages them to set daily targets and to manage their risk on a daily basis in order to reduce the possibility of losses and increase the possibility of profitability.

Setting a target enables you to size your positions and determine how big the incremental steps have to be toward reaching the target. It also enables you to recognize the necessity of keeping your losses down to reduce the burden you must bear to realize the goal. The target forces you to ask the powerful question of what is missing from your present infrastructure or strategy that is essential for reaching the target. Everything is focused on the target and all that you need to realize it.

To follow this method, you must be willing to do what it will take to produce the result. Taking into consideration your daily target helps answer the question of how big you have to be and what kinds of losses you can tolerate. It also helps you to see what behaviors need to be changed to accommodate the goal. For example, if you are a contrarian like Martin, discussed in Chapter One, and are losing too much money because that strategy is out of favor, you have to change your approach no matter how much it hurts. If you typically make money the first week of the month and then lose half of it the second week, you need to examine your risk management skills and whatever else will keep you focused on the target. You have to keep tweaking your behavior to maximize your performance. To the extent that you are driven by the objective, you begin to see what is necessary to play at this advanced, proactive level when you consider what is missing from your performance.

This approach is based on the notion that you can create your results in part by deciding on them in advance and then designing your trading strategy around the concept of producing these specific results rather than relying on what the market will give you.

This approach is to be distinguished from the more traditional, value-oriented, fundamentally driven approach of longer-term hedge funds and mutual funds where the focus is more on beating a "bogey"—some index like the Russell 2000 or the S&P [Standard & Poor's] 500—rather than in producing outsized returns such as I have been writing about.

There are obvious philosophical differences between these approaches, and it is worth noting what these are, since the short-term, catalyst-driven approach points up the possibility of *creating* the results rather than *accepting* results that mirror the market action.

As discussed in Chapter One, longer-term, value-oriented traders do the fundamental work on a company. When they buy a position, they have no problem if the position drops in price. They often believe that if the information is good and their analysis is correct, that it makes sense to buy more when the stock drops. This is how they garner the most value from the stock. The cheaper they can get it, the more interested in it they are. They buy more as it goes down. They buy it at a dollar. Then it is worth 50 cents. Then it is worth 40 cents. They buy more. In effect, they are inclined to buy more when there are dips or sell more when a short goes higher.

This view differs from the short-term, catalyst-driven approach where the objective is more often to get out of losing positions (even if the fundamentals are good) and to start buying the stock back only when it starts moving up.

Although long-term value investors tend not to think about goals and profit targets in the same way as the shorter-term traders do, they are by and large receptive to the notion that they can use a goal to focus their trading better by considering how they can make 2 percent or 3 percent on their money in a month. I encourage them to try this by doing such things as:

- Getting bigger in their bets when they have the conviction based on their fundamental understanding of the company.
- Getting smaller in companies that have already run up a maximum amount and are not likely to continue to climb.
- Getting smaller in their short positions where there is limited liquidity.
- Being more selective in putting out shorts so that they don't lose so much in their short positions.
- Getting out of positions where there are limited reasons to be in the positions.
- Focusing on short-term events (usually viewed by them as "noise") where there may be opportunity to make money (by trading around the position) even if the trade is in the opposite direction to the direction they intend to follow over the long haul.

The goal in working with long-term, value-driven portfolios is helping the traders to maximize their profitability by adding the powerful component of goals to their strategic planning. This tactic represents a shift from what is ordinarily a more passive trading approach in which the traders are waiting for the market to give them results.

In traditional environments traders focus on what they need to do to raise capital to get to a certain size. They rarely, if ever, think in terms of what they need to do to produce specific results. Moreover, they often become focused on understanding the fundamentals and are not as focused on producing profits. Therefore, it is more difficult for them to produce outsized returns on a longer-term basis, because they are not getting the same intraday volatility and relatively lower risk of the shorter-term trading approach.

One trader, Melvin, commented on long-term traders: "At a company I worked at, we felt that if you understood what variables will make the stock work, for example chip sales as they related to the price of capital equipment stocks, you didn't know what price the stock would go to, but you knew that it would go up. You didn't set a dollar target, but you had a mental target based on a change in the fundamentals. You stayed objective. You knew why it worked. If the reason why it went up changed, you changed your position. You sized your position based on your understanding of the company and supply and demand features, not in terms of the price. You bought it because demand for semiconductor chips was picking up. The demands should pick up as the stock goes up. If you saw a quarter where it was not as good as you thought it would be, even if it triples from there, you would say, 'I'm done. My assumptions have been reached.' Even if the stock continued to go up because of the perception of the value of the stock, if your reasons were not there, you would get out of the position."

When long-term traders move to a goal-oriented strategy, they often approach it differently. According to David, a long-term, fundamental analyst-turned-portfolio manager, "Your goal is determined by your price target, which is determined by what you as an analyst think you know that the rest of the world does not know. If I think a company that is currently 32 is worth 50 in 12 months, how do I capture that 50 percent move in 12 months? How many shares do I need to have? If I produce one idea every two weeks for 24 ideas a year and each makes $2 million, that gets me to $50 million. How do I go about finding those ideas, and how do I size the portfolio right? The day trader focuses on how much money he wants to make in a day."

"The brilliance of the short-term approach is in its relatively lower risk to the markets as compared to the long-term portfolio management approach," explained another trader. "Setting the goal of returns forces you to define a daily strategy. It is too hard to set an annual goal of returns in a long-term portfolio because you are subject to too many market vagaries and events that cannot be controlled. In the short-term account, you can trade around the news events and announcements in what amounts to a less efficient marketplace. The day is the only quantifiable period that you can have. Once you go to a year, and not think of it as 250 trading days, then you are into long-term prognostication, and you are off the game. That is beyond your control. There are hundreds of variables in that time frame, and productivity is unknowable. When you get to a day, there is no time loss of productivity, and the variables are easier to manage. It is out of the box. The conventional world thinks in terms of the box.

"The one-day goal can force anyone to become an outstanding trader. It forces the issue. There is no other alternative. In this world, the result is what is critical. You have to give up the intellect and look at other things."

The goal gives you a set of guidelines with which to determine what you must do to align your trading with your trading objectives. You toss the ball out in front of you and then you swim towards it. You declare your goal, promise the result, and then you trade in terms of the promise.

Case Study on Using a Goal

The following dialogue illustrates how the goal can be used as a lens for illuminating the more subtle components of a trader's trading behavior. It also points to the fact that these principles apply to all traders irrespective of the instruments they are trading. Fred is a relatively young foreign currency trader. This dialogue explores the links between goal setting and trading strategy:

Fred: I have been feeling the markets better, running my risk/reward better, and taking my profits early. I am less influenced by the environment and opinions of others and not discouraged by losses.

THE PSYCHOLOGY OF RISK

Kiev: What are your goals?

F: I assume that some days I will not make money. So, I try to make $25,000 daily to get to $50,000 by the end of the week. This week I made $5,000.

K: What happened?

F: I lost money the first few days of this week and then I got off my game. Yesterday I was short dollar/Swiss, and I didn't reach my target. I then went short euro/sterling. As the euro goes down the Swiss generally goes higher. Since my view on the market changed, I should have taken off my position or moved my stop down to break even. I was trying to stick to my risk/reward profile. I should take off the position unless I am five or seven ticks from my stop. I had 60–70 ticks in the trade. It cost me 50. It was one to one. Last week and the week before I was really confident. This week I only made $5,000. I was at $37,000 two weeks ago, and last week I was at $48,000.

K: What did you stop doing this week when you made $5,000? What dropped out of your trading methodology?

F: I think the losses threw me off my game on Monday. So, I started to trade smaller sizes. Today I could have done two units on both trades that I did. I would have made $30,000 today. I had one trade on this morning, and it went against me a little bit. I should have bought more. I didn't do that. Certain trades I need to be bigger in size.

K: What changed?

F: It's the size. I was too small and was getting out too soon or a combination of both those things. You can't get smaller just because you go down.

K: Does the goal put pressure on you, or does it help you to focus on what you are doing to see whether you are deviating from your strategy?

F: The target isn't putting pressure on me. I am trading better. I don't force myself to trade. I need to stick with my position size and hold it longer. I lost $12,000 on Monday and $7,000 on Tuesday. I got gun-shy. I sold cable (British pound) and was worried that there would be intervention. So, I did half the size I normally do. I sold on the cable trade and was offering more above and didn't sell them. If I had gotten filled I would have done better.

I am getting confidence from being focused and having a few winning trades and trusting my instincts. Even this morning, I sold cable, even though some of the senior traders thought it was going up. I had my stops. I knew I was right.

K: Given your approach, how big can you get? Can you trade more units? What is the number of units that scares you?

F: I can do up to ten units staying within my guideline. I am trying to make $200,000 a month and only risk $125,000. I base it on the risk. If I have 14 straight losers, I don't believe it will happen. It is just a question of risking more. My trading style might change after 10 lots. Right now I am doing one or two lots.

K: How many trades can you do in a day?

F: I need to do 2 to 4 trades in a day to reach my numbers. There are days when I don't do any trades. I could never do what Mark does. He has 7 trades of one-half to one lot. They are all correlated with one another. They are all saying the same thing. It ends up skewing the risk/reward. It works for him. I couldn't do it. He does 12 trades in a day and I do 1 or 2.

The essence of this discussion is how a trader like Fred can use the goal to stay focused on the size and frequency of his trades, his use of stop losses, and his need to maintain discipline in the face of losses. He can use the goal to keep alert as to whether he stays with his methodology or is scared out of it by a few losses or even how he might get off his game if he does too well and loses his discipline and concentration. He can use the goal as a benchmark to measure his current degree of involvement relative to those times when he met his target. In general, when the trader veers from his targets, he has stopped doing something that has worked for him and needs to regroup and prepare for the next trading session by making sure he has all his ducks in a row.

Practical Steps

Most of the time, traders do not *create* their results proactively. Rather, they are inclined to passively accept the results the market gives them and to think, "This is what I want, but I really don't know how to do it" or "I don't think I can get it, so what's the sense of trying?" This book is intended to help you achieve your daily targets by defining them, envisioning the future, and then doing what you say you are going to do.

To achieve this end, you must be willing to take a risk by declaring or promising a specific result and then being willing to do what it takes to realize that result, bypassing any kind of anxiety or negative thinking that is likely to appear in the process. Difficult as it is, you have to be able to say: "This is what I want. OK, now I'm going to figure out how to get it."

Although you can't act contrary to certain universal laws like defying gravity, incredible things still are possible just by declaring them and living out of a powerful vision of the future that you have the power to create. As you do this, you will become aware of the power of your own thought processes and how they influence your perception of events and will begin to be able to take full responsibility for the way you trade.

You have the capacity to reframe your interpretations of events so you can trade from the perspective of being fully absorbed in the moments before you. Commitment enables you to overcome the self-limiting expectations of your automatic thinking that creates doubts and puts a ceiling on the possibilities for achievement. A daily target can create a new order of consciousness that redefines risk for you. Commitment enables you to sustain momentum by focusing on immediate actions rather than long-term results. You will stop living expectantly, waiting for fulfillment in the future and will begin to find meaning in the day-to-day events.

Understanding the Approach

A significant aspect of the process of commitment is to notice how much your rational mind interferes with the process of commitment and how it finds all kinds of reasons why you can't do or shouldn't do what you want to do. But here I want to emphasize that commitment is not about being rational, but about creating your life by promising it and then living in terms of the promise. In doing this you are best served by defining your objectives, being assertive, and then being willing to concentrate on the details of specific activities. You have to focus on specific aspects of your actions that provide you with direction and incentive toward realizing your objectives. You must also stay focused on these actions rather than on the self-limiting preconceptions and self-doubts you have, based on your past experiences. If you dig deeply enough into these, you will soon discover that many of these beliefs about the way things are have little real relevance to the trading tasks at hand.

A daily target narrows the focus of attention to the reality before you and functions like a set of lenses through which to see the world. The more you can narrow the focus of your own thinking and the less dependent you are on external cues or supports, the more readily you can enter into the flow experience or the centered state.

How can you construct a setting that facilitates commitment? Consider the following questions:

- What financial objective would you like to obtain this year? Be realistic but not limiting. Remember that the most likely tendency is to understate what you want because you underestimate what you are capable of doing. After developing a yearly goal, divide that out into daily terms. What will your daily goal be? If you are making trades that last several days, you can divide the goal into two- or three-day goals or a weekly target.
- What is standing in your way of reaching that goal? Why do you think you can't reach that goal?

- What attitudes, emotions, and life principles are interfering with your efforts to realize that goal?
- Are you willing to commit yourself to the stated goal without any guarantees or certainty about how you are going to do it? Are you willing to step forth on faith, to create the result to which you have committed yourself?

The elements of commitment include a clear definition of your objectives. Writing down the answers to these questions in a notebook and then tracking your progress as you move toward these objectives will facilitate the process of helping you to realize your objectives. Keeping this kind of diary will help you to increase your capacity to choose your vision and keep risking yourself by taking on the commitment.

Keeping notes each day about your goals, your results, your trades, what you experienced, your fears, your doubts, and the like will help you over time to own your experiences and master the fears and self-doubts that impinge on your trading success.

Visionaries are those who create a concept of the world in their own minds and then bring reality into line with their visions of it. By keeping a daily diary of your experiences, you can develop this skill of visual imagery rehearsal, so that you can empower your actions by mental or visual preparation of the events before you enter into them. More importantly, you can bring reality into line with your concepts of it.

PART TWO

THE PROBLEMS OF RISK

CHAPTER THREE

HANDLING YOUR EMOTIONS

When I was studying for my boards in psychiatry, my neurology instructor, Geoffrey Osler, said something about human beings that I will never forget. Professor Osler began the study of the central nervous system with a diagram of a single cell. Each week he added more nerve cells to the single cell until he had built a spinal cord and then a primitive brain and finally the cerebrum, cerebellum, and the various specialized lobes of the brain, including the all-important frontal lobes.

The frontal lobes, he noted, were designed for the integration of information, perception, and conceptualization, to capitalize on large memory banks of information about past events, to prepare one for the future, and to develop coping strategies, enabling humans to adapt to a complex and often dangerous environment. The problem with human beings, Osler said, was that the frontal lobes sometimes "fell in love with themselves," leading humankind to become preoccupied with our "magical" and "divine" powers and unable to adequately assess and deal with the world around us.

This counterproductive property of the frontal lobes often accounts for much of the fear that human beings experience. In our efforts to protect against fear, we fall in love with our old habits of thought and behavior and cannot see reality as it really is. Efforts to protect against fear lead us instead to ignore our own contribution to the events of our lives, to deny responsibility for our own fears, to project blame onto others, and in the end to search for easy answers and magical formulas for the resolution of our problems.

Defining the Life Principle

Formed early in life in response to the influence of parents and teachers, life principles are beliefs that function as ideas by which your life is organized. They govern what you think, what you perceive, and how you interpret the world. They govern your feelings, your behavior, your imagination, and your expression. Yet because they are largely internalized, you are not generally aware of them.

The life principle, in effect, is the largely unconscious template around which you organize your life. Yet if you are unaware of it, you are very likely not able to change your life in any significant way because the tendency is to try to change elements that you *can* see. Moreover, to the extent that you keep responding as an adult in a way you learned as a child, you may be responding in ways that are no longer appropriate to the current situation. Therefore you need to recognize the life principle so that you can free your thinking to respond more appropriately and less automatically to the events of your life.

As a result of the life principle, very little happens to you that represents a direct interaction between your self and experience. All experiences are filtered through the life principle such that all present experiences are built on past experiences. Relating to events through the life principle effectively leads you to interpret events in terms of your preconceptions, not in terms of the actual experiences themselves. To let go of this template is to let go of a familiar and predictable way of seeing the world. When and if you let go, you are likely to come face-to-face with the dormant fears behind the life principle itself.

Handling Your Emotions

In order to develop the capacity to take risks, you must learn to trade by interacting more directly with the reality of the marketplace rather than through the filter of your life principle. To do this you must relinquish those life principles that both create and perpetuate your underlying fears.

Many traders I see in consultation repeatedly search for satisfaction but have difficulties recognizing how much they are creating all the conflict and dissatisfaction in their trading. They don't understand that changing the outward elements of their approach to trading will not produce inner peace.

Different life principles trap you in different ways. For example, if you are governed by perfectionism, you delay your decisions so as to avoid error or the risk of being overwhelmed by commitment. You also may be inclined to doubt your successes, believing that they won't last. If you are an intellectual, you may be trapped by your thinking. If you are a martyr, you are afraid to act out of fear of being vulnerable. Afraid of being manipulated or losing your autonomy, you may find it difficult to trust, to let go of control, or to become part of a team.

While life principles are not formed with any purpose (but only in reaction to events), they are the basic ingredients of your functioning and self-concept. The belief that the past will be repeated sets in motion a self-fulfilling prophecy so that what you believe will happen usually does or what you are trying to escape from keeps returning. This belief reinforces the notion that you must wait until everything is handled before you take action. When you live in a state of paralysis, terrified by the anticipation of fear, you are unaware that the other side of the action you fear is the freedom you most desire. If you can step outside this paralytic state and take action, you will discover that certainty is not necessary for living your life or for trading successfully.

You get outside this state by becoming familiar with your automatic, magical, and stereotyped thinking so that you can be aware of your thoughts and can notice your automatic reactions to events. This heightened awareness will help you to learn to stop reacting compulsively to events.

The mastery of fear involves tossing out old habits, customs, and attitudes that are kept in place by your automatic thinking. This means relinquishing your natural dependence on such things as the opinions of others and on your perfectionistic need to overcomply with rules, schedules, and demands of the past. As you let go, you will become more in touch with your present experience, the flow and context of the events, and the circumstances of your life in the trading arena.

By leaving behind the pressures of the fearful voices, you will be freer to plan, organize, and implement significant changes in your trading. You will be able to relinquish various cultural myths that mirror your own thinking mechanism and dominate your trading—the search for the Holy Grail, fame, fortune, domination over others, and the like—all of which are designed to overcome some sense of fear but which in fact only reinforce your own lack of authenticity. The realization of your own intrinsic worth and lack of deficiencies will open up possibilities for you at an exponential rate. Once you can accept yourself as you are and can stop beating and second-guessing yourself, you will be free to take appropriate risks, free to assert yourself, and free to create your own reality based on genuine conscious choices.

Examining the Emotions of Trading

The first step in mastering risk involves a willingness to create a larger vision for your trading success and to define specific concrete goals related to your vision. At this point, most traders initially face their own resistance. To focus on the essential tasks associated with your goals means to let go of your habitual way of doing things. You must begin to act in new ways required by your goals, which in itself often creates a sense of uncertainty and anxiety. If you can ride out the anxiety or can get comfortable with uncertainty, you can remain longer in the gap between where you are and where you want to be, discovering in this process what is necessary to realize your goal. However, if the emotional tension is too great, many traders lower their sights or avoid entering into the gap in an effort to feel comfortable. They may abandon their vision, even rationalizing that they didn't want it in the first place. Other traders begin to pressure themselves with thoughts about the present situation as a negative motivator.

I often see this in long-term traders who are trying to adopt a shorter-term, catalyst-driven model of trading. While they are very positive about the value of setting daily goals and reducing risk by taking advantage of intraday volatility, they are often very reluctant to give up their long-term strategy of buying value stocks cheaply when prices dip. They are also hesitant to take profits in response to short-term moves in their stocks. This kind of focus on daily goals seems to create some internal conflict with their long-term buy-and-hold approach.

Other traders resort to psyching themselves up with the use of positive thinking and more hard work. All of these efforts only serve to keep alive the notion of underlying powerlessness so that nothing really changes and they don't really develop mastery. These efforts also may lead to exhaustion and burnout.

Let's face it. Once you are committed to an objective, you are going to encounter internal resistance, external opposition, superstition, pain, fatigue, and self-doubt. You may even encounter negativity from those who lack the courage to do the same thing on their own or from those who feel that their own performances are challenged by your actions. You may experience self-doubts during the extended period of time it takes for your specific goals to be reached.

Anticipating the reactions of others, or the repetition of a past experience, or even worrying about the meaning of your actions triggers fearful thoughts that can distract you from full concentration. This distraction can produce errors, which in turn can lead to more fear, tension, distraction, and eventually, more errors.

Just as your thoughts occur randomly and lack any substantive meaning or certainty, the same may be said of your feelings. But your feelings are rarely the problem. The problem stems from your automatic *reaction* to and your *interpretation* of your feelings.

It is critical to distinguish between your feelings and your reactions to them so as to create fewer problems for yourself. Focusing only on the actions before you reduces the impact of distracting thoughts about the past.

The capacity to break out of your automatic reactions and to view your experiences as another type of information rather than as proof of failure enables you to start producing breakthroughs instead of breakdowns. This reframing approach allows you to keep incorporating what you learn into your way of trading. This perspective supports spontaneity as sources of limitless power.

I do not mean doing what you are already doing or doing more of it. If you solve things by trying to do more of what you have been doing or doing the opposite of what you have been doing (two characteristic ways of dealing with problems), you are actually likely to perpetuate the problems rather than solve them. I mean breaking out of limited concepts of yourself and trading courageously in terms of your commitment to an expanded vision of trading itself. I am talking about making a decision to act in the face of fear, to confront those obstacles that frighten you and stand in your way. I am talking about committing yourself to objectives on the other side of the fear and by the process of commitment to action, gaining the necessary confidence to ride through the fear.

To become fully engaged in your trading, you must learn to ride out the anxiety while maintaining consciousness and continued involvement. You can do this by learning to float with events, to let go of the pull of ambition and other distractions. You may also need coaches to help you through situations that you never have been through before or to stay on track in the face of your natural inclination to sabotage your best interests.

According to Joseph Campbell, anthropologist and author of *The Hero with a Thousand Faces* (Princeton University Press, 1949), the lessons of the world's myths are clear: The more challenging the situation to be affirmed or experienced, the greater the stature of the person who can assimilate it. Believing this, you can let go of the notion that you are helpless to steer the course of your trading. When events occur that seem to be beyond your control, choose them and become more involved in taking responsibility for how they are handled. Be guided by commitment to your vision and not by your life principles or your concern for appearances, social expectations, egotistical pride, or your irrational fears of catastrophe.

Case Study on Trading with a Vision

You can choose to put on a trade even though you're afraid. You allow yourself to experience your fear. You acknowledge your heart is beating fast, and you notice other physiological effects, but you don't assign meaning to these effects. Your heart is just racing, and your breathing is just fast. It doesn't mean anything about you. And it doesn't mean anything about what will happen. It just "is" and need not limit you from taking action in terms of your vision.

James was a successful currency trader who contacted me because of his keen awareness that his fear of losing was creating a real obstacle to his trading success. He was very anxious to take a profit and invariably got out of his positions too soon.

"I can't tolerate the volatility," said James. "I get out of my positions too soon even when my ideas are good. When I set goals, I often press and overtrade and force ideas instead of waiting for them to become clear. My hit ratio was 75 percent, but I wasn't making much money. My short-term goal would screw up my long-term goals, and my process would break down. I would have a vision of a move to X, and I would put on a long-term option position and start to make a lot of money. Then I would hedge it up because I didn't want to give back some profits when I was sensing a correction coming, and I would miss the trade. I didn't want to take the pain of having my profits diminished. I found that more painful than just taking a loss."

James obviously didn't know how to use a target to help him to hold his positions longer to increase his profit. He was more invested in being right and comfortable than in doing what it took to increase his profitability. His fear of losing was interfering with his ability to take enough risk to reach his targets.

"I am not comfortable ignoring the volatility. My short-term trading is excellent, but I don't tolerate enough volatility in it and tend to get out too soon because I can't take the heat of the price dropping. My stops are too far or too tight, and I don't run the positions. When I start to make a profit, I grab it too soon in order to get my confidence going. I am afraid of losing. In my intermediate-term trading, the pain threshold triggers withdrawals. I read the market correctly, but then I don't make much money because I am scared out of the volatility periods when things are going against me. The ideas were good but I didn't run them. I wasn't willing to lose more to make more. I have to be willing to be stopped out more and run my positions."

As you can see, James's fear of losing played out in terms of not always waiting for the best entry point and in terms of taking profits too soon. But, James noted that it would be easy to adjust his trading style to increase his profitability, if only he could deal with the loss side of the trade.

"I hate losing money in short-term trading. That induces me to make stupid exits way too soon. That is a weakness. You would say that I am not committed enough to my goal. Otherwise, I would take the pain. I pick great levels. Even when I know the exit I get out too early. It is a vicious circle of trading badly, losing money, and feeling pressure—which reinforces bad money practice."

What James needed to learn over time was to lower his weekly target to a doable number. By lowering the target, he was able to explore what was keeping him from reaching his number, and he was able to stay in longer. This lower target ultimately had a significant impact on his trading. The target should not pressure him but should help overcome his fear of getting it wrong.

Handling Your Emotions

As James learned over time, you do not have to be held back by the emotions you are feeling. You can simply experience them, and the quality of your trading then becomes a function of what you create. You simply do what you decide to do and allow yourself to experience the totality of the experience.

In order to manage your risk, you have to accept the negative emotions you are trying to suppress. You have to create a space for yourself to be and not attribute any significance to negative feelings. Since you become what you resist, you experience more anxiety when you try to resist it, and you become more fearful when you resist fear. Your emotional reactions should be part of the experience of creating a context for risk taking, but they should not be the limiting factor.

This new approach will not be without fear and anxiety, particularly when you let go of the familiar ways you now have of doing things. Rather, it is creating a more powerful way of trading.

In other words, the vision provides a framework in which to uncover the potential within you by defining it and acting consistently with it. Trading in a risk-controlled way requires that you find this optimal flow experience, leaving your preconceptions and prejudices behind and engaging in calculated risk-taking behavior such that you begin to trade in a way that you never did before.

Your feelings do not have to mean anything. If you simply allow them to be—allow your own automatic thoughts, physical symptoms, and emotions to pass—your reactions will pass as well and will not be carried into the future as if they had any significance. When something unpleasant happens, notice your thoughts and reactions to what happened. Notice your opinion. Notice the automatic decision you make to react, to withdraw, to decide never to trade again, and how much all this relates to a lifelong, underlying life principle or guideline for perceiving the world. Then consider the alternative way in which you can view the event or the same factual issues or problems. The more you do this, the more skilled you will be to relate to the events and problems of your trading, not in the old, automatic, and habitual ways but in a new, more creative and innovative way where you will not be dominated by your emotions.

Practical Steps

Consider how conscious and unconscious memories of past, unsuccessful trades impede your efforts to achieve new goals. How much do old concepts and the recurrent thoughts or fearful conversations in your mind about the way you are inhibit you from trying new things? Consider how concerned you are with the opinions of others and how afraid you are to act contrary to what you imagine their expectations to be. For example:

- Are you excessively dependent on others?
- Do you constantly seek approval from others before acting?
- Are you afraid to speak up because of repercussions?
- Are you unable to plan something without involving other people in your decision?
- Are you unable to keep from talking about something you've accomplished?

If your answer to any of these questions is yes, it may be that you are overly concerned about the opinions of others and reluctant to act without approval. If you can become aware of the automatic patterns of dependency when you are acting in terms of it, you will be able to see how much of your trading is the reflection of built-in attitudes that maintain the repetitive nature of your trading, giving you little choice over how your trading goes.

Consider to what extent you are locked into fixed and obligatory ways of behaving such as those manifested in a tendency to be too concerned with the opinions of others or to be afraid to act in terms of your own self–interest. How much do such patterns reflect your fear of asserting yourself for fear of repercussions? How much do you stay locked into habits out of fear and are afraid to change because of early established fears and not reality?

As you question yourself, you will begin to understand how much fear keeps you from becoming the trader you want to be. An honest inquiry into these questions will set in motion the forces of change in your trading and enable you to start moving toward new and more meaningful objectives.

Understanding the Stress Response

The stress response is the body's automatic internal response to a threatening situation. It is a survival mechanism triggered by a threat that occurs in all animal species, including humans. Often called the fight or flight syndrome, the adrenaline response charges us up when we need it most, thus enabling us, with the added hormonal energy that the response provokes, either to cope with a dangerous situation or to run away from it.

The stress response is accompanied by increased adrenaline production, which increases blood flow to your muscles and brain, raises your metabolism, and heightens alertness. All of these physical responses have value in threatening situations as well as in other situations where some kind of action or performance is required.

The stress response is not only triggered by actual events; it can also be triggered by thoughts. Then the peculiar nature of the human brain can wreak havoc with the fullest expression of our creative potential. The combination of fearful thoughts, the resulting stress response, and the patterns we have learned to use to protect ourselves can lead to a cycle of negative, self-fulfilling prophecies.

The first time a fear-provoking event/thought happens it may be unique; but when its recurrence is anticipated, the fearful response initially caused by it also recurs. The thought pattern becomes set, and unless your thinking changes, you are likely to be convinced that you are going to repeat the error. You react to events/thoughts as if they had the same significance as past experiences. You anticipate events on the basis of the past perspective of your life principles. Therefore, present situations continue to trigger reactions that may have been appropriate in the past but now are maladaptive because they limit your freedom to choose your reaction in the present.

Depending on the situation and the individual, the stress response can range from mild to severe and can be of a brief or protracted duration. You can experience it totally, in which case all your adaptive mechanisms are brought into play, or you can experience it only partially, in which case you can still function normally on most levels.

This response is a drain on your system, and the intensity and duration of external stressors determine the amount of wear and tear your body experiences. The more often you experience this response and the greater the magnitude of the external stressors, the more vulnerable you are to negative reactions. If stress increases without a corresponding increase in your ability to control it, your adaptive mechanisms begin to break down, and you experience nervousness and decreased confidence. This negative aspect of the stress response is a factor in explaining poor performance, sickness, and in some cases even death.

On the positive side, the stress response can be appropriate, adaptive, and even lifesaving. In the Nazi concentration camps, for example, the fortunate few who survived the ordeal, despite forbidding odds, did so not just because of circumstances but because they made a positive response to extreme stress. They were able to make the appropriate physical and psychological adjustments to a situation which, by all objective standards, was utterly intolerable. The stress response also works to our advantage in less extreme situations, enabling us to work faster under pressure and giving us extra physical and mental strength when needed.

From this perspective, emotions can be viewed not as a reason for distress but as a normal response to the uncertainty of risk taking. Inexperience, fatigue, and increased pressure all tend to hamper efforts to concentrate naturally and spontaneously, and they inevitably lead to an intensification of effort and further increased fear and tension.

For example, Darrell Pace, an Olympic gold medalist in archery in the Montreal Olympic games once told me he wished he hadn't won a gold medal, because whenever he practiced archery afterward the persistent thoughts of being a gold medalist kept intruding on his consciousness and raised the level of his expectations and, therefore, his fears. When he was aiming at the target, this intrusive imagery kept interfering with his capacity to find that clear state of mind that would enable him to perform at his maximum level.

Darrell's experience is not unusual. Your thoughts influence the events of your life and how others respond to you. You may have various explanations for why you haven't succeeded or why you can't continue to succeed. You may think you need to do more or to do less or to do something else. You may think others have to change. One thing you are not likely to have considered is the fact that you may have unconsciously chosen what you have.

Creating a New
Life Principle

At the beginning of every workshop or seminar that I give to traders, I invite the participants to think the unthinkable and to consider the extent to which they don't own their lives and that the goals they pursue are not their own. This exercise invariably has a shock effect because everybody believes that they are in control of their life and that they too know exactly where they are going.

I have asked you to consider your goals and whether you have a larger vision for your trading. I have asked you to consider how much you are not living in terms of what is best for you because you are dominated by automatic thinking and by the beliefs and attitudes of others reinforced by the culture.

Admittedly you have a concept about yourself, an identity that has been formulated in the course of your life in response to the demands of your parents and society, and no doubt you make decisions and choose goals in keeping with this identity. Consider these, even more difficult, questions:

- What if this identity is no longer valid?
- What if it is merely what you intended from your childhood?
- What if you could change your identity?
- What if you could decide now as an adult to create your life in line with your own conscious choices?
- Might this not tap creative energies at the core of your self?

In other words, you may not be living your life in terms of your own natural interests and talents because you may have focused more attention on improving your weaknesses than identifying and developing your strengths. Rather you may be pursuing goals related to your identity or social persona and for this reason may not feel good about your goals even when you achieve them. You may even be hindered by your goals, reluctant to let go of them because they are tied to your defensive image of yourself.

You need only recognize that your concept of yourself is inaccurate, that you are an enormous bundle of human potential, and that your experience of risk is based on visual images you can choose and that you can choose whatever images or purpose for your trading that you wish. The only limit is your reluctance to let go of your preconceived concepts.

Handling Your Emotions

ʹ If you can live from the context or goal you have created, you will be able to allow yourself to experience fear and anxiety without attaching meaning to them and will be able to master the challenge of taking risk. The very act of committing yourself to a meaningful objective will give you the courage to ride through and accept the anxiety that may appear from time to time as your risk profile increases.

ʹ To master risk taking successfully at the highest levels of effectiveness, satisfaction, and fulfillment, you must learn to handle your own automatic thoughts and emotional responses. Those automatic responses lock you into fixed patterns that may actually increase the riskiness of your trades and prevent the free and unencumbered flow of your trading potential in a variety of situations.

When you become aware of the habitual, self-imposed psychological responses that color your trading responses and act as obstacles to maximum effectiveness and trading success, you allow events to unfold in a way that will minimize stress. Such awareness and the mastery of some of the principles outlined in this book will help you to handle risk with less fear and emotional reactivity so that you can maximize performance and improve your overall functioning.

Living beyond your history and your past identity (which are based on the repetition of past patterns of behavior), you will discover enormous potential in yourself for creating trades in front of you. If you can stand still in the face of anxiety and ride it out, you will pass through the internal barrier, which is the root cause of fear and which is what keeps you locked into a habitual image of yourself and unable to take risks. Ultimately the mastery of risk means to ride out the anxiety, not to mask it.

The mastery of fear enables you to approach risk as a naked presence, where nothing is meant or justified or prescribed, where you enter the trading arena unrestricted by your identity or various restrictive habits of mind and behavior conditioned in the earliest years of your life. The key to this mastery is to be able to live in the present, to see every situation as an opportunity to hit a home run, to give it your best shot, and to keep focusing on immediate targets relating to the broader objectives.

Notice how your misinterpretations keep you from being nurtured by your experiences and keep you from taking risks. One way to master fears is to confront past errors consciously. Facing up to those experiences that cause fear and comparing them to other fear-producing stimuli may reduce their stimulus value. If the sources of fear can be itemized and described, they will become more manageable.

Conversely, defenses against fear work against satisfactory functioning. In fact, psychological defenses such as total withdrawal, denial, regression, rationalization, and excessive preoccupation with physical symptoms such as headaches and backaches may lead to avoidance of work and achievement altogether.

Admitting to fear is often a more effective tool for reducing it. Reducing the effort expended to hide fear effectively eliminates it. By concentrating on how specific feelings feel, how long they last, what thoughts are associated with them, and taking responsibility for them, you can dissipate the fear and anxiety that come from trying to suppress feelings. Concentration, even on those things that cause fear, has a strong effect on reducing ambivalence, indecision, and weakened efforts; it can thus be of great help in averting stress.

Although you cannot stop thinking, you can learn to observe (and therefore stand apart from) how your life principle leads to the avoidance rather than the acceptance of fear. You can substitute positive thoughts for negative ones, but the ultimate mastery comes when you can remain focused on meaningful objectives and are not caught up with concerns about winning and losing or concerns about failure or rejection.

You do not need to feel compelled to retreat at the first sign of discomfort or distress. You can learn to let negative thoughts pass so as not to get stuck in excessive thoughts of pride over winning or disappointment over losing. You can learn to ride these emotions out until you are in a calm space and can manage your risk by the actions you take in the present.

Case Study on Using Consciousness to Overcome Fear

Because you've been sensitized by your past experiences, you give special meaning to specific events and your reactions to them. This meaning frightens you. You believe that you shouldn't be frightened because this emotion is incompatible with your image of self-control, and you view it as a precursor to losing control. So, instead of dealing with an event as an event or your rapid heartbeat as a physiological response to an event, you view such experiences against a backdrop or value system that puts a high premium on being symptom-free. Therefore, you judge your symptoms critically, getting further upset about the event as well as your reactions to it.

Risk taking requires constant consciousness. Therefore, one of the techniques I recommend to traders is to keep track of their trades so that they can measure today's performance against the backdrop of the last several weeks. This tracking serves several purposes. It reminds the trader of her objectives when she is putting trades on, and it keeps raising the level of her consciousness about what her targets are and how to meet them.

For example, I taught one trader named Sean to time his responses with a stopwatch and keep notes about his experiences in a journal. By doing this he learned that the anxiety was time-limited and that it would soon pass. He regularly found that the anxiety lasted a much shorter time each time he experienced it. He also found that he could adjust his level of anxiety by reducing the size of his positions. Doing so enabled him to hold his positions longer and then gradually scale up the size as the positions worked in his favor.

Another trader named Grant started keeping a diary at the end of June 2000. Within two weeks he was able to increase his capital usage from about $10 million per day to $18 million. On Wednesday of the first week of July, the day after July 4th, he made close to $500,000, a recent record for him. His Sharpe ratio and win/loss ratio was so good that there was no reason that he couldn't keep increasing his capital usage and profitability.

By writing things down, you cannot hide from the truth. Keeping a record of your emotions and your trades, very much like keeping a food diary, reminds you of the size you are taking and how much farther you have to go to meet your targets.

Owning Your Responses

When you deny your responses instead of owning them, the stress response tends to increase rather than decrease. As the tension escalates, you set yourself up to experience an uncontrollable and exaggerated panic response. Rather than recognize and heed your body's signals by slowing down, resting, relaxing, and regrouping so that you can accurately assess and handle the reality before you, you are caught between the escalation of symptoms that you cannot deny and your need to stay in control. The more panicky you feel, the less willing you are to let go and allow yourself to experience the feelings. Finally, when the controls break down, you experience full-blown panic characterized by a pounding heart, shortness of breath, a sense of imminent doom, sweating, numbness, tingling, trouble swallowing, racing thoughts and a sense of imminent death or that you are going insane.

Interestingly, there are many who regularly seek out experiences that trigger the same basic adrenaline reaction caused by panic. Daredevils, parachutists, and others who engage in thrill-seeking sports and adventures do so in part because of the adrenaline rush triggered by these experiences. Adrenaline is the natural response to both real and artificial dangers as well as to symbolic dangers. Indeed, the adrenaline response is quite understandably associated with a feeling of intense liveliness, and many people who seek out such experiences often encounter a diminution of vitality when the adrenaline excitement subsides.

The adrenaline response in smaller doses also accompanies less dangerous sports like jogging or ordinary, everyday activities in which we challenge ourselves or accomplish our objectives. Generally, most of us actually enjoy the feelings associated with the positive stress of challenge and novelty. By the same token, although we don't enjoy the experience of negative stresses (such as divorce, illness, or loss of a job), most of us still ride out the discomfort and distress associated with these experiences. So, what's the difference? Why do we enjoy and even tolerate the stress of some situations and allow stressful emotions to control us in others?

Again, a pervasive need in all human beings (which is often the source of panic and anxiety) is to be in control. Much of our early socialization training has to do with learning to control ourselves and to behave properly. This makes sense. It enables people to gain mastery over their emotions and behavior and to learn proper habits of thought and conduct which enable them to function effectively in their particular society. But, often the lessons are learned too well, and these habit patterns begin to control and dominate behavior and limit self-expression.

Controlling mechanisms often lead to the denial of feelings and the minimization of the body's natural responses to stress. Powered by a need to look good, you may deny your vulnerability and keep pushing yourself when you would be well advised to slow down and admit to your distress. I see this most often in panic patients with accompanying depression. These individuals are especially prone to minimize their depressive symptoms or try to cover them up. They fight to save face or to appear stronger than they are, rather than admit to the feelings, own them, and ride them out.

"All my life I've tried to be in control, to be the master of my emotions and the world around me," said one trader. "I've continually manipulated people so they would conform to my expectations. I'm afraid to face up to the fact that I'm a coward, and I keep putting up this strong, dominating front so I won't get hurt."

This need to control and to manage your feelings often leads to the repression of feelings, which then percolate below the surface as your hidden or secret self, covered by an outer layer or social persona of being calm, cool, and collected. The great fear is that these emotions will be revealed, defeating the public image you have learned to display. For example, Ric won't allow himself to show any weakness and will not ever cry, no matter how sad he feels. "I don't want to appear weak," he said. "I learned as a child that men don't cry."

You too may have learned your lessons so well that you cannot comfortably abide the surfacing of any kind of emotion. The slightest hint that emotionality is surfacing generates anxiety and panic, particularly because you have not learned to accept the normalcy of your emotions and bodily sensations.

These feelings can become so terrifying that it becomes impossible or near impossible for you to relax into the feeling, to allow the waves of adrenaline to course naturally through your body and produce a wonderful state of excitement or euphoria. In fact, rather than notice the feelings and go with the flow, you are likely to attribute the problem to specific situations that you assiduously learn to avoid. This leads to a pattern of avoidance or phobia which is itself a problem.

You may try to avoid whatever stimuli you believe caused the panicky feelings. Of course, avoidance may not seem like a bad idea at the time. You are likely to believe that you are smart to avoid triggering situations that seem to be capable of producing panic. Rarely do you realize that you are establishing a routine that may be even more limiting than the anxiety symptoms themselves.

The goal, then, is to discover the feelings you are avoiding are inevitable and natural accompaniments to creating your life in the here and now in terms of your creative vision. Instead of trying to eliminate anxiety or get to an anxiety-free state of nirvana, you need to own your responses and learn to cope more effectively with anxiety so that you can begin to trade in terms of your own interests and abilities.

Practical Steps

The more you can notice your emotions and let them pass, the better you will be able to see that you are not your thoughts or your feelings. You are a source of power in the universe and can create possibility in your life irrespective of your thoughts, feelings, or circumstances. Notice your emotions and let them pass. Then, you will see how your experiences are simply another part of life and your trading experience.

Here I've outlined one useful practice that may help you learn to stand outside your experience and observe your feelings and your thoughts without putting any special interpretation on them.

- Consider the situation/event that you find problematic. *For example, you failed to get out of a losing trade quickly enough and lost X amount of dollars.*
- On a piece of paper, write down all the facts of the situation that you find frightening and would like to change. *You find it frightening that you held on too long and want to learn how to get out of your losers faster.*
- Now write down the typical emotional reaction and bodily sensations you experience in relationship to the situation. *You were afraid. Your hands were sweaty. You were trembling. Your head hurt. You felt as if you were going to pass out.*
- Write down what the situation means to you. What is your interpretation of it? What do you think will happen? *You are afraid that you will lose all your money, be fired, or embarrass yourself.*

- Consider how much your perspective on the situation is a long-standing one, a point of view that you developed long before the present situation became a problem. You think *"Everything always turns out bad." "I have no real control over the outcome of my trades anyway."* How much does this fixed, historically based perspective color the facts so that you don't see reality as it is but through the lens of this principle?
- Create a new principle or interpretation of the facts so that you can separate the problem (based on your perception) from the facts. *You decide that you do have control over your life and your trading decisions. You can make a difference next time.*
- Notice what the facts look like when you view them through the perspective of possibility rather than the perspective of imminent doom. *You decide that you want to learn from this experience—learn how you can get out of your losers faster.*

When you shift your frame of reference to a new perspective, you begin to interpret events and bodily responses differently and are freed from the trap of your history and past anxieties. Events are neutral. It is your interpretation that makes an event problematic. Once you learn this distinction, you can be freed from many of the thoughts that now frighten you.

Case Study on Escalating Emotions

This case study illustrates the way in which tension and anxiety can escalate into panic under stressful circumstances.

Derek was facing enormous pressure at work from a falling market. In addition, his wife, increasingly on the attack and criticizing him for everything, was giving him no support. His secretary left. His father got sick.

"All of a sudden I felt like I was trapped," he said. "The more frightened I became, the more I tried to handle everything. I was running scared. I knew I was handling a lot, but I believed that I should be able to handle everything. I lost my appetite. I suffered from headaches. I became inde-cisive on the job. I started asking everyone for advice and noticed that I was becoming more and more suggestible and afraid to trust my own judg-ment. I wanted to run away, but to do so would have been cowardly and an admission of defeat. I had been raised never to give up.

"I kept going until one day I totally panicked and went into a state of paralysis. It started with some ordinary tension. Then my heart rate began to speed up. I found I was getting short of breath. All along I had a feeling that something terrible was about to happen as if I was going to die or ex-plode or go crazy.

"I tried to swallow and was unable to do so. Now, I thought I was really in trouble. Then I noticed my hands and feet were beginning to tingle and grow numb, like a pins and needles sensation. I could see no way out. This was the end. I was going to die."

Derek's emotions, though frightening, were actually normal and not unique to him. He needed to go with the flow and admit his reactions in-stead of trying harder and harder to take things on while covering up his re-sponses. Instead, his reactions kept him locked in a vicious circle. If he had known what was happening to him, if he understood the bodily and emo-tional responses of stress, he could have relaxed and allowed the re-sponses to pass and then gone about his business. Instead, he perceived the events of his trading from the perspective of fear and anxiety. He ex-perienced an overpowering feeling of impending doom. This made him more frightened and more desperate. He began to compulsively do more and more until he was totally overwhelmed with panic and the conviction that he was going to die. Eventually, Derek collapsed in a state of total paralysis—shaking like a leaf.

I spent some time with Derek trying to help him understand the source of his panic and teaching him relaxation techniques so that he could ride out tense moments in the market when such feelings of panic were being triggered. As with other traders, I also encouraged him to time his re-sponses and keep a notebook of his feelings so that he could gain per-spective about his experiences. Gradually over time, he took control of the experience so that he was no longer creating a vicious circle of ever-increasing anxiety in the face of the tension, and after several weeks he was able to report considerable success.

"What I realize now," he said, "is that my responses to stress are uni-versal responses shared by all human beings. They don't mean something disastrous is going to happen. What I see is that these responses color reality so that when I am in a stressed-out state I don't see reality as it is, but as the projection of my own fears. If I can only let these feelings pass without reacting to them, I will once again be able to cope. The more I can accept my bodily responses and automatic thoughts and not assign any special meaning to them or see them as who I am, the more powerful and effective I can be in designing my life."

Derek's experiences and observations illustrate how crucial it is to objectify emotional responses to situations so that your interpretation of stressful situations and emotional responses do not escalate and create more of a problem than necessary. Once this skill is learned in one situation it can be applied in a variety of other situations, facilitating the capacity to cope and stay on target with increasing skill and flexibility.

Dealing with Anger

The changes in the body that accompany anger resemble those of fear and anxiety. They are the typical manifestations of increased adrenaline. In fact, the only difference between anger, anxiety, and excitement is in the interpretation of the physical experience—how you react to the experience. Sometimes you may feel frustrated at your inability to act or to just be angry. You may become annoyed with yourself because of your inclination to avoid situations. Therefore, it is useful to consider what is frustrating you and how you can deal with it so that tension doesn't build, leaving you preoccupied with thoughts of revenge. It's also useful to consider how much resentment you are still holding from the past. Consider how much energy goes into covering up these feelings or acting in such a way as to keep others from knowing what you are feeling.

The problem with pent-up anger is that it is invariably misplaced and exaggerated when it is expressed. Something happened a long time ago that you never resolved. Now, you carry a tendency to keep generating anger and resentment by holding back. In addition, you have a marked inability to express these feelings specifically. So, when someone steps on your toes or makes unreasonable demands of you, you go along out of habit rather than being clear about what it is you want. Then the anger builds up again. When it is expressed, it explodes and generalizes to a variety of issues rather than to those specifically at hand. This leads to an escalation of conflict and drastic actions rather than the resolution of issues.

Once you can get in touch with and express your repressed anger in appropriate ways, without fear of retaliation or disapproval, you will no longer need to act in terms of other people's expectations. In fact, once you allow yourself to verbalize the fact that you are feeling angry, you will discover an enormous freedom to be and a liberation from the need to act with a cover-up of earlier experienced emotions that have kept anxiety, panic, and depression alive.

In effect, once you learn to experience your anger as well as other feelings, you will be less afraid and less in need of having to suppress your responses. You will gain a greater capacity to express your feelings directly without concerns about losing control.

Practical Steps

In order to deal with your anger, it is useful to be clear about what you want, what you are willing to do, and what you are not willing to do rather than go along grudgingly. When something does get you angry, you are well advised to express your dissatisfaction in words, letting others know what doesn't work for you rather than exploding. Getting angry doesn't necessarily mean screaming. While that can sometimes be cathartic in the context of a therapeutic workshop or even in the privacy of your own home, it is often sufficient to clearly state: "I am angry about that," or "I am very annoyed or irritated," or "I feel a lot of tension and internal agitation." The key is sharing your feelings and not stifling them. This takes practice. The following exercise may help get you started.

- As a first step in handling your anger, make a list of past events that frustrated you.
- Next make a list for current events. Select some people with whom you are now angry, and write them down.
- Either continue in writing or find someone willing to listen to you express your frustration, resentment, and anger. Try to be as clear as possible about what you are angry about, what your view is, and what you want. You may find some of this uncomfortable because it is sometimes easier to bottle the feelings and then explode. But this reaction is a way of not taking responsibility for the feelings, because explosions are often attributed to "a temper."
- This next step may be a novel one for you. Forgive each and every one of the people on your list. Remember, forgiveness is something you choose. It is not a natural reaction but a positive step that you take in moving on with your life.
- Next, try to consider the details of a specific experience involving each person. What happened? What else happened? What was your interpretation of the experience? Had you ever made such an interpretation before? Is it possible that your prior experiences had so conditioned you that you anticipated what would happen and were dominated by your preconceptions?
- Look at the event through another perspective. Is there something you can now see in the other person that you couldn't see before? Can you consider why they may have been reacting the way they were? Can you see that it is possible to let go of your own resentment of others and view things from a new perspective?

When you hold on to anger and self-justification, you keep yourself separate and apart from others. You suppress the expression of creativity, and you are able to justify your failure. Resentment blocks the fulfillment of your vision and the capacity to support others and to seek their support for yourself. It uses up energy and keeps you locked in a vicious circle. Anger toward your symptoms and anger about your circumstances further locks you in and keeps you from realizing your potential. Once you understand how invested you are in your anger, how much it represents an attitude or posture and that there is not, as you may imagine, a reservoir of anger that must be contained or discharged, you can devise various ways to behave independently of it.

Case Study on Trading Without Regard to Emotion

This case study is a dialogue with a new trader, Alan, and revolves around the kinds of issues I focus on in the initial interview with a trader.

Once you learn to make money and learn to observe your own responses to the market so that you can control your emotional reactivity, you can readily expand the size of your portfolio. This discussion, therefore, points to the importance of understanding the emotional factors in trading so that you can monitor your own responses to your trading and learn to maintain objectivity in the face of losses and successes.

Alan: I panicked on the opening today. There was a catalyst last night. I came in long. There was a speech from the CEO about the problems in a company I was buying. I felt that he wasn't going to shoot himself in the foot and that he would make it as rosy as possible and that we might get a bounce off that. He didn't do that, and it was down this morning. It was heavy on the opening. I waited. At 10:00 it was still heavy. I have seen 25 percent moves in the sector. The group was down four points. My group is getting more volatile as time goes on. I felt uncomfortable being long. I got out. Five minutes away from the bottom, it rallied two points. Where I sold these things, they sold. At the time it looked like it might keep going down.

Kiev: This is good risk management. You want to keep your losses down.

A: I wanted to stop myself out on a $25,000 loss per day too.

K: In the long run, that is more valuable than not. That it went up, then it was time to get back in.

A: I haven't done that. I keep beating myself about missing the trade.

K: Are you inclined to second guess yourself?

A: I do.

K: Notice that you do it, and realize that it won't help.

A: There are times when you can take some pain, and instead of cashing out, buy a little more.

K: You ought to have a general rule that if it goes down a certain percentage, you will get out just to keep your losses down. It could have kept going down, and it could have been worse.

A: I need to learn that.

K: Unless you really knew something, that it was going down for erroneous reasons and should have held on or bought more.

A: I didn't.

K: You have to recognize that getting out of a dropping stock is a good risk management move. If it goes up, you have to decide whether to play it or not, but you can't flagellate yourself for getting out of the stock before it moves up. There are two separate moves here, the defensive risk management one and the decision to play it on the bounce. You may want to consider why you were reluctant to get in. You may still have been thinking about why you hadn't stayed in, but it is important to note that the market keeps giving you opportunities to respond to new data sets and new perspectives. It is a dynamic process, and you have to be prepared to keep adapting to the changes in the tape.

A: I can't paralyze myself because it is bouncing. I have to get in motion and buy some stock. Stay in motion. If I don't, I miss 5 percent moves and start flagellating myself. It is a new gig for me.

K: If you do well there is another set of challenges. You are always reacting to something that is coloring the way you respond to the next opportunity. Besides fear, another problem is how you respond to success. If you didn't get out and the thing reversed and went up, you might have felt like a hero when in fact you were really lucky. Then you may do some stupid things. You want to track your responses so you know how you respond and can correct for emotional responses, which are not good strategically. You have to learn more about yourself in this area so that you can develop a trading style that corrects for your bad habits and builds on your strengths and natural proclivities. You can't let your feelings interfere with your trading. The target forces you to increase your size commensurate with your goals and to watch your losses.

Alan's experience underscores the importance of trading on the basis of what you *know* rather than on how you *feel*. His description of his own responses suggests that he has to learn how to manage his trades when he is euphoric and tending to overestimate his chances. Not uncommonly this tendency toward overconfidence is coupled with a tendency to beat himself when he is wrong. He has to learn to observe these tendencies and then try to steer a clear pathway between these emotional extremes.

Remember, your own observations of your responses will be more critical for your ultimate success than how much money you make. What separates one trader from another is self-awareness and good discipline and good habits developed early on in his or her trading career. Once you own your responses and understand how to make money, you can multiply your results by getting bigger. You want to learn how to track your emotions so that you can use self-awareness in your trading.

Maintaining Your Concentration

Few things in life happen by chance. Most things happen because of a persistent and continuous effort made by a motivated individual who takes responsibility for selecting relevant goals and doing what is necessary to accomplish them. You must be able to focus only on what is before you and to notice, but not be influenced by, the automatic self-doubting, self-destructive, and self-sabotaging thoughts that so often are generated in the face of stress and that so often influence your outcome as a goal is approached.

Concentration links discipline, desire, motivation, and satisfaction to achievement and may be the single most important integrating quality in any sort of achievement. Concentration resembles a meditative state where you can experience the split second, when no external world exists for you save for the activity in which you are absorbed. In this state there is, according to St. John of the Cross, an "annihilation of memory." Augustine Poulain describes this state as a "mysterious darkness wherein is contained the limitless Good, a void, other than solitude."

When you are totally concentrated, you experience a similar detachment from externals, a reduced dependency on images, objects, and the consequences of events. This state has value in any goal-directed activity because it focuses on what can be controlled—namely, your efforts.

When you concentrate, you assert yourself when necessary and are neither inhibited, resentful, nor given to explosions of hostility. You maintain a state of calm in the midst of chaos and do not become frozen in your efforts to control your emotions nor allow them to overwhelm you. Concentration enables you to face reality without shrinking from it and without letting self-doubt intrude on your functioning. It enables you to maintain your focus of attention and relaxation in the midst of pressure without becoming distracted or too self-absorbed.

If you are in a particular situation, you have to ask yourself what is it you are doing that is creating the result. What must you do to change the world you have created? On what must you focus your attention? Invariably the answer is to get back to concentrating on tasks before you that are consistent with your vision.

Handling Your Emotions

Concentrated action means focused efforts. It does not require impulsive actions done without preparation nor perfectionist caution that results in avoidance of your goals. When you concentrate, you examine the situation carefully before acting but don't get so caught up in details as to be unable to act.

By focusing on the intricacies of the activity, you can perceive more accurately what is going on around you so that you can establish a more realistic strategy for producing effective results. Focused on the details, it becomes easier to ride out discomfort, pain, and other negative feelings.

Concentration favors efforts that are tempered and gentle, slow and easy. Effortless movement in fluid drive is the key. Concentration enables you to achieve a harmonious state of functioning where mind and body, effort and object, are integrated and you are moving in a self-fulfilling way toward a meaningful objective.

Nowhere is concentration on the task at hand more important than in a tight situation where you are under pressure and are becoming preoccupied with feelings of inadequacy and fears of failure. Concentration enables you to keep plugging away, totally focused on the activity at hand. Remember, you are capable of a wide range of feelings and can choose to focus only on the useful ones.

You can also improve your concentration by learning to control a number of factors. Obviously, a calm mind and body facilitates concentration. You can also improve concentration by focusing on one mental image at a time. Focusing on specific tasks can help you to minimize the distracting effects of intrusive thoughts and external stimuli, much as focusing on a mantra provides a symbolic focus for concentrating energy in yoga. Concentration is also made easier by finding something about an activity that is interesting and captures your attention so that it can be done effortlessly and with an empty mind, free of distracting, egotistical considerations.

In continuous activities it is useful to look for a break in the action, such as a pause between sentences or paragraphs in a speech or a pause between strokes (as in golf and tennis) where you can catch your breath and think a little bit further ahead. In these instances, it is useful to focus on some aspect of the action that will enable you to impart more energy to it, rather than thinking in general about how you are going to do it or what you are going to do.

Paradoxically, excessive efforts to concentrate or focus can also lead you to focus too much on a single object so that you lose awareness of the larger context in which an activity occurs. You can avoid this result by learning to shift back and forth from the specific item to the general background or context in which you are acting. In this way you will not become so absorbed by the specific that you become distracted and lose touch with the realities around you.

Additionally, you can practice shifting your concentration from a narrow to a wider focus, for example, focusing on this word, to focusing on the room you are sitting in, and then back from a wider to a narrow focus. This exercise will teach you to sustain concentration on a single, narrow set of objects or activities for an extended period of time and help you to stop shifting unconsciously from one object to another. It is also useful to practice shifting back and forth from internal thoughts and sensations to external sensations and events. The more you do this, the more you will recognize your own best concentration skills.

Concentrating is very much like flying an airplane or steering a car. To turn left in a small plane you need only concentrate your thoughts on turning left, and you will gradually shift the steering wheel to the left. Similarly in a car, you are always making slight adjustments with the wheel—not drastic or rapid movements—to steer around a curve or to make a left turn.

When you trust your instincts, you are able to become one with the activity. You make small adjustments instinctively but spend little time thinking about how you look or what the outcome will be. The same applies to trading in a risk-controlled way. You take your mind along for the ride. You allow yourself to be with the experience and try not to control it. When you can do this, you will be more fully engaged in the moment and therefore trading at the maximum.

Concentration enables you to determine how much preparation is necessary for particular situations and fosters confidence in your abilities. It minimizes fear of competition and shifts your concerns from beating someone else to doing the best you can do. It reduces your need to keep proving yourself or changing your game plan in response to every new circumstance. It allows you to persevere in the face of obstacles, changes, and complications that trigger fear and un- certainty. At the same time, it does not keep you so inflexible as to be *unable* to adjust to changing circumstances when a new strategy is in order. This is particularly important when you have to learn new ways of trading after the development of new skills and perspectives changes the way you approach other aspects of your trading.

Case Study on Redefining Your Focus

One long-term values portfolio manager, Danny, spent considerable time learning how to short stocks while keeping his losses to a minimum. Even- tually he became so risk averse and good at preserving capital that he began to take his profits too soon. Clearly, he had learned the lessons of cutting losses too well and had to redefine his focus so that he could ride out the impulse to take his profits too soon and thereby maximize his prof- itability. Talking about one stock he had traded, he noted:

"This should be a 300,000 share position instead of a 60,000 share po- sition. It's $20\frac{1}{2}$. It was at 23. I got short before earnings because I believed they were going to be bad. The stock didn't go down much. So I covered. Looking at a longer time frame, it was 28 before earnings, and now it's 20. That's a 40 percent return on the short side. I shorted at 24, 25. I know it is a bad story. I am not as big as I should be because I keep covering every time it goes down two points. That's not how I can make bigger profits. I am afraid it will go back up, and I will lose my profits. It didn't go down for three or four days. I started to think I wasn't right. I came very close to buying it back today. Now I am waiting for it to play out instead of getting bigger."

The stock was starting to go back up, but nothing had changed. The fundamentals were still terrible, but the market activity kept driving this and other stocks up because of short-term market sentiment or psychology. Danny wanted to play that but didn't want to get hurt. The ultimate challenge of trading is to catch the right trend at the right time, even though the long-term story may be bad (as in the case of shorts) or good (in the case of longs.)

Danny was perturbed about his inaction and asked me: "The stock is going down. My instinct is to cover. Are you saying that now is the time to short more?"

"The master trader will do that," I replied. " You have to be able to read the price action and the amount of activity in the stock. Is it liquid?"

"It trades 10 million a day, but I am all caught up in being angry with myself because I know I should be bigger here," he answered.

This opportunity allowed me to discuss with him the importance of letting go of anger so that he could concentrate on the trade. I told him to stop focusing on his mind-set. Danny needed to ask himself about the opportunity here. He had a valuable lesson to learn—don't get invested in emotions.

"Don't beat yourself so that you can unconsciously praise yourself for recognizing that you have done something wrong," I said. "This behavior may be something you learned as a child to demonstrate to your parents that you were learning right from wrong, but often adults use it as a way of gaining internal praise for expressing guilt over having done something wrong. It has little place on the trading floor and is totally irrelevant to your profitability. Instead, determine the next move."

Once you tell someone you are distressed or angry about your trading, there is an unconscious need to keep feeling that way, especially if they come back and ask about your distress. Again, it is better to notice those feelings and then let them pass. You don't want to let this demon become an entity. You want to disconnect it from your trading.

When you concentrate, you are not dominated by your impulsiveness or by your inhibitions, self-criticism, and fault-finding principles. You can tune out these conflicting inner demands and realistically focus on the reality before you. You can accept the fact that the world isn't fair. You can let go of the belief that you don't deserve to succeed, or that you must succeed. Concentration will give you the capacity to postpone short-term gratification for long-term benefits, to resist the inclination to overreact to pressure, and to maintain your focus on the critical steps needed to reach your goals.

Concentration enables you to keep giving your all, even when it appears that you are not going to achieve the objectives you have set. It enables you to produce maximum performance rather than to focus simply on winning. It is what enables you to keep doggedly working at winning even when you are losing.

When you concentrate, you are more relaxed, alert, and receptive to what is going on in the world and therefore are better able to respond to the events around you. New bits of data are seen as if for the first time, and many bits of information and stimuli ordinarily ignored can be incorporated into your actions to enhance performance.

Practical Steps

Most people use up much energy trying to acquire objects or symbols of success that will give them the appearance of adequacy or a feeling of completeness. Learning to maintain concentration involves accepting your vulnerability and the need to distinguish between your basic humanity and your interpretation of it. When you have lost your concentration and are in some kind of breakdown, it is useful to see what is stopping you. Consider the following questions:

- What are the recurring issues that keep you from moving forward in your trading?

- What are you afraid of?
- What is the life principle that gets in the way of action?
- What are you afraid will happen that keeps you from staying on track?
- How does your personal history hold you back in your efforts to accomplish things?
- How do your recurrent self-doubts limit possibility?
- Were you unwilling to commit to the results as if there were no alternatives?
- Have you wittingly or unwittingly allowed failure to occur by not being clear about your objectives?
- Have you failed to focus attention on critical issues or not functioned like your word mattered no matter what?
- Have you taken on too many details or not been tough-minded in making certain that your objectives were realized?
- Did you fail to make the plan of action clear to others or establish a structure of communication with your teammates with intention, instruction, and discipline to ensure that the trade was set in motion?
- Have you failed to take responsibility for the result from the start and allowed others to take it on and not achieve it because of their own self-doubt?

Most traders take themselves out of the game by reacting to their emotions and their emotional interpretation of events rather than sticking to their strategy based on their commitment to their vision. You can do it differently.

You will make the most progress if you take responsibility for the problems you are creating. You must be in an open, ready, and alert state of mind, in which you let go of extraneous images of success, failure, resentment, competition, and envy which can distract you from your target. You must be totally concentrated, with your attention focused on the steps necessary for expressing your vision.

Handling Your Emotions

You can learn to ride out the whole range of mixed feelings from anxiety to euphoria. You can learn to make observations and track your feelings to give free reign to the desire for success and spontaneity that characterizes maximum performance.

Although negative, fearful thoughts are not going to stop, you can develop the ability to stand outside yourself and observe such thoughts so you can function in the world without excessive consciousness, self-criticism, or a concern for the opinions of those around you.

Notice your feelings. Be with them, own them, but stop trying to separate yourself from them. When you struggle to separate from yourself, the market looks more frightening and unpredictable. If you can accept yourself and your fears, your fears will soon pass.

CHAPTER FOUR

LEARNING TO
LET GO

I am always looking for metaphors from the world of sports to help explain the subtleties of trading. Skiing is one of the best metaphors, because the ultimate challenge is to master the art of sliding gracefully down the mountain. To accomplish this you must let go of control at the same time as you are balancing the out-of-control act of sliding. The natural tendency of most beginning skiers is to try to control the sliding. But when they do that, they tend to fall. As you master skiing you learn to control the out-of-control feeling associated with sliding by progressively learning more and more skills. With more maneuverability you can allow for more free fall and allow gravity and the sliding to take over. To experience the exhilaration and mastery of skiing, you have to let go of the urge to control the slide or the holding on, which generally leads you to fall.

Trading is very much like skiing. Letting go of the controls, participating in the process, and accepting a little bit more of the phenomena of the trade itself are all important steps in learning to take more risk. As the trade is going right, you must learn to relax, to go with the flow of the trade and be able to hold your positions longer or get bigger instead of getting out and taking your profits.

. The better traders take the risk, rather than micromanage it, take small profits, and lose big pieces of the upside. Trust your instinct. Go with the flow, where you allow yourself to experience the phenomenon as it is happening. Listening to the market is like looking for the sweet spot in tennis. Watch the ball, not anything else. Don't think of the last shot. Don't watch the stands. Focus on what is in front of you and swing.

To the extent that you can let go and just participate in the experience, you are likely to succeed. Many traders start to get a trade right, where it is making money, where something that they have bought is moving upward. Then instead of going with that, and getting more data to support their efforts to get bigger in the position, they get scared and take their profits.

Auto racing also offers another metaphor for trading. Gary, a successful portfolio manager, first learned to manage risk while racing autos and finds great similarities between trading and auto racing.

"The challenge of racing, like trading, is to allow yourself to go outside the comfort zone," he said. "When racing a car, you make a decision early in a turn and then relax, let go of control, and go along for the ride. By the time you get to the turn, you will know whether your decision was the right one. Once you are initiated in a turn and are committed, you can't alter your line. The car is at the limits of adhesion. If that decision was wrong, you can't change the path of the car. If you are not on the right circumference, you can't change your path before it is too late. You will have an accident if you made the wrong decision early on. But you have to take that risk in order to win.

"There comes a point in both racing and trading where you have to let go of control. The trick is to get to the point where you make good decisions before you reach the point beyond your control. If you are good at making the initial decision, then you will do well. It can also be compared to ski jumping. You are really going fast before you go off a jump, and you have to be properly positioned. Once you are in the air, you cannot change your trajectory. In trading, you have to learn to make wise decisions and then to let go. That is the equivalent of letting go in racing.

"When I started racing, I was going 100 miles per hour. Now I can do 160 miles an hour. Letting go is similar. Theoretically you can be an Indy driver if you keep letting go and keep honing your skills. The same thing is true in trading because the downside gets greater and greater, and you need to be able to tolerate that better. You have to learn how to crash in racing and how to lose in trading. You have to lose some money, let go, and get ready to make money again tomorrow. Getting to the next level involves psychology."

While learning to let go in a controlled way seems to be critical for mastery in trading, as in other high-risk activities, it is more common to encounter a variety of defensive responses triggered by the uncertainty of the marketplace and which color the way traders respond to the markets. In fact, no amount of rational argument may be enough to convince you that you can do it—that you can let go and learn to function with this seeming lack of control. Rather than acknowledge your feelings and ask for help or learn new skills to master the situation, you may be inclined to deny your discomfort and attempt to handle things in old familiar ways. In your attempts to avoid anxiety, you may actually develop a number of self-destructive behaviors.

Currently, your trading may be affected by a variety of psychological defenses. Habits, long-standing beliefs, emotional reactions, and personality predispositions influence how you see opportunities, how you make decisions, how you handle time and money, and how you are able to postpone gratification in the present for a future outcome. These factors manifest themselves in a range of maladaptive behaviors from perfectionism to paralysis to hoarding.

In this chapter, I examine some of these behaviors and their psychological underpinnings. Once you begin to recognize your responses for what they are, you will be better able to handle the uncertainties of risk taking in your trading.

Battling Perfectionism

"If I can't do well, I don't want to do it all." I'm sure you have heard this statement before. Perhaps you have even said it yourself. This kind of statement reflects a philosophy of trading centered around perfectionism. Although perfectionists want everything to be just right, their unrealistic expectations actually lead to a myriad of problems and can stifle their trading success.

For example, the self-centered nature of perfectionism often shows itself as an inclination to obsess about potential problems as well as the attitudes, responses, and anticipated criticism of others. Underlying this obsession is a basic motivation to avoid risks while appearing to be doing the right thing. Perfectionists are cautious, reluctant, and too concerned about being exposed.

Often these traders want to wait for everything to be "perfect" before they pull the trigger. Fearful of entering the realm of uncertainty, they romanticize the past and forget that they were once willing to take risks.

Andrew, for example, is afraid to pull the trigger and thinks in terms of "shoulda, woulda, couldas" and other rationalizations for missing trades or taking positions that in retrospect proved to be too small. In one trade, he shorted only 15,000 shares of a major credit card company when it gapped up. He kicked himself afterward when the stock went down. The same was true with a European telecom company which (after it spun off a subsidiary) went from 195 to 155. He knew there was a trade there, but he was reluctant to take it. He is also disinclined to take the initiative in developing a specific portfolio and is waiting for his manager's endorsement as opposed to getting the endorsement by doing it.

"I get antsy. I don't have a gestalt. I don't have a context," he said.

Again, this reluctance is reflective of his fear of risk taking and his fear of making decisions, lest he be wrong.

For some traders, perfectionism is characterized by a tendency to get bogged down in too many details and too much analysis. In the face of ambiguity they cannot act.

Case Study on Overcoming Perfectionism

Eric, an analyst who started trading in the volatile bear market in the first part of 2001, wanted to gather as much data in his sector as possible even though this amount was overwhelming. Given his analytic propensity he was having a hard time tuning out a lot of the stuff going on around him.

As Eric said: "If I hear a conversation in the room about anything related to my sector or my companies, I am going to listen. I am definitely overloaded with ideas, and it is creating decision distortion for me. I am moving, but the overload is creating problems for me, and I have little ability to tune out any additional incremental data, even though I probably don't need all of it to be successful. I am being distracted by all this data."

Being selective about ideas is a problem for someone who is introspective and attracted to them. Eric is attracted to data for its own sake and then must sift through more and more to get to tradable or actionable ideas. One solution may be to find a room off the desk where he can think. But in reality, he needs to learn to put on blinders. He has to learn to walk away from conversations. However, this is very difficult for perfectionists to do because of their propensity for being polite.

Eric: Can I tell these guys to leave me alone when I sense we are getting into an area that is messing me up? I don't want to listen to 10 minutes of data about things I already know.

Kiev: Can't you walk away?

E: It's kind of rude.

K: You are in a Darwinian trading environment. For this environment to work, you have to excuse yourself from these conversations and focus on your work. Can you imagine what your passivity is doing to your psyche? You are obviously frustrating yourself and are thinking, 'Why did I listen?' And for 10 minutes you are taken out of your game.

Eric's insatiable need for more data, coupled with a need to be polite, has led him to situations where he is paralyzed by too much input with little ability to separate himself from the situation. He wants more details because he feels he never has enough, and at the same time he cannot bring himself to be more self-protective because he is concerned about the image that he presents. So, he finds himself continually boxed into non-productive situations.

Practical Steps

Many perfectionists need to get bigger to be able to reach their targets but are reluctant to do so because of the fear of making an error or of losing. They often wait to have all of the data available before taking a trade.

Do these battles remind you of your own? Consider the following questions to see if you are a perfectionist:

- Are you self–critical?
- Do you view your own efforts as insignificant or insufficient and allow the anticipated criticism of others to get you off your strategy?
- Do you find yourself caught up with a range of time-consuming activities that absorb energy and attention and distract you from taking responsibility for the full development of your trades?
- Do you characterize yourself as tentative or anxious?
- Are you easily scared out of trades when you are not sure of your assessment or the uniqueness of your perspective?

If you answered yes to most of the questions, then you too may be battling perfectionism. Your strength is your intellect, but your weakness is your investment in your intellect. You have to learn to be comfortable with uncertainty and not make risk taking harder than it needs to be.

A master trader has zero investment in the intellectual assessment of the facts or the analysis of the data. You may be invested in your models and the correctness of your intellectual product. He is not. He is interested in the profitability. You may be reluctant to get into a trade because you lack certainty or may get out of a trade before it fully develops. The master trader is willing to get in on a trade with less certainty and stay the course longer as the trade develops thereby maximizing the opportunities for profit. He realizes that he can learn a lot about how a stock is doing from the trading action itself.

Uncertainty and discomfort are inherent in the trading process, and over time even a perfectionist can learn to deal with them.

Case Study on Letting Go of Excessive Attachments

When perfectionists become overattached to their intellectual formulations, they often fail to take appropriate action when it is necessary. Manny had successfully traded crude oil and natural gas for more than 20 years. In the process of expanding his risk profile, he came face-to-face with a tendency to hold positions, despite his instinct to get out of them to reduce losses and maximize profitability. In April of 2001 he told me:

"You have to read the tape as well as the market. Sometimes you miss something in the underlying market fundamentals, and the tape tells you what to do to get ahead of the curve. If the tape isn't conforming to your analysis, it is either an opportunity or you have missed something. That is the hard part to do.

"In the past two weeks, I read the geopolitics of crude oil very well. I caught this last big down move that coincided with the equity market meltdown. The crude market went with it. The OPEC [Organization of Petroleum Exporting Countries] meeting came. The market went down, and I made money on that, but I only took off half the position at the bottom, even though I had a queasy feeling that something was happening and that I should get out. Then the oil guys started buying oil, and there was a huge short covering rally. The market ran against me, and I lost everything that I made in the initial trade because it went up twice as much as it fell. That was a lesson.

"The problem is I am always worried that I might get out too soon because I want to take the money off the table. If I don't like the way the tape is acting, and I am spooked, I have to accept that. I was not playing it safe by leaving risk on the table. Playing it safe was to take it all off. The real issue or obstacle was my unwillingness to admit that the play I had been thinking about was over. There is no glory left in it at that moment. I have to be dispassionate about my ideas. It took a lot of research to put on these positions. It was an unpopular position. I argued with a lot of people, putting on a short on the OPEC meeting. I was right and somehow I felt that it should last more than a half a day."

Like Manny, many perfectionists keep believing their story even when the tape says they are wrong. They need to be nimble and learn not to be trapped by their beliefs in a stock or commodity such that they fail to liquidate their positions and thus cut their losses in response to the market action.

If this example hits home with you, you may want to think about handling your own perfectionist attachments. You cannot become too attached to your side of the argument. You have to learn to hold two opposing ideas at the same time and still retain the ability to take action. You can do this by objectifying both perspectives and acting in terms of what is most profitable, because ultimately you can never recover what you lose when the position reverses itself. Manny and other traders who become enamored with their perspectives must realize that it is OK to second-guess their original theses when the data points in another direction, rather than not acting or compromising by holding on to half of the position so that they can ostensibly have it both ways.

"I said to myself, 'Well I did take off half the position,'" continued Manny, "but that's not good enough, because the markets just tear you apart for whatever you leave on. I am just coming to grips with this. I need to withdraw from the battlefield and do it proactively instead of leaving stuff behind."

It is possible to deploy your analytical skills in analyzing your trading behavior. You need to review current circumstances and the tape action as well as the original facts that led you to take the trade in the first place. You have to learn to let go of the perfectionist's need to always be right the first time. Remember, the goal is not 100 percent accuracy. It is to make more money than you lose.

Overcoming Mental Accounting

Mental accounting is the tendency to value some dollars more than others and to treat equivalent amounts of money differently, sometimes with detrimental results. Although we *know* (at least intellectually) that money is money and that it should all be treated with absolute value, we don't always treat it that way. An example of this is the way people treat a tax rebate as compared with how they treat their weekly salary. A tax rebate is often thought of as found money—money that can be blown or spent recklessly. The same can be said of gambling winnings.

The premise goes like this: To cope with the daunting task that we humans face in regard to comparing the cost of every short-term transaction we make against the size of every long-term goal we have, we put our money into mental accounts. These accounts are created according to their significance. Petty cash, for example, is not treated with the same regard as a mortgage payment. Although mental accounting can be beneficial in some instances (such as the protection of retirement savings), it can also be very costly insofar as you may be too quick to spend money that you undervalue, not astute enough to hold on to found money, and somewhat too cautious when you trade because you look at stock prices in relative dollar terms rather than in absolute terms.

For example, traders may value unexpected profits that have been earned from one trade as money that can be risked more easily in other trades. Suppose a trader has 10 names in a portfolio, and one of them is losing money. If the trader stays with that tenth position longer because the others are financing it, then he is trading in terms of mental accounting concepts. The truth is, if the other 9 trades were also down, the trader would kick out that tenth position without much consideration.

Case Study on Maximizing Profitability

Mental accounting is often seen in traders who fail to maximize the profitability of their successful trades. For example, Chris whom I mentioned in Chapter One, thinks the money he loses in losing trades is more valuable than the money that he makes in winning trades. He therefore holds positions as they are dropping, hoping to regain his loss or make more in instances where he believes the fundamentals warrant further investment. Moreover, he plans to buy more of the stock when it starts to move up. In actual fact, because he has suffered so much pain on the way down, he is relieved to get out of the stock when it finally turns and moves up—sometimes to less than where he got in. Instead of adding here or holding for the real profit, he gets out and therefore misses the upside move. He is gambling on the way down, and getting out on the way up when he should be willing to risk more at this point. Even when he scales in correctly (based on good fundamental analysis) as stocks are moving down and takes the pain, he gets out very rapidly after the stock has run up again and before it takes off—which is what he was waiting to do all along. Therefore, his basic objectives need to be to learn not to lose heart and to stay in the trades longer after he takes the pain.

This is an example of rationalizing losing positions in terms of fundamental analysis (sometimes justifiably so) and being too slow to add to positions when they are moving in the direction of your choice. The aversion to loss carries more significance than expanding the potential for profitability.

Learning to Let Go

Using profits to finance losses was a problem for one long-term, value-oriented hedge fund manager named Ron. His basic approach was to buy undervalued companies which would increase in value over a two to five year period and short overvalued companies which would deteriorate over time. This approach made perfect sense in terms of his analytical skills and yet he was less than satisfied with his profitability. A closer review of his efforts revealed that he was often more concerned about the correctness of his fundamental thesis than he was about his return on capital.

Ron often got caught in long and painful short squeezes when the stocks he was shorting kept going up far longer than he had ever anticipated, eroding the profits he had made in the long positions that had worked out and demoralizing him at the same time. In effect, he often was trapped by his belief in himself as a fundamental value player and therefore averse to make trading decisions related to profitability. He had no profit targets and was not maximizing profit opportunities. He focused only on his expectations that undervalued companies would increase in value over time while overvalued companies would deteriorate over time. Additionally he was in many illiquid, old economy stocks which were cheaper to buy and hold for the long haul.

Through the lens of profitability we considered whether it made more sense to find liquid bigger cap names in the tech sector or in more active sectors where he could make more money. Through the same lens we also considered the fact that he was not inclined to think of cutting his losses or his positions when the catalysts were no longer available or when the story had changed; nor was he inclined to get bigger when things were working.

A review of his positions revealed that his short ideas were not as well developed as his long ideas. He thought of shorts as short-term bets but had not applied his fundamental analysis to them. He was in shorts in which he had little conviction about the negative story. In the past he had shorted a lot of tech too early when it still went up too high. He got out of tech early and lost a lot of money and was reluctant to get back in later on when his thesis was beginning to work.

As a result of our discussions he began to tighten up his approach to trading. Since he realized that his biggest profit came from his biggest bets with the most conviction, he began to get out of weak stocks that weren't rallying with the market. He also stopped looking for price inefficiencies in terms of illiquidity and began to find price inefficiencies in more liquid stocks that could rally.

He began cutting positions that weren't working to preserve capital and stopped holding on to things simply because he believed in the long-term value of the stock. Cutting his losses in the short term was a good way to increase his profits. He also realized that he could reduce the size of his biggest bets where he had the least conviction.

He was feeling better, more productive, more centered, and not thrown by the market. Indeed the drop in the markets in the early months of 2001 was a boon for him because he could buy good value stocks more cheaply.

Further efforts to tweak his trading approach led him to take more profits in his shorter-term trading positions when the stocks moved up or down. These profits added considerably to his confidence and sense of accomplishment and started helping him to finance his longer-term portfolio. To the extent that he could take advantage of the trading market that existed in the last half of 2000 and the first part of 2001, he was able to consider what trading stocks to get into and how to trade them from a short-term viewpoint. Here he began to trade around his longer-term positions in companies with short-term catalysts and trading events or news. He also began to cover his bad shorts.

Thinking for the first time about trading in terms of profit targets, he began to reduce the number of positions he was following so that he could do more of his intensive fundamental work on those he held. He looked for better shorts that he could trade in a more timely fashion, got bigger in his good shorts and bigger in his good long positions. He also began to get smaller in defensive shorts and find good longs. With this new strategy he expanded control over his portfolio instead of justifying his failures in some stocks by his successes in others and feeling beaten down by the inertia in his portfolio.

Practical Steps

Some traders rationalize mental accounting errors by saying that they don't want to devote too much time to their losing positions. It is easier to just leave them alone. Others may be acting out of a fear of missing out, holding the trade in the case that it starts looking profitable again. But in reality they are doing the same thing with their trades that many people do with their wallets—carelessly spending their petty cash without regard to its actual value.

Do you find yourself in the grip of mental accounting? Answer the following questions to see:

- Do you find yourself easily justifying your losses in some stocks by your wins in others?
- Are you prone to make trading decisions (such as whether to buy or sell) based on that day's results in another trade?
- Do you tend to view smaller trades as less important than larger trades?
- Are you more conservative when dealing with larger amounts of money?

• Remember, a dollar is a dollar and should be treated as such. The basic premise of holding on to winners and selling losers still holds true regardless of whether you have 2 or 10 other stocks that are doing well, whether you are investing $100 or $10,000.

In other words, every trade should be a stepping stone to helping you draw closer to your financial objective. Make your trades in terms of which actions will be profitable, not which decisions appear correct.

Combating Paralysis

Although a master trader knows how to balance the scales and make his decision based on the weight of the issues, many traders do not. Data overload sometimes leads to decision paralysis in traders who get caught up in their own labyrinthine thoughts.

In fact, behavioral economics experts explain that the more choices we humans face, the more likely we are to do nothing. Called the theory of choice under conflict, this theory helps to explain why traders may be unable to take action. The more attractive options that you have, the more difficult it is to choose where to spend your money. Of course, if you defer action long enough you may miss out on the profit potential all together.

Case Study on Overcoming Paralysis

George is an analyst turned trader who was paralyzed by indecision and overanalyzing. Basically, he was afraid of being wrong and wanted to constantly feel in control.

"Ideas are intellectual—although there is an instinctual element," said George. "The execution level is instinctive and psychological. I have good ideas. I am poor at executing them. I tend not to act on a lot of my thoughts, and a lot of them work. My first instinct is right, but I don't act on it because I think I need to do more work. I am not being selective. The idea is to create a lot of positions and then pick and choose. Add to the good ones. Get rid of the bad ones. If I could act on my instincts I would have more positions. But I overanalyze and act too little. I need someone to give me a push. I lack confidence, and I feel frustrated."

The purpose of knowledge is to acquire additional leverage in your trading. George is not really seeking more facts as much as he simply wants a feeling of understanding about a trade—more than just an idea. Given that George has already done the appropriate homework and has enough data, he could write down and rank his ideas, make a limited number of phone calls about each, and read *First Calls* to help give him the added confidence and power to help him make his move.

After considerable discussion, George began to use his analytical skills to build a balanced portfolio. By taking on more risk in a risk-adjusted way, he gained greater control without losing the ability to move.

Practical Steps

Are you a victim of decision paralysis? Consider:

- How often do you second-guess your decisions and pull out of a profitable trade too quickly as a result?
- Do you have a habit of missing trades because you are overanalyzing the data and unable to make a decision?
- Do you consider yourself an indecisive person who is always seeking the advice or approval of others.

• Most traders try to manage their anxiety by trying to control a situation—doing more analysis, waiting for more confirmation. But that is not the answer. In fact, it only creates more data, more indecision, and more paralysis. A better way is to learn to let go and experience the anxiety by timing it, keeping a diary about it, and over time becoming the master of your anxiety.

Additionally, it is useful to diversify and run a balanced portfolio to keep your risk down. It also makes sense to start small. Take one step at a time. Eventually you should be able to do more.

Learning to Become Flexible

Sometimes traders become so locked into a characteristic or habitual way of trading that it becomes a limiting factor in the present (even if it was successful in the past.) When this happens, you may not adapt as readily to changing market circumstances, as was the case with one trader I know.

Case Study on Adapting to Changing Markets

On April 11th, 2001, Chase was way off his target for the year, a fact that he attributed to the "directionless, trendless market," which was being dominated by negative macro sentiment about the consumer rather than by fundamental valuations of companies. Looking at these companies on a microfundamental basis (which was Chase's style) was no longer helping him to make money. Traders who had been invested in safe haven retail stocks were moving back into cheaper, but highly valued tech stocks, and these retail stocks were going down rather than up.

Chase: What's good is bad and what's bad is good. It's double thinking. The fundamentals don't help. Looking at these companies on a microbasis doesn't help make money. The way this market is working, the trends are very limited. If you are at the wrong spot, you get pushed around. You have to think one or two steps ahead of the Street.

This month I got stuck in a consensus short. I could have limited the amount of loss. Instead, I doubled up on the short as the stock was going up because I knew it was going up for the wrong reasons. The expectations set by the management team, given the present environment, were not realistic. It was counting on the back half of the year for things to be better. The whole world was betting on a miss. It didn't happen. The trade became crowded, and I got caught in a classic short squeeze. Now I have to ride it out until the short covering is over with so I can piece it back. Fifty percent of my loss resulted from being stubborn and 50 percent was due to being caught in a consensus trade. Thirty-five percent of the loss could have been eliminated by admitting I was wrong, covering it, and looking to come back. I didn't do that because it was a consensus short. I knew I had to get through so many days of short covering and that the stock would come in. It hasn't. Now, I will cover on pullbacks and trade around it. It is a core short. It has gone to a price that will not go higher. You can't stick around in the consensus trades in these markets. It will kill you.

I am susceptible to this. I was too narrowly focused on the microfundamentals of the company and missed the macro sentiment that was the driving force behind the stocks. A master trader uses the analysis of the companies as a small component. He looks at individual groups, takes a view of the market, and moves in and out of the market. He applies specific information about companies to the sentiment on the group and the macro sentiment on the market and figures out how the market will react. He is one step removed from knowing too much. If you know too much, you have so much conviction that you are clouded by it. If you are too focused, you may miss the forest for the trees.

Kiev: If you had used the goal as your lens and asked what you needed to do to make your goal, would that have led you to look for what was missing in your method? Would that have gotten you to look at the macro sooner?

C: It is easy to say I need to make x dollars per day. The equity market is about stories. It is hard to turn the stories off and pay attention to the goals. If I make 65 cents on 100,000 shares, that's $65,000. I need to have x number of those on the sheet to offset any losses.

I have been in conditions in the marketplace that have rewarded you for knowing secular data in individual companies. I could get by on that. Now the market has changed. This is where real portfolio risk management skills shine through. I have these, but I need to refine them—how big and how long I have to hold as opposed to knowing the story. I have to know when to size the bets. In this market (especially if it is going sideways and in a range in a group) I will need to have 10 stocks in the group to make sizable profits. Until now I haven't been doing it that way systematically. Until now, I would have been trading ideas for halves to points and trading them with levels. Then I had good fundamental stories that I wanted to play big in. Then I would have hedge vehicles to protect my downside. I didn't design this in terms of producing a specific result. It didn't have to be. I was up 125 percent in my capital last year in longs and shorts. But I wasn't systematic. This year [2001] I am going to have to be more systematic and spread my bets across the portfolio.

The market is constantly changing, so traders like Chase constantly have to reevaluate their risk. They need to look at how changes in the market have affected their current positions.

Ideally you always want to know why you are in a trade, so that if it looks like an event is over or something has changed, you can get out of the trade. You have to be able to recognize what has changed and alter your plans accordingly.

Practical Steps

Traders often fail to assess the market realistically and then act (or fail to act) as a result of these incorrect assumptions. Many of the topics we have already discussed (such as mental accounting and loss aversion) are a manifestation of this underlying problem.

Do you have a problem adapting to a changing market? Consider:

- Are you often caught holding on to losing trades?
- Do you wait too long to get into a trade and miss much of the profit by the time you decide to make the trade?
- Are you reluctant to change the volatility of your portfolio even though you know you need to take more risk to gain more profit?

Traders cannot assume risk on the basis of how they feel. They have to step back and take an objective look at the events around them and try to logically sort through the processes at hand.

Case Study on Adapting to Changes

Spencer's story demonstrates the inability of the inexperienced trader to adapt to changing market conditions. He consistently loses money in certain names and certain trades because he buys stocks that he should be shorting. He repeatedly has tried to pick a bottom in one communication company, and invariably it has gone down. He is afraid to lose money and has always approached the short side as a hedge against his long positions rather than as a place to make money. As a result, he has not selected stocks that were weak and shorted them aggressively. When the best traders were making money on the short side in the fall of 2000 and the first part of 2001, Spencer consciously avoided the short side because he didn't want to be part of the crowd. He wanted to be different and held to his long bias, even though his analysis and his instincts told him that a number of single-product technology companies were going to disappear with the end of the Internet bubble. He is very invested in having a "unique thought process" and does not want to be considered a copycat.

For these reasons, Spencer holds on to a lot of small positions that are going nowhere. He gets cautious about being too long because everyone is short, and he believes that the market is going too low. For example, he was short 20,000 shares of one large technology company when another trader was short 250,000 shares. He realized it was a good idea, but couldn't short more because he hadn't done enough work. He spread himself too thin in too many other ideas. He didn't want to look like a copycat, even though it was his idea to short the stock originally. The solution for Spencer? Limiting his trading to ten names, learning to tolerate bigger positions, and making a conscious effort to cooperate with others.

• To manage risk most effectively, you cannot be worried about what you paid for a stock or what your losses have been. You have to treat each day as a separate day from other days and each trade as separate from others. You must be ready to admit when you are wrong. You have to be quick in getting into the winners and steadfast when sticking with them. To succeed you must be able to maximize the trade and not become fearful when circumstances or information change.

"I lost focus and got defensive," said one trader. "Every time I had a loss, I took the loss, but I didn't want to hear about it. I would then decide that I liked the position and get back into it and got long again. I ran around in circles."

Remember, the idea of a goal is to provide a framework for the ever-changing markets. If the way you approach the goal throws you off the game, the solution is not to abandon the goal but to consider what you must do to handle the goal better.

The goal is a directional signal and a guide to help make decisions about what is important and what is not. If you are taking yourself out of the game because of your inability to adapt, then it is critical to slow down and pay attention to the way in which you are responding to your trades.

Hoarding Stub Ends

Hoarding stub ends is a form of stubbornness and resistance to change. It occurs when traders retain a portion of a stock after they have sold off most of a larger position. They hold on to the so-called stub end of the trade for no other reason than to have at least a little piece of the stock in the event that it turns into a bigger opportunity. This habit ties up a large amount of capital that can be used more profitably elsewhere and may also be the source of additional losses if the stub end continues to move downward.

Case Study on Letting Go of Stub Ends

Vern, a trader who holds on to stub ends, must learn to manage this problem as a way of increasing his profitability. He also has to learn to respond to changes in the market and not be trapped by his resistance.

"My problem," said Vern, "is adjusting when I am wrong. Bigger is easy. I am comfortable doing that. The problem is getting out when it is wrong—getting out of the stub ends. For example, with that oil trade. I wasn't completely out of it. I had one huge position in one stock. But I also had a lot of smaller positions that were distracting me and were setting me up to lose some of my profit. Instead of being long 100,000, I was long 25,000 in a number of positions. There are too many other things going on to be wasting time in such small positions. It wasn't a significant part of the

P&L [profit and loss]. It's a matter of focusing. That is what I need to do to get to the next level. I have to clean them out. I can't hold on to them on the chance that they may continue to go up and give me some more profitability."

"The critical issue is why am I losing money. It's not up or down. It is not price action. It is data analysis. I need a reason for being there. If I don't have a reason to be in a stock I shouldn't simply hold on to a small position in case things turn around. The end result of what we do is to make money. It is about not getting caught in the one bad trade. It is about having risk management so that when you are in a bad trade, you are able to get out of it and not hold on to a little bit of it. It is how you react when you are wrong, what you do to cut your losses."

A successful trader can't be indecisive about his or her decisions.

Practical Steps

Hoarding stub ends is a costly strategy that you may be holding on to because of intellectual arrogance. If a stock is not profitable, you have to take the market's opinion as an indicator that your thesis has been proved to be wrong. Face the truth and get out of these positions.

Here the strategy is to start using stops so that you can protect your profit before the stock moves down below where you bought it and becomes a loss. Ask yourself the following questions when you are holding on to stub ends or weak stocks:

- How much are you down in your biggest position?
- Is it time to reduce the position size of weak stocks whose stories seem no longer to be as substantial as when you put on the positions?
- How much more work do you have to do in order to get bigger in your long-term positions or to get smaller in longer-term positions that aren't working or where your original thesis is no longer working?

Remember, when you hold on to a stub end, you are in essence holding on to yesterday's trade. Although it is difficult, you must remain unemotional about stock movements and prices and trade them objectively. That is the key to successful risk taking.

Considering the Herd

Until now we have been observing a variety of maladaptive behavioral patterns of trading such as perfectionism, decision paralysis, mental accounting, and hoarding, which affect traders in varying degrees. In some way all of these behavioral patterns reflect the inability on the part of the trader to let go of control in the same way as the auto racer lets go of control once he has made the decision to follow a particular course or the ski jumper lets go after he has launched his jump. Because of this inability to let go, the attempt at adaptive behavior, be it more analysis, more preparation, or excessive cautiousness, often leads to trading problems rather than trading success. Moreover, because of these problems, traders are often drawn to what might be called herd behavior or what Chase described as "consensus" trades.

Wracked by indecision, it is often easier for these traders to follow the crowd to get some kind of reassurance about their trades, especially in unstable markets, which are hard to predict. Moreover, they lack the kind of flexibility that allows the master trader to trade counterintuitively. In contrast, he opens himself up to reading the forces of the marketplace (the decisions and opinions made by other traders) in order to get a sense of the way in which things are happening so as to trade counter to the herd mentality.

This all relates to what is known as game theory. Created by a man named John von Neumann, this theory gives new meaning to risk by explaining that uncertainty really lies in the intentions of others. The complexity of this kind of approach has been characterized by Bernstein in his excellent book *Against the Gods: The Remarkable Story of Risk* (Wiley, 1996, p. 232):

> From the perspective of game theory, almost every decision we make is the result of a series of negotiations in which we try to reduce uncertainty by trading off what other people want in return for what we want ourselves. . . . Choosing the alternative that we judge will bring us the highest payoff tends to be the riskiest decision, because it may provoke the strongest defense from players who stand to lose if we have our way. So we usually settle for compromise alternatives, which may require us to make the best of a bad bargain.

The whole thing can get rather complicated, but let's try to outline the general premises a little further. Let's say there are two or more players in this "game." Each has a choice of two or more strategies, and each set of choices generates a set of rewards. That's simple enough, right? But there's a catch. The reward of each player depends on the choices made by the other players, not only on his own decisions. Therefore, the players have to make their choices independently (without knowledge of what others are doing) but also based on their anticipation of what the other person(s) will do.

The best example of this is known as the Prisoner's Dilemma. Let's pretend you are watching a popular television police show. The detectives drag in two suspects who they believe collaborated on a crime. They place each in a separate cell. After a short round of good cop/bad cop, they tell the suspects they have a deal for them. They tell each one that he will be released if he rats on the other and the other does not rat on him.

So, if only Suspect A rats on Suspect B then Suspect B will get five years and Suspect A will go free (or vice versa). If they both denounce each other, both will get three years imprisonment. If neither rats, the police still have sufficient evidence to send each to prison for one year.

Now, pretend you are the suspects. Of course, the results are largely based on what the other suspect does as well. You could wind up free, or you could go to jail for one to three years. What would you do? One thing is certain. Your decision will be, in large part, determined by what you think the other suspect will do. This is the essence of game theory.

How does it relate to your risk-taking decisions? Although it is unwise to make your decisions based *solely* on what others are doing (i.e., to sell just because others are selling or to buy just because others are buying), it is equally unwise to trade without considering the actions of others. There is no way to get around the simple fact that the actions of other traders do matter and affect the way in which your trade moves. Therefore, the master trader makes his decisions about what to do based on his assumptions about how others are going to interpret market signals and information.

The master trader gains the information and then factors in how others are going to respond to the data and trades based on certain assumptions about the stock and the likely response of the market to the data and analysis. He is not simply buying the stock based on news that it is going up, and, most important, he is not trapped by his perfectionism, decision paralysis, mental accounting, tendency to hoard stub ends of positions, or other behavioral constraints. A wise trading decision is based on a combination of the fundamentals (which gives an understanding of the stock and company), an assessment of how others will assess the fundamental data, and an understanding of present market conditions.

This type of thought process takes a remarkable willingness to let go of ego and tune into the sentiment and psychology of other traders who represent the marketplace and who are likely to influence the movement of stocks. The first derivative thought process is focused on what the other person is thinking; most people (the so-called herd) think this way. The second derivative thought process employed by the master trader tries to decipher what the other person thinks the rest of the world is thinking. This process is seen in Keynes' oft-repeated example of a beauty contest with one hundred women, and you are supposed to pick the six that are the most beautiful. The trick in picking the winner of the beauty contest is to pick the six that you think the rest of the country is going to pick. The same principle applies to stock selection. That is how you can develop trading mastery.

If you are a longer-term investor, you are relying on the fundamentals and not on the changes in the herd psychology. But short-term trading is often about assessing the changes or rates of changes in crowd behavior or in a particular security and trading on that basis. To do this requires that you get past characteristic behaviors that limit the trading mastery of the vast majority of traders.

Case Study on Trading Out of the Box

Drew is a master trader who is particularly good at evaluating the markets in order to manage his own portfolio more effectively. He profits by seeing the positive openings in stocks when there is no follow-through. He pays close attention to the momentum created by the crowd and to capital flows and trading enthusiasms when making his trading decisions, but he does not put too much credence in what the crowds believe.

In effect, he pays attention to the herd's response to the markets and tries to be one step ahead of it. If the crowd believes the hyperbole of a stock, he may assume that a stock may move today, but that it is a short-term move, and he gets out before the momentum stops and it runs its course. In effect he discounts the momentum movements caused by crowd behavior in making his trading decisions.

Drew is psychologically objective and in control of his emotions. He uses his own emotional responses not to react to the market but as an indicator of what others are feeling and thinking and doing. This is a second derivative type of trading wherein he makes decisions based on how he believes others are likely to trade and the direction in which the market is likely to move.

He uses a minimum of denial and rationalization. If he is wrong and the market tells him he is wrong, he gets out. If he is right, he presses his bet. He is not invested in being right or having his thesis proved. If the data suggests he is wrong, he moves on. He is agnostic and doesn't buy into his emotions or beliefs about companies. He is always looking to factor in certain assumptions about how other people are likely to trade or interpret information bits.

Drew is able to interpret what others are doing based on how he sees others trading in the room, how he feels, and how he anticipates others will feel. Everyone is reacting to the price move. He is reacting to their reactions and making his decisions based on among other things, how he thinks they are going to act or how they are already acting.

According to Bob, a highly experienced trader: "The whole apparatus of Wall Street focuses on explaining what happened. They never tell you what is going to happen. Drew is trying to anticipate what will happen and makes probability bets on his predictions based on a number of factors, not the least of which is the way the crowd is likely to respond to the data. He is asking what is the chance that others will interpret the data in a certain way. What effect will this have on the market? How can I trade the stock or the option based on this assessment? He is always looking beyond the data to a level of interpretation in terms of how others are likely to respond to the data, and on the basis of this he decides on an actionable thesis. This is a second order of abstraction. He is distilling what he thinks will be relevant for that stock and how others are likely to respond. He then decides whether to buy or sell."

Bob continued: "Most traders don't ask themselves what a trade will look like in the future. Most people are reading everything at face value and are being reactive. Most people don't make the distinction between what is real and not real. Drew is able to have his hand on the pulse and really get the distinctions. He knows when to buy and when to rent."

The ability to read the psychology of the crowd also shows up in a similar ability to read below the surface in understanding company reports. Underlying the popular story there is often a more rational explanation. Drew sees something happening and tries to understand the implications of events. He is looking for the real explanation of what is going on. He wants to understand the underlying dynamic issues in a situation and the implications of a lot of subtle events. He is looking for a variant perception that will explain things beyond the balance sheets, because numbers can be manipulated and there may be better explanations of what is likely to be going on.

Drew regularly does this kind of second derivative analysis. For example, semiconductor chip or DRAM prices go up every day. The supply and demand turns, but Drew doesn't see signs that things are failing. There are pressures in the market, and he sees problems developing that would limit the upside and create the conditions for the downdraft in semiconductors. His analysis demonstrates the beginning of fractures in the market. But as long as the market believes in the stock, Drew is taking the stocks up. The intellectual formulation that the companies are failing is just that. Drew, therefore, keeps buying these stocks while waiting for real evidence of a turn.

Remember, momentum created by crowd enthusiasm may peter out. The master trader recognizes capital flows and trading enthusiasms and factors that into his trading decisions but he does not put too much credence in what the crowds believe. He pays attention to it and sometimes goes with it when it seems justified, but he is always objective. He has his own set of objectives. He reads the mania but does not necessarily act on it. He doesn't necessarily care if he is *right*. He is trying to capture the profit inherent in the move created by the momentum and the herd.

Therefore, when it is to his benefit to follow the herd, the master trader does, and when it is to his benefit to buck the system he does that as well. The objective is to understand the psychology behind herd investing and use it to your advantage.

Releasing the Rationalizations

Many of the problems discussed in this chapter are in one way or another related to rationalization, a mental process whereby you try to explain away your losses, or focus excessively on details and miss the forest for the trees. Excessive intellectual efforts are often focused on minute irrelevant details and rationalized as strategic considerations. Attention to these details interferes with performance by reducing involvement in the critical or essential tasks necessary to reach the goal. At the same time this obsessive activity creates an illusory feeling that you are in control. It's another manifestation of perfectionism. By focusing all your attention on extraneous details which are often given magical significance, you stifle your intuitive skills.

The more you allow yourself to be dominated by these demanding, self-critical voices, the more likely you will hold back and ultimately not tap your hidden potential or achieve your objectives. When you stop your self-criticism, you will have considerably more confidence to master enormous obstacles and increase your chances of self-fulfillment. One trader who stopped this self-criticism reported: "I didn't feel the same urgency about making money. I enjoy my work, but I seem to be approaching it in a more relaxed way, as if I know it will work out because I'm good at it; I don't have to try so hard so that I'm drained at the end of the day. I seem to be able to enjoy the opportunities before me and don't have to manage things so compulsively."

Practical Steps

Freedom from compulsive effort and a need to accomplish things in order to prove your worth is one of the many liberating features of taking risks in accordance with the principles outlined in this book.

Before you address the solutions that we have discussed in this chapter, it is key to frame the issues. Consider the following five questions:

1. What is the emotional impact of the trade?
2. What does the trade mean?
3. What does it represent?

4. Why does a trade have different results each time?
5. How does my emotional makeup impact the outcome of the trade?

By identifying certain habitual behaviors that are interfering with your risk-taking ability, you reduce the tension and frustration caused by trying to suppress these aspects of yourself and, as a result, experience a greater sense of wholeness. In fact, risk-taking means to become fully engaged and absorbed in activity without holding back or being concerned with your image or the opinion of others. When you understand this and get comfortable with the discomfort of taking risks, you will be able to become more fully engaged in your trading activities. As I have repeatedly stated, the key to doing this is to become fully engaged in the next moment through committed action to your vision, which will free you from the trap of rationalization and all the defensive maneuvers you have created to protect your ego.

Acting Now

The potential to realize your vision is within you. You need only let go of the constraints within yourself, which keep you from expressing your potential. You can facilitate this unfolding by surrendering to the vision or the context you have created without managing events or dominating others. You surrender by not holding on to the past by not resisting change. When you do this, the potential within you will begin to unfold.

To learn white-water rafting it is necessary to ride the rapids. Although you may need to do this with a guide, you can only experience the unpredictability of the ride, the sense of being at risk, and the importance of following the rules from actually taking the ride, not from reading about it or preparing for it.

The unfolding of your creative potential comes only from interacting with the reality of white water. What you discover about yourself can only emerge from participation in the event itself. As a result, something emerges from within you that was not present before the event. This new sense of self and the possibility of creating your life emerges from responding to the events themselves.

A critical distinction exists between the preparatory and analytical thought you may have about events and the actual complex action and responses that occur in response to events. The value of action is that it enables you to see an aspect of reality quite distinct from your concepts of reality. Action breaks through your fixed way of seeing things. Action lets you see the truth between the cracks before ideas about the event are fixed and become part of a concept about the experience.

Essentially, you need action, motion, change, challenge—to see beneath the facade of reality. This is essentially what the Japanese mean by satori—a space in the world that you can't see until you take action consistent with your vision so that you become at one with what you see.

PART THREE

THE PERSONALITIES OF RISK

CHAPTER FIVE

PROFILING PASSIVE TRADERS

Ultracautious. Insecure. Timid. Anxious. Do one or more of these words apply to your own trading style, either often or occasionally? If so, you're not alone.

Many traders allow their feelings, rather than their strategy, to dictate their actions. Doing so often makes them passive—either too fearful to make a decision or so insecure that they constantly seek reinforcement from others. Passive trading is not the way to master market uncertainty.

In this and subsequent chapters I discuss specific examples of various trader profiles so that you can more easily identify some of your own trading patterns that may need improvement.

Cautious Traders

There are several types of passive traders. A cautious trader likes predictability and stability. He doesn't like risk—not on a physical level or in his decision making. He is more likely, for instance, to prefer the weekly gym routine over adventuresome exercise habits like hiking or mountain climbing. He prefers the certainty of regularly scheduled developments in a familiar setting. He likes to have everything under control and pays attention to details, which is essential for first-class analysis.

But sometimes this same caution can inhibit the ability to pull the trigger and take the risks required for trading success.

There is a self-centeredness in many cautious traders that also shows up as an inclination to obsess about potential problems as well as the attitudes, responses, and anticipated criticism of others. An obsessive trader is reluctant to pay up for things and is concerned about being too exposed.

Like the perfectionist, the cautious trader has to learn that trading does not amount to executing with perfect information. In fact, successful risk taking actually forces traders to act with less-than-perfect information in an unpredictable and volatile market.

Successful trading relies on the appropriate amount of risk—not too much, but also not too little. Like a good adventurer, a trader who is seeking mastery will learn to enjoy conquering difficult situations but will understand the importance of preparation. He will find the place between high and low risk where there is challenge enough to stimulate but not so much that it is overwhelming.

Case Study on the Dangers of Extreme Caution

Jeremy is a cautious trader who gets out of positions as soon as they have moved up a point or two or down a half point. Psychologically he has trouble holding his winning positions longer because he is afraid of losing. He is also afraid to use more capital for the same reasons. Here his cautious, sensible approach has become a limiting factor, preventing him from adapting to the markets and from expanding his performance. What's more, he blames himself for not being prepared rather than recognize that it's his attitude, not his lack of information, that is hurting him.

"I don't know that company well, but today I heard that the company is splitting," said Jeremy. "They're spinning off their coal company, which has been basically a wait. The stock was up four bucks. On the opening I was short 25,000. It came in a little bit. I covered. The fact is that even if I was right, I should have known that was a possibility. I was completely blind-sided because I didn't do enough work. That was an $83,000 loss. Everyday I am down 20 or 30. There are many names I am not being thorough about."

"I do the technicals, and I do some of the work fundamentally. I have a reason but not a strong catalyst. It is just not clicking. I am not making the kind of money I want to make. I am frustrated. The lesson is I have to do more work. I need more of an edge. My timing has been off a little."

A closer look at one day of trading revealed Jeremy's inclination to brood over yesterday's indecision coupled with an inability to take action in the present because of a reluctance to pay up for a stock. As much as he tried to justify his unwillingness to act, the purpose of the dialogue was to explore the possibility of taking action in the here and now.

Jeremy: I got up to my numbers and got a lot of 50s on and felt good about it. Then the stocks just faded and did not react the way I wanted them to. So, I sold half of my positions. Of course, today they are being added to recommended lists of the brokerage houses, and they are going higher.

Kiev: You can't get back in?

J: I can get back in, but they opened up too high relative to what I should pay for them. I don't want to pay up for them. I was looking at it yesterday, and my entry points were good yesterday. I sold them yesterday but did not get back into it today because I thought the price was too high. Today they opened above where I bought them yesterday.

K: Was there still room for it to go up today?

J: The thing is, it opened higher and I did not want to pay those prices. If they come in, I want to buy them.

K: The prices are too high?

J: They just did not come in to where I wanted to buy them, but they are acting OK. They are acting well relevant to the news that came out yesterday. The market is acting awful, but these are acting well today.

K: So what if they go higher?

J: I don't know. That is a good question. If they go higher, should I go ahead and just buy them?

K: If they go higher, then you are going to say, 'Well, should I have gotten them today as opposed to yesterday?'

Although Jeremy's remarks reflect a clear-cut ability to control his risk, the purpose of my questioning was to underscore how much his extreme cautiousness trapped him. He failed to capture as much profit as was available to him in the trades he was taking because of his inclination to get out of winning trades too fast. To help him overcome his internal constraints, we began talking more precisely about sizing his positions in line with his monthly statistics. The key was to help him examine his trading statistics and then define a sizing pattern that was within the constraints of his Sharpe ratio (a measure of risk-adjusted returns based on a ratio of returns to the volatility of returns). In order for him to make a larger sum of money, he needed to put on more risk, that is, increase the amount of volatility in his daily trading.*

The power of the Sharpe ratio (which is based on performance history) is that it tells you how much you will make for every unit of risk that you put on. A Sharpe ratio of 6 indicates that for every dollar of risk, Jeremy will get back six times as much on an annualized basis. To get to his goal of $25 million, he would have to triple his risk size.

There is a stability to his Sharpe ratio very much like a baseball batting average. If he is a .300 hitter, he can expect to get 60 hits if he comes to bat 200 times. If he is at bat three times more often or 600 times he can expect to get three times as many hits or 180 hits.

The same applies to how much profit Jeremy wanted to make. To make more profit, he had to put more money at risk. But this is where Jeremy's psychological barrier came into play. He hesitated to lose more money in his daily swings even though if he were to use more money (given his Sharpe ratio), he would make more profits.

---

*Jeremy's Sharpe ratio was 6. His daily profit and loss (P&L) fluctuated about $84,000 which is measured by standard deviation. When he multiplies this number by 16 (which is the square root of 252 trading days), he gets an annualized standard deviation of $1.3 million. Multiplying his annualized standard deviation of $1.3 million by 6 gives him a potential annual income of $7.8 million, the amount of money he can make given his present statistics.

The first step in helping him was to demonstrate what was required mathematically for him to reach his target. Next we developed an incremental plan wherein he was encouraged to increase the size of his positions by 25 percent and then 50 percent and then increase the number of larger positions. Then he had to learn to hold his positions for longer periods of time and to put more positions on his sheet. Eventually, he teamed up with an analyst who helped to do more analyses of the companies he was trading. Additionally, to help control his anxiety I urged him to keep a trading diary and a time chart so as to get greater control over his underlying urge to get out of positions too soon.

Fearful Traders

A more extreme form of cautiousness can be seen in traders who are so afraid of losing that they fail to get into a trade on time or they pull out of a profitable trade too early. This common pattern of trading not to lose is known as loss aversion. Despite the rationalizations that fearful traders present, trading not to lose doesn't lead to real satisfaction. Instead it leads to a sense of quiet desperation. The trader, trapped in his own self-protective habits, is afraid to risk more. As a result, when he does go for broke he is often off-kilter and loses more confidence. Even when he succeeds, the fearful trader doesn't feel terrific because he isn't getting the joy of swinging or trading full out. He knows that he can do better, but he has self-protectively taken himself out of the game.

Of course, not all traders who are fearful trade cautiously. Some, like one of the traders discussed in Chapter Six, trade more recklessly as a result of their fear. However, as a general rule, most traders who are extremely fearful trade too prudently as a result of their fear. Let's consider some examples.

Case Study on the Limits of Fear

After a series of major losses about 10 years ago, Jake has been trading scared and has not been able to utilize his know-how to his best advantage. His fear stifles him and he holds on to positions for too long. Thus he doesn't take as much profit from his trades as he can.

Somewhat like the compulsive gambler described in Chapter 6, Jake takes shots. Finding it hard to postpone action and wait for better opportunities because he cannot stand the tension of waiting, he impulsively buys things. He is overly preoccupied with the end-of-the-year result which creates anxiety for him. He is unable to differentiate between long-term and short-term trades and to assess when a trend is still happening. He cannot hold his currency positions long enough to profit or extend the range of his stop positions below the buying price so that he can withstand some of the volatility of the trade and not be stopped out too soon.

"It's much easier to deal with the problems when you're up," said Jake. "When you're losing, you just pray."

Jake is familiar with the concept of commitment to a specific goal and is not afraid to put on the trade. He just isn't maximizing the trades. He claims that his investment banking background predisposes him to take profits when he can and go on to the next trade.

"I was never sure how to quantify goals," said Jake. "My performance never matched my ideas. I would always subject myself to extreme bursts of optimism and excessive risk taking and would get hit and have to work back up. If I had a long-term goal, my short-term goal would screw up my long-term goals, and my process would break down. I don't want to take the pain of having my profits diminished. If I set goals, I would often press and overtrade and force ideas instead of waiting for them to become clear. My hit ratio has been 75 percent, but I haven't made much money."

Jake started to take control of his trading once he faced up to the underlying reasons for his behavior. Once he could acknowledge his basic, underlying fear of loss (hidden behind a mask of superconfidence), Jake gradually began to take incrementally bigger positions, to hold them longer with wider stops, and to use his goals to prod himself to greater success.

The first step in taking on more risk was to place stops at a distance from his trades so that he wouldn't be forced out of trades too soon. Holding trades longer, he could ride out the fluctuations and increase the profitability of his trades.

A second step was to adhere more conscientiously to trading targets in order to overcome his preference for being right as opposed to being profitable. Over time he began to use the daily target to help define a strategy for increasing profits. This meant giving up his emotional investment in his hit ratio. Listen to the following conversation that we had regarding these changes in his trading style:

Kiev: If you are trading on a daily basis, why can't you have a daily number? How much can you make every day in spot trading?

Jake: It depends on how much pain I can take when I am wrong. I should be able to make $40,000–$50,000 per day. If I were running my ideas for a day or two and were relaxed, it would be $200,000 per week.

K: Can you set up to make $50,000 a day?

J: I can identify 10 trades a day. I would have to run bigger positions with fewer trades, and hold them 6–12 hours longer than I am doing now. I can do spot trades as well.

K: Do you typically line things up that way now?

J: I focus and passively watch the market. I try to get a feel for interesting things. Something gets my attention, and then I go through the charts. I am good at identifying good entry points that will have a good risk/reward first stop.

K: How many can you find in a typical day?

J: Three or four.

K: What are you not doing now that keeps you from doing this successfully?

J: I am not always waiting for my entry. For example, when the Dollar/Swiss traded at 173, I thought we could get back to 175.70, and that would give me great entry for a short. The high was 175.75, and it collapsed from there. And I am not short now. I started getting short too soon. I got uncomfortable. I tried going short at 174.50 and got out of synch. I took a small loss. I didn't want to get back in. It is down 100 points now. It is 174.75. Even if I did two units, it would have been $30,000. There would have been no pain. I didn't wait long enough. It threw off my timing. I was out of synch.

Last night I picked a level of 94.40 in euro/yen to buy. I wanted to get long. I thought the stop would be so close that it wouldn't even get below 94.20. I bought it at 45. The low was 42. It went straight up 80 points. My stop was 20 points away. I grabbed the profit instead of running it. It would have been 80 points. Instead of a $10,000 trade it would have been $70,000. This happens every day.

K: Can you tweak your trading style so that you can increase your numbers to make $200,000 per week?

J: It would be easy to do if I could deal with the loss side of the trade. I hate losing money in short-term trading. That induces me to make stupid exits way too soon. That is a weakness. I pick great levels, but even when I know the exit, I get out too early. It is a vicious circle of trading badly, losing money, and then feeling pressure which reinforces bad money practice.

K: Then lower the number to $100,000 a week. Whatever the number, it should be doable. It will help you to explore what is keeping you from doing the number. If you modify this number, it will make a significant impact on your trading. Just staying in longer is all that you have to do. You have to begin to get a hold of that by having a target. You don't want it to pressure you.

J: The only thing pressuring me is my own fear of getting it wrong. I do not trust myself even though I have done all the work. It could be one-quarter of a unit or it could be five units.

K: The first 15 times you hold it longer, it may be uncomfortable. You have to keep doing it until you can make the numbers higher. You can learn to do this by keeping a running diary of your entry and exit points, writing down what you are feeling, especially when you want to get out of a trade in a hurry. Measure the duration of your anxiety response so that you will learn it is time limited and will not last indefinitely. As you learn to ride out the anxiety, you will develop the tolerance to stay longer with your trades.

J: The ideas were good, but I didn't run them. I made money in short ideas because of a 75 percent hit ratio. What was not working was that I wasn't willing to lose more to make more. I have to be willing to be stopped out more and run my positions.

K: Profitability is the key, not the hit ratio.

J: My way feels good, but it is not effective.

To overcome such an extreme fear of losing, most traders need to lower their target number. By setting a more easily reachable goal, you can explore what is holding you back. Here the target is valuable. You need to make a conscious decision to hold positions longer to make more profit. You need to let your target influence your trading. This point is critical in using the target to help determine what you have to do in your trading in order to increase profits.

You can't be too invested in your feelings about a trade or the way you view a trade. The critical thing is profitability, and to be more profitable you have to be uncomfortable sometimes. Additionally, you can do what I suggested to Jake: Time your anxiety until you learn to ride out the discomfort without feeling pressured to take action too quickly.

Insecure Traders

The insecure trader always seeks approval. He may be held back by perfectionism, a fear of losing, and a cautious nature as well, but underlying all his actions is a basic need for acceptance, respect, and a pat on the back. He is the master of avoidance and is often caught up in rationalizations, intellectualization, and a reluctance to take the initiative. Before he acts, he invariably checks his decisions with others. When he talks to too many people, he may even become confused and paralyzed.

Insecure traders have an inward desire to be the center of attention and often have grandiose plans. Unfortunately, due to their inability to act, they rarely live up to their unrealistic expectations and then blame circumstances rather than themselves. They are afraid of failure and the critical reactions of others to their performance.

Case Study on Pulling the Trigger

Jason is a prime example of the insecure trader. He is afraid to act and seeks constant reassurance. He is waiting for everthing to line up perfectly before he acts and, of course, is very frustrated by this. He is afraid to pull the trigger and is filled with doubts. He needs to build confidence about taking risk by deciding on a goal and a strategy, and taking action.

"I want the boss's endorsement beforehand as opposed to getting his endorsement by actually doing it," he explained. "I get antsy. I don't have a gestalt. I don't have a context. I am doing stuff big to prove I can do it. It is impulsive. It is not thought out."

Basically, Jason is not making money because he avoids putting on the risk to make money. He is avoiding taking the action.

"I am hoping for someone else to provide the solution," he admitted. "I keep trying to build the perfect desk setup instead of making things happen myself."

Although Jason spends much of his time in introspection and self-absorption rather than action, he is amenable to coaching, "I want to assume risk," he declares. "I want to be involved in everything. I want to be at the epicenter. I don't want to be tangential." Jason can be challenged to get out of his head and to take sensible action. In fact, with some pushing Jason has been able to take reasonably sized positions and has begun to make some money.

Listen as we discuss Jason's desire to become more profitable:

Jason: I want to understand how to better control my volatility and set my portfolio up so that I can produce a certain amount of profitability from taking a certain amount of risk. These conversations with you are helping me to learn how I get nervous and how to conquer that. The trade is the manifestation of individual inputs, wants, and desires. You take out of the trade what you want. There is something about my makeup that wants clarity, but I don't take certain steps to get that clarity, and that is reflected in my trading. My lack of confidence is showing up in my trading.

Kiev: What have you learned in recent months that has helped you to develop your capacity to take risk?

J: Once you are not worried about the size of the loss, you can go for bigger gains. You can't have bigger gains without being able to have bigger losses. You have to be willing to lose $100,000 to make $250,000.

K: What has enabled you to do that?

J: I suppose it is getting some right on bigger sizes where the P&L [profit and loss] was moving.

K: What else have you learned?

J: How my emotions influence my actions and how important it is to override my emotions. The other thing I have learned is that you can't be a big trader unless you take responsibility for your errors. No one will tell you what to do. I was never inclined to do that before. Now that I am taking full responsibility for my trading results, I have begun to listen to my friends differently. I hear their excuses as to why something can't be done. The only person who can get something done is yourself. If you can't get it done, then you have to change.

Rome wasn't built in a day. My conversation with Jason, for example, has been going on for several years. If any of this is applicable to you, you should know that it will take time for you to learn to bypass your insecurities, ride out your anxiety, and give up lifelong habits of excessive dependency on the approval of others. But this is what must be done to help you master the psychology of trading. By learning to separate all stimuli or trading events from your own automatic responses and interpretations, you can respond to the market in new ways from the perspective of your trading objectives. In this way you can learn to respond not passively but proactively by focusing action toward your goal. Moreover, you can learn to overcome your natural tendency to be risk averse.

Practical Steps

When there is a choice between a certain and uncertain profit, the tendency of most passive traders is to be risk averse and to take the profit available right away, getting out of trades too soon and leaving money on the table. But when the choice is framed in terms of how much more can be lost in a losing trade, the tendency then is to be more adventurous, to gamble in the hopes of doing better. This action leads passive traders to get out of winning trades too soon and to experience even more loss in their losing trades by holding on too long. In other words, passive and less experienced traders are usually more conservative when it comes to locking in a sure gain and are more willing to take risk in order to avoid a sure loss. This tendency, of course, is the complete opposite of the two basic precepts of trading success: to *hold winners* and *sell losers*.

Are you too cautious or risk averse? Consider the following questions:

- Do you find yourself holding onto losing trades in hopes that they will turn around?
- Do you reframe your losses in an effort to feel better about them or justify them in terms of another win?
- Are you extremely cautious when trying to get into a trade, perhaps investing smaller amounts in the beginning to be on the safe side?
- Do you pull out of winning trades too quickly in order to lock in your profit and then miss out on the bigger move?

• Risk aversion and passivity can often be overcome with good fundamental analysis. The more detailed analysis you have of a company, the better informed you will be to make a decision, by seeing all sides—the pros and the cons. In this way, you can overcome any tendency to hold too narrow a viewpoint.

But even more important as a key to trading mastery is your willingness to commit to a result.

Committing to a Result

To take risk requires a willingness to go to the edge of the abyss and to act in line with your objectives without any guarantees or certainty about the outcome. This means to be able to go past your self-doubts and any distractions that compete with the pull of the vision. To be fully engaged in risk-taking in an experiential way means opening yourself to the trading experience and acting consistently with the opportunities available to you without being run by your needs, wants, desires, or life principles from the past. It means acting in terms of your untapped creative potential and doing what is necessary and consistent with reality in line with the perspective of your consciously chosen trading objectives that takes you beyond your preexisting interpretation of the markets and puts you in touch with the markets in a more psychologically centered way.

It doesn't mean waiting until the last dregs of self-doubt are gone. It means acting in the face of these demons so as to discover the power of focused action directed toward your objectives. Only then will you learn the value of specific targets as directional and motivational signals helping you to overcome the most terrible of anxieties.

Committing to a specific result instead of resigning to things as they are is a more powerful way of dealing with reality, because it invites you to take risks in the present moment from the perspective of your vision, recognizing that the gap between where you are and where you will be when you realize your vision points to the actions that need to be taken in the next moment.

When you put on more risk, you will experience bigger losses than you did when you were running smaller amounts of capital.

These losses may raise the level of your anxiety, self-consciousness, and panic—all of which you will need to learn to manage. But these are not reasons to avoid trading in terms of a specific target. It is just part of the learning process.

As I mentioned before, I encourage you to keep a diary and to time the duration of your anxiety. Invariably, once you know that your anxiety is time-limited, you will find that each time you experience it, it lasts for a shorter span, until eventually it hardly ever occurs, even under the most trying and stressful situations.

. I have seen this over and over again. Once you realize that anxiety, which can be timed and then overcome, is stopping you, you will be able to increase the size of your capital usage, holding periods, and, ultimately, your profitability. In addition, as you build confidence, you will be able to get out of losing positions much more rapidly and move on to the next trade.

It is also important to remember that the failure to realize your vision does not mean anything about you and should not be taken as proof that you cannot succeed. It is only information about the trade and an opportunity to learn more about what you need to put into place in order to succeed.

While profitability is the end result of trading, don't fool yourself into thinking that profitability is synonymous with happiness. The purpose of the goal is to help you tap more of your hidden potential, not so much to fulfill yourself. Efforts to achieve a goal to fulfill yourself often derive from a life principle of insufficiency and the erroneous belief that you both need and can get something you didn't get as a child. The fact is that you cannot get what you didn't get, or what you perceived you didn't get and efforts to do so only create a vicious circle of efforts that intensifies feelings of inadequacy and incompleteness.

True vitality begins when you realize that there is nothing to seek, that you are already whole, that everything you need is already within you, and that efforts to complete yourself by reaching a specific objective only intensify feelings of incompleteness.

True empowerment begins from where you are. You commit to a vision and take actions in line with the vision in the face of opposition and your own internal resistance. True empowerment begins when you realize there is nothing more to seek and you give up all those activities that produce this internal splitting and sense of inadequacy.

• True empowerment begins when you realize that the power to take risks means becoming all that you already are, in other words, becoming your vision by taking action consistent with it. When you do this, your trading becomes a way of expressing your vision in the here and now by doing all that is missing from the full realization of your vision.

Most of your distress comes from covering up your feelings and thoughts, not from what was said or done. By speaking the truth, you release yourself from the past and enter the next moment.

If you are fearful, feel the fear. If there is sadness below the fear, notice that and allow it in. Allow yourself to be fully alive to whatever you are feeling in this moment before you. The moment before you is all there is, and the task is to be able to bring all of yourself to bear in the moment before you and to allow the contexts you have designed to create the challenges and requests that lead you to become engaged in the moments before you. This is the essence of true risk taking.

• To enter the next moment you must appreciate and acknowledge yourself and recognize your trading as being an expression of who you really are.

Keep reminding yourself to stay on target, using the goal or vision to help define a purpose and a sense of direction and way of seeing the markets. Remember that more than likely everything is unfolding as it was meant to unfold. So, you can relax into the next moment in the contexts you have created and stop running around needlessly.

If you are open and receptive, you will find that the next moment contains a multitude of trading opportunities related to your objectives. As you let your self-doubts and fears pass, you will be able to face uncertainty with greater equanimity, engage more authentically in the events of the day, and tap into the beauty, power, miracles, and energy in the markets.

Choosing What You Have

If you are a passive trader or are troubled by self-doubt and insecurity, it is critical for you to learn to choose what you have, by which I mean to let go of judgments and interpretations about yourself. Choosing what you have means finding the resources within yourself to make your trading work. Choosing what you have reduces the pain, struggle, and waste of energy that come from looking for something you do not have and ignoring the strength that you do have. By accepting yourself and focusing on the moment before you, listening without judgment, and letting go of superstitions, you are able to move beyond the psychological comfort zone to a creative realm of being where you will be empowered to take risks. Choosing what you have facilitates surrender to the moment before you. It enables you to get past your social persona of appearing competent and in control, or your need to be liked, or your inclinations to preserve the status quo, and your reluctance to see the truth and to speak it.

In essence, the real issue is whether you are willing to take the necessary actions associated with risk taking. Waiting for the right answer before you act traps you in abstract notions and locks you out of experience.

In other words, you may think you are doing something when you are deciding on the right way to go or the right path to choose. In fact you actually may be trapped in your thinking. From the perspective of commitment, the issue is to choose or not to choose—not choosing the right answer. In order to take risk, you must take action and not live your life on the dock waiting for the right answer.

The more you take action, the more you will discover that trading success is not something to be grasped or gained or to be realized through achievement but is something to be lived fully in the present. In effect, you can only trade in the next moment. Trading mastery is not about gaining something in the future. Rather it is a time and space in which to be present to the opportunities available to you by functioning in terms of a conscious decision about choosing what you have and *trading fully in the moments* before you rather than searching for something in the future to give you a sense of security.

Discovering What Is Missing

A trading strategy is the organization of risk-taking actions that you design that allows you to produce the results you are committed to producing. When you create a strategy, you focus on what's missing and what more you can do. You don't assume your goal will be realized by itself without close monitoring. You maintain a level of consciousness and intention toward your goals such that you are constantly experiencing the world through the perspective of your objectives. Therefore it is necessary to create a large enough goal or vision that you can keep working toward, so that your trading becomes a form of practice designed to express the vision. To tap into your potential and to keep the challenge up, your vision should be bigger than your ego and bring you far into the future. It should not be readily attained in the next moment.

All there is to do is to take risks in the next moment consistent with your vision and to design a structure or strategy that will enable you to focus moment-by-moment on the incremental steps leading to the objective. Insofar as you can only do one thing at a time in the moment before you, it is useful to decide on what steps you need to take to express the vision, including relinquishing certain expectations, habits, and thoughts, as well as taking positive actions.

Figure out what is not yet present that must be present for your vision to be produced. This method does not imply insufficiency or inadequacy but rather recognizing that all the requisite factors have not as yet been tapped or utilized. Only by acknowledging what elements are needed (but are not yet present) can you bring them to the fore. You must be willing to trade with a willingness to face the truth. When you have begun to move toward your objectives and to run into obstacles or errors, you must be willing to listen to what is missing and what needs correction and be willing to fine-tune your actions consistently with your objectives to produce the results.

· Whenever you commit to a specific objective in your trading you will run into resistance, old habits, and ways of seeing the world that run counter to pursuing your vision. This is natural. It is possible to free yourself from identifying with your automatic thoughts and life principles as well as your physiological responses and defensive decisions made in moments of reactivity so that you can trade proactively in terms of a larger purpose. Allow yourself to be vulnerable. Notice your reactions and your physical responses without interpreting them. While your responses are triggered by events, you can let them pass rather than overreact to them. Listen to events. Notice your physiological responses, emotional reactions, and automatic thoughts, and keep creating your trades consistently with your vision rather than with your preconceptions and behavioral ways of responding.

What you have, including your circumstances and your handicaps, are challenges to assist you to tap into the courage and creativity within yourself. If you resist what you have, you will create a split within yourself and be trapped in your thought processes. Choose it, and thereby heal the split within yourself. Create a vision of a goal and begin to do what you can to express the vision, and when it is bigger than you are, you will tap into more of yourself.

CHAPTER SIX

PROFILING THE HIGH-RISK TRADER

When you read Chapter Five, did you say to yourself: "Passive? That's not me at all. I'm more likely to gamble, to be daring, to stick my neck out, to go for broke." Usually, the willingness to take risks is a good thing. But it can become problematic for traders who take risks just for the sake of taking them. Among such traders, the urge to take risks, which is a necessary ingredient of trading success, overpowers the need to take thoughtful precautions. High-risk traders, like those with a gambling propensity often seek the action or euphoric effects of trading more than the production of a steady profit. Just like a drug addict has to increase his usage over time in order to maintain the same "high," traders who manifest this tendency need to make increasingly larger bets or take larger risks in order to produce the desired effect. The emotional impact of the trading, therefore, takes on more significance for these traders than the steady profitability associated with more measured risk taking.

Case Studies on High-Risk Trading

A trader with high-risk propensities may have difficulty in cutting back or cutting down when he is in drawdown and is at risk of blowing himself up as well as the firm. He may experience irritability, restlessness, and even depression in the effort to control his impulse to get bigger, even when the risk manager is asking him to reduce the size of his capital and cut back on his risk-taking behavior. He often cannot be objective and when in drawdown may abandon any semblance of trading strategy and start trying to get the losses back in one big bet, which frequently only gets him further into a hole.

"I am very anxious to get losses back and to start making money," said Dustin, a bright young trader with an undisciplined impulse to go for broke. "I hate coming in and giving it all away. I never appreciate the money that I am up. When I am up, I say 'whatever, whatever, whatever' and take some shots and give it all away. I am not excited about making money. Perhaps I am too complacent. Whatever it is, I go home and come in and do it all over again. I am still anxious to get the money back the next day. I can't seem to get off this treadmill."

A knowledgeable observer opined about Dustin. "He is not managing or hedging his risk. He is dollar weighting too much of one bet or too much of several bets in too few positions and failing to figure out how to protect his downside should the market change dramatically. He may put all of his capital into his three best ideas all in a single direction, say long, rather than hedge out the position in a way to protect himself, or he may have $30 million of long positions and $10 million of shorts—small number of bets, highly concentrated dollar amounts, and not hedged.

"The reason Dustin was as good as he was in the years he was good was that his sector benefited from a lot of money flow. Dustin would keep adding to his positions when he believed in something. He didn't realize that he might be missing something or that there might be some potential downside to his trade. Some traders like Dustin get so huge in a position that they keep discounting the fact that they could be wrong. If you don't run a hedged position by having something else short, it may work seven out of eight times, but it only takes that one time to wipe out all the profits of the previous seven times."

Commenting on his own experiences when he was in drawdown, this particular trader said: "When we were in drawdown, we decided to moderate our expectation, to come in with a game plan. We set a goal of $ 1 million a month. Instead of shooting for three points, we decided to hit layups or easy shots. Dustin wanted to be down 30 points at the half and come back and hit all three pointers to win the game. He put himself in the situation where he was down, and he wanted to come back and swing his way out of it. This year (2001) the critical thing is to survive. It is the hardest tape that people with 20 plus years have seen. If you make a lot of money, that is great. The critical thing is not to blow up trying to force something. Don't try to make something happen out of nothing just because you have a credit line. Don't make ill-calculated bets.

"The high risk trader goes out there and swings. Some traders with a big appetite for risk can swing, but they have better control and are likely to be more hedged and are good at identifying when something is not working. When something isn't working the master trader will go to the relative peers and start to make the bet on the opposite side to protect himself."

Another observer commented on Dustin's risk-taking appetite: "He was just not putting any thought into the process. He was playing the slot machines. He had no idea why he was in the positions he was in. He just listened to what people were telling him to do, and he would do it big. He rarely had the patience to stay with his winners long enough to maximize his profits. And he would defend his position by holding on to losing positions or doubling down as his stocks were dropping, hoping to get his losses back in one fell swoop. Sometimes you do buy more when things are going down, but generally, especially from a short-term viewpoint, it is a losing proposition."

Unfortunately, if a trader like Dustin *does* succeed in reducing his losses by taking shots, he often forgets about his lack of discipline and his repetitive pattern of losing. Instead he thinks of himself as a successful big player and believes he can keep reproducing the big wins. Then the next time around he exposes himself to even greater risk.

"If you get it right you look like a genius. That is the gambling part of the trade. The not gambling part is having good information. The gambling part is the intuition," said another more profitable and risk-controlled trader who had a feeling for the distinctions here. "Intuition comes down to risk management and judgment. You need to put risk out there to make money but not so much that you are going to be in trouble. It comes down to confidence. When you are losing money, you are likely to take shots and gamble more than when you are making money."

Nathan is another high-risk trader, and he knows it. He can't stand the boredom of trading. He can't tolerate the "mundane nature" of going for a fixed target and then slowing down after he reaches it. Generally, when Nathan is ahead he gets euphoric and overconfident and starts swinging for the fences and, more often than not, blows up from doing this. Consider these tendencies:

Nathan: I am a compulsive gambler, and I have to work at it every day. I should take my cash and run, but I don't take my profit soon enough. I get greedy and try to make more. I made $250,000 three times this year. I made $100,000 a couple of times. But I am losing 40s, 50s when I am up money. I am getting greedy and want more and more, and then all of a sudden I am wrong. The market can kill you. I should get the profit and get out of the trade. One month ago, I was up $890,000, and in the last four days I lost $490,000. If I don't change the way I am, I am never going to make any money. The problem is that I keep getting bored out of my skull.

Kiev: Why are you bored?

N: There is nothing to do. I am just sitting here. I am making calls. I am not trading. Things are quiet. Earnings come later. I am an action junkie. I am sitting in front of a screen where I can be involved with the market.

K: If you were to do enough work so that by Wednesday you had work on 10 stocks and were working them, you ought not be bored.

N: I am bored.

K: You get bored if you are not trading?

N: I know I shouldn't, but I do. I should be engrossed in setting up, but I feel like I have to be involved.

K: Preparing isn't being involved?

N: It is not the same.

K: You are looking for the . . .

N: Quick fix. It is bad. I am an action junkie as opposed to a trader who is trying to get the edge. It is tougher to find the edge than being an action junkie. It takes less work—being a junkie.

K: How does it feel to be playing it when you are playing it based on information?

N: It feels great, but it is horrible when you get hurt. But to salvage something when you have been hurt and turn it around and make something—

that is the greatest feeling. That comes from what you know and what the street doesn't know . . . I think I am a better trader than my P&L [profit and loss] shows.

K: You are no better than your P&L.

N: I am holding myself back from being a good trader. I am being a gambler. Greed and the quick fix are what kill me.

On the face of it Nathan appeared to understand what his problem was, but when I suggested that he do more work (talk to more analysts, talk to the companies whose stocks he was trading, do some technical analysis, and learn more about the markets and the stocks he was trading), he resisted. He believed that he knew all that he needed to know and didn't see all the opportunities still available in the market. He didn't understand all the interesting things that he could be finding out about his companies that would make the trading more challenging and also combat the high-risk trading tendencies that caused him to constantly seek action.

Fortunately, Nathan felt so much pain from losing relative to his friends and colleagues that he finally realized it was critical for him to get control of the urge to get bigger and greedier. He eventually took control of the problem and began to do more work so that he was able to harness his intellect to the trading process, increase his degree of preparation, and begin to understand the complexities of trading. He also learned painstakingly to take his profits until he had a succession of successful days—after which he began to take larger positions and tried to make more money.

Practical Steps

High-risk trading is especially problematic when, instead of reducing their risk, traders take outsized risks in the face of drawdown. These risks only increase the chance of a blowup. Although this tendency usually occurs in traders who are already predisposed to gambling, it also may occur in anyone who has experienced a significant loss. Sometimes when a trader is down, he becomes emotional and starts flailing about trying to take shots at things in the hope of getting back what he lost. This is a recipe for disaster.

Consider whether high-risk trading is problematic for you:

- Do you have problems with denial, superstition, and overconfidence?
- Are you constantly seeking a sense of power and control?
- Are you competitive, restless, energetic, and easily bored?
- Do you find yourself avoiding work or not giving it your all until you are pressed by others or circumstances to do so?

The psychological motivation behind high-risk trading is actually a form of anxiety coupled with a low tolerance for uncertainty and an inability to postpone gratification or the reduction of anxiety by doing more work. You can't tolerate uncertainty and don't want to wait to see where a trade is going before you step in. Too eager to anticipate the market, you get in too soon and don't properly assess risk parameters. You are quick to act, hoping to get the big result as fast as possible without doing all the work required to succeed in a systematic way.

If any of this is true for you, then you may want to think seriously about how to gain control over your trading rather than wait until you experience so much pain that you are forced to cut back (as is so often true for high-risk traders). You have to decide to commit to making a significant change, to take the opportunities before you, and to not be so cavalier as to lose everything because of your compulsive need for action. You have to recognize that the trading waters are treacherous. You need to apply caution and cautiously guard profits. You also have to be aware of certain trading strategies to which you may become drawn because they appear relatively easy.

Case Study on Picking Tops and Bottoms

High-risk traders are drawn to quick profits, and picking tops or bottoms is a form of trading that looks like it might lead to a home run and enable them to get ahead of the competition. For high-risk traders, picking tops and bottoms is an emotionally satisfying way of trading because there is a feeling that when the "last fool was buying, you were selling." It gives an emotional and intellectual thrill to those who want to be unique, go against the crowd, and seek adventure.

Some traders try to pick a top when shorting a stock. If a trader thinks a stock, which is moving up, is about to hit its top and turn around, he may short it in order to get as much profit as he can before the price of the stock drops from its high. Picking bottoms is just the opposite. A stock may be moving downward, and a trader, thinking that the stock is about to turn, will buy it near what he thinks is the bottom of the range.

Picking tops means the trader is starting to scale into his short positions as the stock is rising, anticipating that he can make more profit from the trade by getting into it early while others are still buying the stock and pushing the price up, so that when it comes down he will make more money. He is trying to get bargain prices and in so doing is taking a greater risk—even though psychologically he may be convincing himself that he is putting himself into position to make more profit than he would if he started shorting the stock after it turned. In fact, the risk *is* greater because he is also losing as the stock moves up and ultimately may experience so much pressure that he is forced to cover his shorts before they turn, thereby losing money rather than making it. The same occurs at the bottom of the market.

The problem with picking tops and bottoms is that no trader can know in advance where or when a stock will change direction. If a trader picks a top and sells short, but the trade continues to move upward, then the trader will lose money. If he picks a bottom and buys a stock that continues to move down, he will also lose money. Therefore, both these moves can be very costly.

Other traders pick tops and trade on the long side. Their goal is to maximize profitability on the up end of the stock's trajectory. While it makes perfectly good sense to keep buying a stock as it keeps going up, the danger with this strategy is that unless the trader has set a profit objective and has defined an exit point for himself, he may fail to get out of the position when the stock stops going up or starts to go against him. For example one trader I know, Michaly, kept holding on to his stocks, hoping to make more money even though the stock movement was telling him that his strategy was no longer working and that it was time to get out of the position. As he later admitted in hindsight: "Holding the stocks wasn't wrong as the stocks were going up. That is good. Not selling them when they turned against me was wrong. I have to recognize when I am wrong more quickly."

Unfortunately for many high-risk traders, getting out at the right time is very difficult. They seem to have a predisposition for holding too long in hopes of making more. They don't buy/sell because they don't want to miss the additional move and end up losing profits. Then they beat themselves when the stocks start moving in the wrong direction. The problem is often compounded when they become paralyzed by the losses and fail to get out of their losing positions.

Interestingly enough, top and bottom pickers are also somewhat inclined towards heroics. They often want to be the first one into the trade. They want to take the trade when the odds seem against them. They relish being ahead of the crowd and sometimes even being against the crowd. They also often take themselves out of the game before the stock starts to move. They run out of money or they can no longer take the pain, so they don't stay in the trade for the full duration as they had originally intended.

So, is there any rationale to picking tops and bottom? Picking tops and bottoms is often a successful strategy with cyclical stocks that over time fluctuate over a range and is not an uncommon strategy in long-term, value-oriented portfolios, especially when the managers are confident about their fundamental understanding of the company and have self-assurance that things will eventually turn around.

According to Mark, a fundamental analyst turned trader, "I like stocks when they are bombed out or have bottomed. I don't mind being early before they turn upward. Hopefully they turn up. I don't mind losing money in a position on a particular day. What distresses me most is not having enough of a position when it is really the right time. I need to work on my speed in entering and exiting positions."

Although there is a valid rationale for buying stocks cheaply and even a little early before they have bottomed and turned, this strategy can become faulty if you run out of capital before things turn around. For example, Long Term Capital, a huge hedge fund that included several Nobel prize winners on its board, failed in 1998, according to one observer, because of their strategy of doubling down (which was a form of picking bottoms).*

What is it about a dropping stock that turns high-risk traders on? Why are such moves appealing to them? For some it is because the drop looks like an opportunity to pick up a bargain. For others it is a chance to make a real killing. The person who picks tops and bottoms wants to beat the system. He wants to get it before it turns in order to be unique and distinct.

However, while picking the bottom of the market is an appealing intellectual task and one that looks like it will be extra profitable in the long run, it is based on an unreasonable expectation. You not only have to be right about the assessment of the market direction but also right about the timing of the market movement as well. Like all analytic efforts, the emphasis in doing this far too often becomes a concern about being right rather than about maximizing profitability by trading the stock after the direction and the momentum has become apparent.

---

*Doubling down is a strategy whereby you keep doubling your bet until eventually you hit a winner and get back all your losses and make profits in one huge bet. The danger is that you will run out of money before the odds turn in your favor or the stocks that you have been buying as they have been dropping reverse and start moving upward.

Case Study on Trading to Be Different

A variant of this same overvaluation of ideas is the contrarian need to be different from the crowd. For example, Tim is one trader who invariably prefers to buy stocks when others are selling them and sell them when others are buying them. In fact, he admits that he gets an adrenaline rush by taking a position opposite to everyone else in the market. This search for excitement was no doubt related to his incredibly high tolerance for pain and what seemed like an unconscious willingness to take on the additional burdens of drawdowns. As Tim observed about himself:

"I like to be in the hole to start with. The psychological pressure about being in a hole never bothers me. In fact being in a hole is actually inspiring. The problem is that it is very costly in terms of time and effort. If you have a $10 million loss, you have to make $20 million to get it back. The time value of losses is disproportionate to the amount of capital."

An aspect of Tim's inclination to be a contrarian is his visceral aversion to being part of the crowd or to piggy back on the trades of others. By this he means that he consciously avoids any trades that others are doing which he considers to be too mundane, even if they are profitable. High-risk traders like Tim receive great intellectual satisfaction from getting things right and put more emphasis on the analysis than on reading the market and trading in terms of the price action.

This was brought home to me by Jack, an oil trader, who said: "I'm an intellectual snob on a trading desk. I have to make money because I am smarter. To make money today isn't right. To make money every day is for guys who are street smart. I have negative ideas about day trading although I love it. Sometimes I find it is coarse. The quality of life on the trading desk is not socially redeeming. I sometimes have ambivalence about what I do. I would rather describe myself as a portfolio manager than as an energy trader. I try to differentiate myself from the screen jockeys, day traders, or guys in the pits screaming into phones."

Digging deeper into these issues, Jack decided to adapt his trading of oil futures to the short-term trading model. He decided to place his emphasis on productivity and profitability rather than simply being right about his analysis. Here he describes some of the lessons he learned throughout this process:

"You have to learn to respect the movement of the tape," said Jack. "The tape is telling you something about reality, and you cannot ignore it because you believe in your story. That is not to say that you have to give up analysis, but you have to live within the tape. While living with the tape, you have to stay flexible in your thinking and put what you do in the context of the reality of the tape. The tape is telling you a story. You have to figure it out. In this model you see intraday volatility not as noise but as opportunity. You shorten your time horizons. This works better than the long-term, fundamental value approach to trading. The shorter-term, catalyst-driven approach is to trade in and out of positions, relying heavily on a market feel as well as analysis and understanding company stories. It is not just staring at a screen or sitting in an office doing analysis. This is a rare model.

"In the past I would have felt I worked really hard for nothing. I would have been frustrated. Now it makes sense. Follow the stories. There is a greater tolerance for uncertainty in this model."

Much of the psychology behind high-risk trading is about self-validation. High-risk traders want to be big when they are right. They could be right for a trade, but it wouldn't get an explosive headline effect if it weren't big. They want the effect. They want support for their intellectual thesis. Read on as Jack expounds on this phenomenon:

"I was absolutely sure this one trade was a fiasco. I was going to hold on to the short position to make sure I was the guy who understood it," he said. "But in the end, I got more relaxed. I finally realized, it was just a trade. Who really cares? I think now I don't want to cut my gains. I want to take my gains. That is what I did yesterday. Now every day I come in and say, 'Are we ready to make money?' We have to figure out how we will make money today. I would never have thought about it before."

Case Study on the High-Risk Addiction

Jason and Daniel are partners who also both fall prey to high-risk trading. Jason seems to like a crisis and enjoys fighting his way back. This may be why he gets in too soon without assessing the risk parameters and does not pay enough attention to reducing losses.

"I like fighting the drawdowns," said Jason. "Maybe I am addicted to overcoming adversity. The best I feel is when I am fighting my way back. Just running along and making a lot of money doesn't do it for me."

Jason likes to buy stocks when they are weak and keep adding to them as they move up. However he often remains in the position long after its price has reversed and come down and he has lost all of the profits he has made on the way up. In late 2000 he was trying to become a more risk-averse trader.

For example, in 2000 he played the cyclicals from the longside. He bought stock in a large paper company and made $20 million riding it up. He rode it up into the Fed meeting and then got short the stock. Then, all his catalysts were gone. Shorting them was a change in strategy that was incredibly hard for him given his inclination to keep buying momentum stocks rather than shorting them.

"It feels like the right thing, but intellectually I can't help asking why I am short this stock at 32," he explained. "There are a lot of cuts. Odds are we are going to go down. If they don't, I'll cover it. It's a very uncomfortable feeling. Earnings and visibility are good. Fundamentals are good. I had $70 million of exposure, but it hasn't worked. I cut it down. It's hard to do that. I just want to buy more. I can't play against the world. If the stuff isn't working, cut it down to be more nimble. I am trying to reduce the volatility."

Looking at some other trades he was making, he commented on the way he and his partner Daniel were always looking for the turn in direction: "We always try to get the inflection point," he continued. "We anticipate something in the fundamentals that is an inflection point. For example, DRAM prices are going down. It is a tumbleweed effect. The costs are going down. They can't afford to make their interest payments. The Korean companies are selling lower and lower. We are buying some of the companies figuring that the lower they go, when the prices get to a certain level, you will get fewer people making these chips, and fewer people buying them. Eventually you get to a huge inflection point or V bottom because of supply. Then you need the demand. We will look for the capitulation down there and hope for the huge turn. We buy it all the way down and then get out as soon as it turns. The smart and disciplined master trader will wait until it turns and then will pay up 20–30 percent and ride the trade up. He'll catch the real move. We are too excited about breaking even after taking pain all the way down. We will get out right after the inflection point."

As you can see, Jason is impatient. He denies his pain, risk, and potential for loss. He plays not to lose and changes his mind too often. He doesn't follow his plan of action. Ideally, he should be comfortable with the idea and size of a trade *before* he trades it. He is stubborn and complacent and isn't conditioned to keep losses down. His biggest problem is that he doesn't want to admit to failure. So when his positions change and he is losing money, he stays in the positions instead of getting out. In addition, he gets too big too fast and stays in certain stocks well after the catalyst has passed. He doesn't like to admit to mistakes. Basically, Jason is not managing his risk because of a concern for his image.

Jason soon adopted a more relaxed approach and felt more comfortable concentrating on not losing money. The next step for him then was to learn to take profits rather than hold on to positions only to watch them drop, swallowing up profits he had made and adding further anxiety and desperation to his trading.

Unfortunately, Jason's partner, Daniel, has a similar problem with his own trading.

"I am the classic home run hitter," Daniel said. "I have always been out on the edge. I lose sight of my own ability. I don't panic, even when things get out of control. If I did maybe I would rein things in a bit. I am overconfident. That is what gets the volatility going. That is why we can lose $25 million in 8 weeks and make $25 million in 2 weeks."

Daniel has no fear of taking chances for their own sake—without doing the requisite work. He is an adventurer who isn't very good at managing his downside risk. His risk-taking personality makes him a good trader but not as good as he could be if he learned to be more circumspect. He has a high tolerance for risk and a high pain tolerance. He needs to cut losses and play smaller. Interestingly while Jason is governed by the need not to be wrong, Daniel is governed by the need to be different.

For example, Daniel picked a top in natural gas and started shorting. He kept adding to the position when it was at the top and then covered the first day it was down from the top. He kept adding to the short position as it moved up, doubling up his position and playing it for the turn. He was less interested in riding out the short than he was in picking the top. He believed that the price action would attract more sellers than buyers at some point. Daniel sees the chart and sees what others are doing, but he is waiting for the inflection point. He is stubborn. By his own personal account, he'll risk his entire net worth to be right. He will put everything on a highly leveraged bet.

The problem with this approach is that Daniel often gets way too big too soon and is forced out of positions before they have reached the inflection point. Forced to cover, he often takes a big beating.

It should also be noted that Daniel is experiencing pain all the way up on a short or all the way down when he is picking a bottom. According to Jason: "I watched Daniel buy corn at $2.20 a bushel. It bottomed out at $1.85 and he was out at $1.95." He is not out after the reversal because he is relieved to be out and not experiencing the pain. He is out because he has only played it for the inflection point or the turn.

This team also had a problem using their goals as a guideline to help them make decisions about getting out of positions to keep their losses down. For example, they have a monthly goal of $20 million but didn't want to think too much about it, lest they press their bets at the wrong time. Until they got a handle on these problems, they had to learn to cut their risk, play smaller, and be more focused on keeping their losses down.

Although Jason and Daniel both like risk taking and the adrenaline rush of their trading style, they both understand how that style is holding them back.

"I like the fight. I like to play. I like to be in the game," said Jason. "But of course, I don't like having to flatten out the book. I don't like getting out of the game. We don't enjoy losing money."

Taking profits is a critical aspect of managing risk, and this team soon realized that "it is so much more comfortable to sell a large cap stock up two dollars when you bought it the day before than to hold it and see it reverse, which is what we used to do. The old way is so painful. We are learning to take our profits and not hold things too long, just to hold on to them. We are trying to have 25 million dollars worth of positions. We have to get out when the stocks are going down and not add to our positions.

Profiling the High-Risk Trader

We need to add to positions when they are going up and learn to play the middle range of the pitch. We also have to take profits when we can."

"We have been watching Brian (a master trader) trade and have asked ourselves, 'Does a master trader ever engage in this form of high-risk trading?' Absolutely, but with the caveat that he doesn't take *unnecessary* risks. He doesn't feel the need to take shots. He is not looking for quick gratification. He doesn't feel the need to buy 2 million of Company B and have it move up $2 to prove he can catch the bottom of technology. He would rather buy it up $10 and have it go up $12. It's the same two dollars with less pain."

The master trader will get involved in the price exhaustion phenomenon for very specific reasons. He is looking to catch the trend. He buys into the shorter time frame. Once it turns he will not chase it. When it is wrong, he gets out of the trade very rapidly. As much as he plays the tops and bottoms, he is not invested in taking these trades as a matter of belief or style. He simply takes such trades opportunistically when the charts suggest price exhaustion.

Jason and Daniel also started to size up their trades when they had big catalysts. They made sure that they maximized their best opportunities in line with the concept that 3 percent of trades can account for over 100 percent of the profitability of a portfolio. This concept, as easy as it is for most traders to grasp, is generally harder for high-risk traders to implement because it flies in the face of their impulse to hold on to losers and to get out of winning positions. Constantly discussing this, Jason and Daniel began to improve their profitability in their best trades by looking for reasons such as catalysts, earnings announcements, news events, and the like to get bigger in trades that were working or looked like they would work. Here they began to consciously try to make more in their winning trades than they were losing in their losing trades. This meant getting out of losing positions faster and holding onto winning trades longer, or getting bigger in winning trades until their profit to loss ratio was 3:1. It also meant paying attention to other factors in the marketplace so that they could make their sale and take their profits before the price dropped.

They also recognized the importance of consciously avoiding high-risk bets that could throw them into big drawdowns. Daniel had gotten very long in a European initial public offering (IPO) and lost a substantial amount of money. In reviewing the trade, it became apparent that he was assuming it was safe to be long before the company prereleased even though he had believed that numbers would be guided down. But he hadn't spoken to enough analysts and was taking too big a bet on insufficient information. He lost money in another big wireless bet based on his own macroeconomic analysis that the companies looked like they wanted to find a level and fundamentals were getting washed out. He believed that he had a window before any prereleases because of a huge wireless conference in Europe that was generating several days of positive news. He was long $40 million of four wireless companies and then another wireless bellweather blew up that night and his positions were down 10 percent.

"I was long $40 million in wireless. That was one-half my capital. It was probably too much capital."

Between the wireless bet and the European IPO, Daniel and Jason were down $15 million, almost wiping out their profits from the earlier part of the year. From this experience they realized that they had to manage their positions better. Instead of a handful of positions, they should have had thirty positions in a portfolio. As Daniel noted:

"I can't have positions bigger than $8 million. I should have 30 positions in a portfolio and they should be managed as a portfolio, not as separate stocks. I have to be smaller, even if I have a home run idea. It shouldn't be more than $8 million. If it is, I should run it by management and have some very compelling reasons to be bigger."

He recognized that he was not paying attention to risk. His positions were too big and he was betting too big in highly volatile stocks that could make very big moves very rapidly.

The Solutions

As you can see from the previous example, Daniel and Jason had to take a number of different steps to begin correcting their high-risk tendencies. In fact, there are many psychologically sound steps to take to correct the proclivity toward high-risk trading. These principles are grounded in the methodology described in my previous books, *Trading to Win* (Wiley, 1998) and *Trading in the Zone* (Wiley, 2001), and have to do with increasing self-observation and consciousness about the actions that you take and learning to try new behaviors that are more compatible with the objectives that you set.

The first step is to recognize the impact of your preconceptions and subconscious attitudes on your trading activities. You also need to develop a metaconcept about your trading so that your trading experiences themselves become the source of the observations that you make, and the changes you can make to gain greater control over the risk-taking processes.

Next step—think about the compulsive component of the urge to trade in a high-risk manner. One move here especially when you are trading just to get an adrenaline rush is to acknowledge the compulsion. It is also important to accept the support of a team, a coach, or manager to help you deal with the compulsion to go against the crowd. You have to learn that it is OK to trade from a more rational viewpoint than in terms of how you are feeling.

Changing high-risk trading patterns is hard to do, because they are a set of habits and attitudes built into the way in which you see the world. To increase your profitability, you have to change your view of the world as it relates to trading. You can be a bargain hunter on the outside. You can look for good deals when you are buying a house or a car, but when you are trading you have to be more flexible, not so stubborn. As I told Daniel, you have to put your intellect in the service of profitability even if that doesn't make you unique.

When you engage in high-risk trading, you are bringing your own reality to the trading arena. You want to deny failure, to be different, to get a bargain, to be first, to beat the consensus. To master this pattern you have to learn to trade to manage the fear of losing and to learn patience and control over your impulses. You need to determine and know the specific reason that you are in a stock. If you don't have a reason to be there, you need to get out rather than ride out the pain for contrarian reasons or keep holding them when they reverse against you.

Currently, the satisfaction of being the first one into a trade compels you to trade early before a turn. It may make sense to learn to hold off and wait for the turn before getting into some trades. It also may be better to take the discomfort of being out of the trade rather than the pain of being in something that is moving against you. Use the pain as an indicator that you are doing something correctly. Additionally, where you have taken the pain of something moving against you, learn to stay in longer after the inflection point and ride it up. In a word, you have to devise a more flexible trading discipline that can help you override your natural inclination toward high-risk trading behavior.

To improve your ability to manage risk, you need to identify the underlying assumptions behind your habitual ways of trading. Doing so can help you control those things which are counterproductive and can give you a greater sense of containing over your ability to handle risk.

Changing habits is the most difficult thing for traders to do because most are wedded to their own approach. First you have to develop a desire to manage risk in a better way and to face whatever resistance you may have.

Another step is to make a conscious commitment to the objective of not getting hurt in your trading. You must take on less risk until you have demonstrated that you can manage it successfully by keeping your losses down.

Recognizing this personality proclivity—your insensitivity to pain, which fosters too high a tolerance for risk—you must consciously seek to temper your urge to take on risk for the excitement of doing so with more focus on data and analysis so that you can make better stock assessments and reduce your overall financial risk. According to one trader:

"I am trying to temper the adrenaline component of my trading so that I am more effective as a trader. My gut check now when I go home is whether I am anxious or worried at night. I don't have to be out of control. I thought that was the name of the game. I was dragging myself along. I was fighting the tape. I have been fighting my whole career. I was putting myself in more jeopardy and now realize I don't have to approach it that way."

Practical Steps

If you are a high-risk trader, then you must give up your stubborn streaks. Having to do things your own way isn't going to help you reach your goals. Do you ever justify your actions by saying, "That's just the way I am, and I can't change"? This statement is common to make when your habit patterns are identified. Be aware that it shows you want to avoid responsibility for your actions and to stay trapped in a set of learned attitudes and behavioral habits. If you are battling with high-risk forms of trading, consider the following:

- Try to become less of a contrarian just for the sake of being a contrarian. Learn not to trade against the consensus, and be willing to give up the need to be different, especially if others are making the right market call.
- Consciously stop trying to play trades for the bounce or the reversal or the turn. Stop trying to be so early to the trade in an effort to get in first or avoid being last.
- Be willing to let go of the need to hit huge home runs or make the big score. Be happy with the smaller but more steady profits that come from trading a smaller part of the curve.
- Use your creativity and talent to focus more on retaining profits and minimizing losses than to be creative and individualistic for the sake of it.
- Learn to react to news faster. If the stock is dropping, get out and cut your losses as opposed to doubling down.

Remember, the master trader is not looking for a thrill. And he is not trying to be a hero. The master trader is always pushing forward.

He takes his capital down when the market is shaky. When he gets big, he is prudent. He trades for profitability, not for ego or an emotional high.

This new psychology of risk taking deals more with your own psychology than with gathering more information about the markets. Of course that is important, but ultimately it is your capacity to enter into the realm of the unknown, to adapt to difficult circumstances, and rise above success and failure that constitutes the essence of trading success. Nowhere is this more true than when you must develop a new way of being in the trading arena that allows you to trade in terms of your objectives rather than in terms of your compulsion to be different.

Ultimately, your success in trading has to do with your ability to be open to the markets, to stay in the present, to be free of fear and ego, euphoria, and grandiosity, and to approach the markets as opportunities for mastery rather than as situations designed to fulfill your basic sense of self.

CHAPTER SEVEN

RECOGNIZING THE MASTER TRADER

Think of the continuum from overly passive trader to hyper-risky trader not as a flat line, but as a bell curve. At the peak of the bell stands a more skillful individual who handles risk with just the right mix of caution and confidence, the master trader.

By choosing to trade for a living, you probably have a greater risk appetite than those in accounting or banking or medicine. Yet some of your colleagues have both more risk tolerance than others and an even greater capacity to objectify what is going on in the markets. Those colleagues should be your role models; they have developed what can reasonably be called mastery.

There are distinct differences between the master trader and other traders, not only in terms of profit margins but in the way in which the master trader carries herself, conducts her trades, and handles wins and losses. All these traits are worth exploring because they create awareness about the possibilities for personal transformation.

Mastery is the capacity to empty your mind of preconceptions about yourself and the market, to let go of your persona, your life principles, and other beliefs and limiting notions, so that you can more fully take risks in the here and now. Mastery is about telling the truth, about not being too egotistical about your success or too depressed about your losses.

To be a master you not only have to make more in your winning trades than you lose in your losing trades, you also have to get past all the values that you are carrying with you from the past and focus on the challenges before you—whether they involve making $50 million or $20 million or $10 million or $5 thousand a day. Throughout this book we have been discussing how to focus, how to follow the strategy and pursue the goal. This chapter discusses the distance between where you are (or have been) and where you want to be—so that you can grow from being an ordinary trader to becoming an extraordinary one.

Defining the Master Trader

In order to achieve trading mastery, the master trader has learned to keep his emotions in check so that he remains calm in the midst of chaos. By doing this he follows his strategy as opposed to making decisions based on how he feels. He is emotionally and intellectually in control of risk taking and is able to differentiate the critical factors that may influence a trade from the noise and hyperbole surrounding it. This ineffable factor was underscored by a trader named Lenny who told me:

"The master trader is listening to an aspect of events that others aren't listening to. He is able to calculate the risk factor in terms of how many people are playing a particular story. This is an intangible skill. He has learned from trading the tape how a stock is moving. He can tell when there is positive money flow into a sector or changes in money flow and the impact this flow has on stocks. He can then question why the stock is moving and explore reasons for it in terms of events going on in the company. Then he integrates his theory with a view of the entire market and what is happening in other sectors.

Recognizing the Master Trader

"Why is company X up three points? Track down some stories to find an explanation. Is the story specific to the company? Or is it sector specific? The master trader integrates this additional analysis with a view of money flows into various sectors.

"A large discount store chain said it saw an uptick in sales secondary to the tax rebates in the summer of 2001. Some believed this was in the stock, and that it was old news. Other people kept watching for the stock to dip and believed that the news wasn't baked into the stock and that it was wise to buy the dip. Then the stocks started to scream and a lot of people started to sell all the apparel-related names that thematically weren't doing well. Department stores were reporting 'bad traffic,' 'missing expectations' and the discounters were reporting 'above plan sales' because of the tax rebates. The malls were showing reduced traffic. The weather was warm and people weren't buying sweaters for the fall. There was a growing dichotomy between these various groups. Knowing what to do in the face of all these diverse reports is mastery—the ability to assimilate facts from various places with the patterns of activity in stock movements.

"The ability to mechanically trade and buy and sell and execute trades is also a component of mastery. It contributes a lot to the overall P&L [profit and loss]. The master trader understands the dynamics between supply and demand in the stock. There are different types of supply and demand. How is the stock acting and what is it communicating to you? Stocks speak to the master trader in terms of money flowing in and out of a stock. He gets a feel of the action in the pit on the floor. He can see the unfolding exchange between supply and demand and where the imbalance is in the crowd. He has a sense of when it is time to buy or to sell."

What are some of the other characteristics of mastery? I asked Ben, a currency trader about this, and he noted: "Being able to marshal confidence after a long period of drawdown, with all the negative implications this has for killing self-esteem. The master trader has been there before, has been prudent in reducing his size, and is able to take a stand to get bigger based on his conviction of the bet."

"The master trader stays with the pain. The ultimate risk management is profit," added another trader. "The key is not taking your profits too soon. That stamina and confidence is critical to mastery. It is masterful when you put the money to work, and you make a lot of money, and you can keep taking advantage of market moves and have the courage of your conviction to trade it in whatever direction it is going.

"The master trader is able to say that the entire market is wrong and he is right. It is supreme confidence that he is better than anyone else trading that stock. He is also a bit more cynical than most traders, which goes along with being successful on the short side. A monkey can be trained to buy low and sell high. The master trader knows when to take the trade off; he knows when he is losing money, when he is breaking even, and when he is making money as well. It is very hard to do."

The master trader uses his own emotional responses not to react to the market but as an indicator of what others may be doing. This is a second-derivative type of trading wherein he is making decisions based on a number of factors, including how he believes others are likely to trade. If the master trader is wrong, and the market tells him he is wrong, he gets out. If he is right, he presses his bet. He is not invested in being right or having his thesis proved. If the data suggest he is wrong, he moves on. He doesn't buy into his emotions or beliefs about companies. While some traders get anxious about being anxious, the master trader maintains balance.

Case Study—An Example of Mastery

Sam is a master trader who admittedly has a natural gift for trading but who has also developed it through a lot of hard work and continuous rethinking of his approach. He keeps recreating himself in response to changes in the markets, changes in his level of capital, and changes in his ability to utilize different strategies and the help of others.

Sam is able to make rapid fire decisions in the face of considerable uncertainty. He always balances the risks against the rewards of his trades and pays close attention to managing his risk no matter how profitable he is. He sees things that others don't see. While some traders react to anything, Sam reaches his own conclusions. He makes a determination and a decision.

Another trader, Luke, describes Sam and his style of risk taking: "Sam looks at things in a three-dimensional way. Not just, 'Are they up or down?' but how are other people interpreting the available analyses so that he is factoring into his own decisions an estimation of what he thinks other traders in the marketplace are going to do. He tries to interpret what they are doing based on how the traders around him are trading, viewing their trading as a proxy for the market. Then, he acts. While everyone else is reacting to the price move, he is reacting to their reactions—making his decisions based on how he thinks they are going to act or how they are already acting. He is looking at the price movement as indicative of something else. He looks at a wide range of data and comes to an actionable thesis."

A lot of people can find reasons to trade specific stocks based on the available analyses but aren't necessarily able to think outside the box. Sam distills from the data what he thinks will be relevant for that stock and decides whether to buy or sell. His assessment tells him what will be an issue. He is framing what could be a focus and the reason for the focus. The second derivative thought is considering how people will react to changes in the market, the sector, and the company itself.

Master Traders Examine Lots of Data

The master trader couples fundamental analysis with trading savvy as he handles risk intelligently in the short-term, catalyst-driven model. He understands the issues involved in assessing companies. He looks for the reasons why a company is working or not working.

Sandor

Whereas an ordinary trader often spends most of his time watching the price action on the tape, the master trader looks beneath the surface and tries to understand more about the fundamentals of a company and the relevance of catalysts such as earnings announcements, brokerage house upgrades or downgrades, and other newsworthy events that may affect the price of a stock. When he sees something happening on the tape, he tries to understand the implications of events. He is looking for the real explanation of what is going on and recognizes the importance of understanding the underlying issues. He wants to know whether a company is managing its businesses well and listens carefully and skeptically to reports of company representatives as well as Wall Street analysts so as to form an educated view about the direction of a company and its stock. He understands the implications of a lot of subtle events, and by his analysis of a variety of bits of data he can get the critical variant perception that enables him to see beyond the balance sheet.

Master traders have an ability to assess fundamental and market data and trading patterns so as to increase the probabilities of their trades. They are always listening for whether companies are managing their businesses well. They recognize when something is wrong despite what the company is reporting. They are always skeptical and try to make appropriate comparisons because sometimes the consensus is correct, and there is nothing to do.

Case Study on the Mastery of Information

An example that I referred to earlier occurred in 2000, when the price for semiconductor chip or DRAM prices were going up every day. Then the supply/demand turned. Sam didn't see any signs that things were failing, but there were pressures in the market. He saw signs that prices were

Recognizing the Master Trader

creeping up and figured that this would limit the upside in semiconductors and create the conditions for a downdraft in prices. In effect he was seeing the first signs of a fracture in the market, but he waited until the fractures actually began.

His view was that as long as the market believed in the stocks and was taking their prices up, the intellectual formulation that the companies were failing was just that. Sam waited until he saw real evidence of a turning in these stocks. He was waiting for the stocks to turn and watching them to see when the beginning fractures impinged on the stock value. He understood DRAMs were about supply and demand, but thought maybe this time it was about supply and not demand. As long as the market was taking the stock up, Sam wouldn't act. He was waiting for it to happen.

The master trader isn't just a contrarian. He understands the business model process and waits for the right moment. He understands companies and where they are moving. As one trader said, "This isn't accomplished by guesses. You need a thought process." The master trader continually asks himself what will the stock look like in the future. He doesn't take anything at face value and is proactive rather than reactive. He continually tries to distinguish what is real from what is not real.

Most ordinary traders don't ask themselves what the stock will look like in the future. They read everything at face value and are reactive instead of proactive. They don't make the distinction between what is real and not real. The master trader has his hand on the pulse and is able to make real distinctions. As one keen observer noted: "He [the master trader] knows when to buy and when to rent."

Another characteristic of the master trader is his ability to look beyond immediate data points. Read how George describes a master trader:

"Most people are aware of company reports and the dates of the reports and the relevance of these reports for trading purposes. The sell side reacts to the information reported by the company on specific dates, and the stock makes certain moves. You build up a chronology of evidence and a time line of probable events and start to make a risk/reward bet into an event, trying to tap into sentiment and expectation. The master trader weighs risk and tries to measure adjustments.

"Ric, a master trader, shorted a large retailer going into an analyst meeting. He considered the incremental data from the meeting and realized that sentiment had started to shift back from being positive. There was no incremental news, and there were whispers that comps would be negative. As a master trader, Ric had the ability to stay short and anticipate that, especially in light of the fact that we were going into a heat wave, it didn't matter if they reported a negative comp and it was believed to be factored into the stock price (as was true for many ordinary traders who got out of the trade, believing it wouldn't go down any more). He believed that there was not much that could get the stock to bounce, especially because the weather was working in his favor. Instead of viewing the analyst's meeting as neutral, he viewed it as the top in the stock and traded from the short side into earnings, expecting that it might drop from 42 to 26 before earnings.

"At the analyst meeting there wasn't a lot of data presented. Several people who attended the meeting said they heard comps in men's wear were negative and stayed negative on the stock. Ric shorted it at 42 and stayed short and didn't cover. Going into comps, other short sellers were shaken out when the stock hit $35 believing that the negative comps were baked into the stock. Ric, the master trader, was able to look beyond the immediate event and consider that there was still more downside in the stock and kept pressing it. He didn't care that the comps were bad. He looked past that data point and assessed the longer-term loss potential in the trade."

"The ability to think several moves ahead is what differentiates the master trader from the good trader. The master trader has the ability to trade as if he were playing chess. He is not just moving his pawn. He is thinking about how to protect his rook and his bishop and is thinking three or four steps ahead of everyone else. He is looking at the board and creating scenarios in his mind of how things will play out. He has an inordinate ability to assess data creatively and develop a story or thesis—continually modifying it in terms of changes in the marketplace or how much attention or lack of attention an idea is getting. He keeps looking for data points that support or refute his theory, in terms of price action, supply and demand, and a variety of other factors affecting the movement of a stock."

Recognizing the Master Trader

Master Traders Tweak Their Own Styles

Master traders come in all sizes and shapes but what is common to them all is their willingness to follow their own style and conviction. To become a master trader, you have to learn to find the edge of the envelope, to set a goal, develop a strategy, and tweak your own style. The key is learning how to work to improve your specific game in managing risk better and maximizing opportunities.

If you aspire to become a master trader, you have to think of making changes in the framework of how you see the world. This is not easy to do for most of us. It is far easier to bask in the notion that we are "doing fine," "don't really need to get" what we were going for, or that "providence will take care of it" or "if it was meant to be, then it will happen." Many such beliefs keep us from facing the truth. But in reality, perhaps you are not as focused as you could be. Perhaps you are not stretching yourself as much as you could. Perhaps more could be done if only you could acknowledge that something is missing, and having recognized that, begin to look for what it is in the moments before you.

One trader describes his struggles in this journey toward mastery:

"I have to learn to use the discomfort and be able to stretch in terms of doing things that would be more profitable and not just comfortable. For example, I had something the other day and didn't use the discomfort. I put on a spread. One paper company was being bought by another large paper company that had an asbestos issue. It has been in their 10K for years. Recently all the asbestos stocks had collapsed and were down to near zero. Now they were going after the large paper company. So, naturally I wondered whether they had financing to do the deal. Another trader didn't think they had financing. There was a $2 spread. I thought, if I lose $10, he will say I was trying to be a pig. So, I took it off. Then they confirmed there was financing. I was upset with myself because I allowed the discomfort and the other guy's potential criticism of me to scare me out of something. Part of having conviction is using the discomfort. If you don't have conviction, then how can you trade?"

- The master trader can endure the internal discomfort associated with the impulse to act for instant emotional gratification. He is patient. He is good at focusing on what he is looking for.

To become a master trader, you have to stop trying to control yourself and the world. You must stop any inclination you might have to look for a confirmation of yourself from other people, or from your material possessions, or from other representations of yourself. Give up all reference points and attempts to prove your identity. You must simply enter into the next moment without regard for what you or others think and feel. If you can do these things, you can be more present to the trading events before you than was ever possible before.

The same guidelines apply if you try to change by copying someone else's strategy rather than choosing what you have and developing your own strengths. Although you can learn from other people's efforts, it is best to consider how they have developed their own resources and how this model might help you to discover your own strengths. Identify your interests and gifts or natural proclivities and focus on them in order to be true to yourself. Then and only then can you become a true master trader.

Developing Mastery

I have outlined various elements of mastery throughout this book. Perhaps the most critical of these is the ability to see reality for what it is with a minimum of denial and rationalization. The more you can see past your own preconceptions and prejudices, the more you can begin to modify the way you experience reality. Freed from the past you can begin to relate to events from a creative perspective, by facing the truth, and continually examining how your life principles distort reality.

There is an invisible realm of the universe that works according to the laws of reality. This realm cannot be seen as long as you function from the perspective of what you already know. When you live in the gap and enter into the realm of mastery, you are open to this unseen reality and will be able to see through to the ground of being in this world. Here you will begin to see new possibilities and pathways.

• Once you are aware of your automatic thoughts or basic assumptions of the world, you are free to choose your response to events and to take risks in a more conscious, creative way than you may have been doing until now. You will be able to trade more creatively than when you are functioning on automatic pilot based on limited notions of your social persona or fixed life principles of the past. This capacity to be aware of your automatic thoughts will increase your aptitude for surrendering those limiting perspectives.

Create a New Perspective

The capacity to alter interpretations of events is what differentiates human being from other species. The power of consciousness enables you to change your thoughts and to think about your thinking. By inventing new perspectives, you can see the world from new angles and thereby transcend the limits of biology and early life conditioning.

Essentially, it is possible to design a new concept from which to perceive the market and then trade from this new future-oriented perspective rather than to be trapped by the limiting perspective of the past. Another name for this new concept is vision, which provides a new way for ordering information and defining experience so as to design your trades in terms of specific results. This vision is not the same as the inclination to live from primary life principles related to survival needs of safety, well-being, sexual satisfaction, and security or secondary life principles pertaining to proper behavior and approval. These life principles may have existed since childhood. Although they are largely unconscious, they influence your perceptions and actions and in this sense lack the power of vision.

The power of vision enables you as an adult to consciously create a new template for your trading that is more consistent with the market than with your preconceived notions of it. Recognizing your power for this creativity can indeed not only change your trading forever but can become a personal, transforming experience. When you reframe your perspective and create a new vision for your trading, you change your underlying assumptions about the market. By doing this, you free yourself from the habitual urge to keep repeating the past and put yourself in a position to take bolder risks, appropriately sized in a measured way to your objectives.

By looking at your trading through the lens of an expanded vision of the future, you will be able to see opportunities in the markets that you couldn't see before. You expand your natural talent by taking on more complex levels of risk so as to achieve more of what you are capable of achieving. The key to mastery is a willingness to act in terms of your vision rather than your old concepts of yourself by taking on new challenges and acknowledging your newly discovered potential as it begins to surface without retreating into the self-protectiveness of rationalization.

Pursue the Vision

When you are totally committed to an action and are totally absorbed in all the steps necessary to produce the desired result, you are likely to experience a sense of exhilaration or high momentum, where everything is flowing appropriately, without any extra effort. I have discussed this throughout this book in terms of establishing your goal and taking incremental steps consistent with it. Focused attention enables you to maintain your concentration on the task before you and to keep yourself free of distracting concerns. The more you stay focused, the more you can avoid overinvolvement with distractions without actually trying to correct or eliminate them. You simply accept them for what they are. Focusing leads to specific results, which will give you a sense of control over your trades and will enable you to bring more energy and attention to your trading. It also enables you to bypass excessive concern about egotistical issues.

When you are completely engaged in an action, it absorbs you so totally that you don't mind what people think about you. You feel relaxed and are enjoying the experience. The more skillful you become in being completely engaged, the more you can bring all of yourself into play in the course of the activity.

Pursuing your vision means to put yourself in the mind-set of the Zen master archer where you can shoot the arrow without even focusing on the target. It means trading and then moving on to the next trade without struggling to redo the past. You notice what you did, and you move on, without trying to perfect what you just did. Notice it, move on, and take another trade.

Between trades (as between serves in tennis) you should relax, exhale, clear your mind, and begin to prepare for the next moment. Visualizing positive steps to take and putting yourself in a positive frame of mind, as well as in a positive physical posture for taking action (sit up straight or walk confidently rather than slumped), prepares you for maximum performance. When you find yourself functioning more effectively than before, you notice it but keep focused rather than focusing on what might have been. The past has brought you to the next moment just as the next moment will lead you to the moment after that. There is nothing to think about. There is only the chance to trade in the moment before you.

Engage in the next moment fully. Recognize that the results are inherent in the structure. Your only task is to create the structure.

Once you have started doing this, don't limit yourself. Keep expanding the space by continuing to create the structures that support the vision.

Release the Ego

Mastery means accepting the possibility that your self is not a solid entity, but a succession of moments or transactions. The ego that you think you are is not a permanent entity but is rather a set of transactions in the moment before you: Mastery means letting go of your false sense of self and recognizing that you can keep taking risks moment-to-moment.

This new view will rid you of certain fixed notions that you have about yourself such as that you are fearful or cautious or precise or whatever you believe is a fixed quality of yourself. This new self-concept will also help you to let go of efforts to convince others that you are indeed the person you believe you have always been. Your long-standing view of yourself may be a social fiction which, however convenient, traps you. Wouldn't it make sense to adopt instead the belief that you are free today to choose a different persona? Wouldn't it be good to feel exhilarated by operating in the world from an entirely fresh perspective?

Currently, you might keep justifying this restrictive concept of yourself, a pattern of manipulation of self and others insofar as you get the world to confirm your concept of reality. Notice whether you have any tendency to be self-denigrating, self-deceiving, or falsely humble and whether you give away your power through such a cover-up because of some unconscious notion that you do not deserve greater achievements or that others will ridicule you for being whomever you want to be.

Cover-up weakens the structural or creative tension between where you are and where you want to be in terms of your goals, either by denying reality or misrepresenting it to you such that you invest in image and appearances and mistake the menu for the meal. If you think that fame and fortune are real, or you are able to convince yourself and others that you have certain powers and put your energy into appearances rather than into action, you will weaken structural tension and consequently weaken your power to create by trading in the zone.

If you can let go of these reference points, you can begin to tune into the power of the moment and the uniqueness and vividness of all the phenomena of the world. Take a stand that you are the trader you wish to be who is willing to take measured risks to produce specific results. Know in your heart what you have committed to and then each day focus on what you can concentrate on in front of you without too much discussion about what you are doing, and you more than likely will be able to produce results far greater than you may have ever imagined.

Practical Steps

The power of trading in the gap comes from your willingness to admit your problems. Once you can admit them, you can begin to trade more successfully. The first step involves distinguishing events from your reactions and inhibitions and learning to label emotional responses.

When it is possible, recollect your past most successful trade. If you don't have one, make one up. It doesn't really matter. The brain processes real and symbolic or invented experiences in the same way. If you can remember it and get into the same mind-set that you were in when you successfully traded, you may soon discover that you begin to feel better. You begin to feel excited. You feel some of what you may have felt when you were successfully trading—a sense of impunity, a sense of being able to see things clearly that you might not see so well when you are feeling depressed or you have been trading poorly.

ᐧ It doesn't matter how you traded yesterday if you can keep coming back to this positive mental state. You accomplish nothing by beating yourself up for having done poorly the day before or on the last trade.

Of course, getting into a positive mind-set does not substitute for the work, but it enhances the way in which you perform. It puts you into the right frame of mind. It permits you to tune out some of the distractions around you that may reduce your concentration and ability.

Once you realize that you don't know what your psychological limits are, you are better prepared to trade in the gap. In fact, the size of the discrepancy (between where you are and where you wish to be) you can tolerate determines the amount of energy you can generate so as to shift your trading into a miraculous realm.

Consider:

- What's missing in your risk taking?
- How big must you be?
- How else might a trade have been handled?
- What can you learn from what happened so that the same mistake won't happen again?

Create a structure context to produce the results. Take action, and then review what was done so you can see what's missing (e.g., data, more work, the right attitude, a trading partner) in the structure that is keeping you from fully realizing your objectives and put that in place.

To trade in the now means to take appropriate risks, sized to the results you want, without opinion and judgment. Nothing that you have rejected is necessarily bad, and nothing you have grasped is necessarily good. You accept events as they are and open yourself up to the opportunity to take risk in line with an expanded vision of your trading objectives.

Allow time for things to develop. Accept the uncertainty of reality, and do not see it as a reflection of your own inadequacy or incompetence. Use the future, not as a place to get to but as a place to come from—as a guide from which to enter into the next moment before you. Trading can be treacherous but with commitment, a proactive approach, and lots of practice, you too can cultivate your practice of mastery.

Assessing Your Progress

Of course there is a tendency to become so enamored of the vision or goal that it becomes an obsessive preoccupation that engulfs you and causes much misery in your life. It is important to realize that choosing a vision is done purposefully to create a guide for action and to draw you into the future. Your vision is both compass and magnet, but it is not an end in itself and ought not to become the total focus of your thought. It is useful in helping you to become as fully engaged as possible, but its realization will not fulfill you.

Efforts to achieve a goal to fulfill yourself derive from a life principle of insufficiency and the erroneous belief that you both need and can get something you didn't get as a child. The fact is that you cannot get what you didn't get or what you perceived you didn't get, and efforts to do so only create a vicious circle that intensifies feelings of inadequacy and incompleteness.

Trading mastery enables you to be free of striving, free of a notion of insufficiency. Indeed, the state of mind I am describing means you are totally present to risk-taking opportunities without artifice or dissembling. To do this you have to recognize and stand aside from your thinking defenses, which cover up your sense of vulnerability.

You need only be where you are. The opportunities to realize your objectives are before you. You only need to listen for them and not be, as in the past, so opinionated, impatient, or quick to respond automatically, or so cautious and perfectionistic that you are trapped by abstract notions that lock you out of experience. You have the capacity to be open to the opportunities before you and do not have to look for answers somewhere else.

The real issue is whether you are willing to take the necessary actions associated with risk taking. This means being able to set goals, create strategies, and keep moving forward, always reviewing what is missing in the gap between where you are and where you wish to be. Once you acknowledge that something is missing, that you don't have all the answers, you will be more willing to look to see what you need to do to produce the results and more open to getting help and support from others. This openness is the essential value of acknowledging that something is missing. It is not a judgment about yourself or a prediction about impossibility. It is the "Open Sesame" to productivity.

Practical Steps

The value of scores or results or statistical measures of outcome is that they measure what you have accomplished in relation to your objectives. Then you can consider what is missing and what more can be done. When you ask what's missing or what more can I do or what dropped out of a strategy that was working, you run into a natural tendency to rationalize results, to explain them away, to justify them.

In fact, the result wasn't produced because it wasn't produced, and the task here is to look more carefully at what needs to be done to produce it.

- How much more attention can you focus on the task?
- How can you change certain routines that you automatically follow?

- What shifts in your thinking or in your routines can be made that will enable you to master the reality before you without getting caught up in self-protective ways of trading?

Resistance refers to the habits, self-doubts, fears, and life principles of pessimism and defeat that lock you into the past. A proactive perspective enables you to take on higher risks and produce the results you have committed to produce.

To master resistance, you need to become conscious of those resistant thoughts, body tension, and reactive process, and then go back to choosing what you have and committing to the strategy you have designed in line with your target. You also want to notice how much your trading is limited by your concepts of the world, thoughts about who you are, and thoughts of what you are entitled to as opposed to trading creatively in terms of an objective or purpose in front of you.

Stop trying to change yourself. Don't try to remove yourself from the action. It is better to choose what you have, to accept the fact that this is it. What you have is what you have. This time is your time. There is no other time and place. There is no need to keep focusing on the future, thereby rejecting where you are. When you get to the future, you will still be in the same mind-set and will still be searching for greener pastures and will miss the acres of diamonds in front of you. You have all the skill and knowledge that you need.

In the same way as you can choose what you have, you can let go of all thoughts or desires of getting something in the future. Design your trading strategy with that in mind, not so much to get to the result but as a powerful way of tapping more of your potential and creativity. Create a challenging vision, design specific goals related to the larger vision, and then do what you can do to express the vision. This is one of the most powerful ways of becoming fully engaged. But as I have said before, the goal is not an end in itself. Therefore, the difficult task before you, as paradoxical as it seems, is for you to pursue goals at the same time as you relinquish them.

' Focusing on the results, on gratification, or on gaining ideas or desires, only uses up energy in pursuing who you think you are rather than enabling you to be who you really are. To tap into your capacity for courage and risk taking, you must tap into yourself and let go of the expectation that external objectives or rewards will complete you.

Once committed to an objective, you are likely to encounter internal resistance, external opposition, superstition, pain, fatigue, and self-doubt. But if you persist and keep adhering to your objective and keep doing what is necessary to pursue it, you not only will experience much satisfaction but more importantly will discover something new in the world that was not there before—a new dimension that you could not see until you passed the obstacles inherent in the challenge.

Of course, you may encounter negativity from those who feel that their own performances are challenged by your actions and who are unwilling to encourage you as you try to perform in a new way. There also are bound to be your own self-doubts during the extended period of time it takes for your specific goals to be reached.

But to get to this new place of mastery you need to let good and bad feelings pass. Don't cover up your feelings, but be willing to acknowledge your vulnerability. In time, you will begin to understand that pain and suffering and even pleasure are transient emotions and that to live at the level of mastery means to go beyond pain and pleasure by noticing them and letting them go.

PART FOUR

THE PRACTICE OF RISK TAKING

CHAPTER EIGHT

INCREASING YOUR RISK

At a recent seminar I was giving to a group of foreign currency traders at a large international bank in New York, one trader after another reiterated the observations of the head trader: "We have no problem in managing risks, "he said. "All our systems are geared toward that. What we have a problem with is getting people to take on more risk and use more of the capital allocated to them."

"Despite the general conception of traders as risk takers, the problem of using insufficient amounts of capital is a fundamental problem for most traders that must be tackled if they are ever to reach a level of trading mastery," I replied.

Since most traders don't take enough risk, it has been my goal throughout this book to emphasize the importance of increasing risk by getting out of losers quickly and adding to winners. Unfortunately, most traders still are reluctant to use more capital to make more profits. Many are afraid to do this because of the increased chances of bigger losses. What they often don't realize is that greater risk almost always pays off.

To increase your profitability you need to increase the volatility of your trading—that is, the range of the profit and loss (P&L) swings you incur in the course of a trading day. If you trade consistently in terms of your Sharpe ratio (or some measure of risk-adjusted performance), then your performance should continue to be the same when you use more capital and increase your volatility. Even though your losses may be greater, if you adhere to the same level of performance, your wins will be proportionately greater as well. Because increasing risk is equally important as cutting losses, this chapter considers the obstacles that traders face when they need to add to their winners.

Understanding the Value of Statistics

Where the traditional risk manager is more concerned with defining and monitoring a trader's risk parameters, I am interested in a trader's psychological parameters—those limitations he imposes upon himself that prevent him from reaching his goals. The risk manager determines capital allocation issues, whereas I focus on helping a trader handle his capital or expand his use of capital by examining anxieties and psychological issues impeding the full implementation of his game plan.

From my perspective, the most critical issue is helping traders to discern certain repetitive patterns in their trading based on personality factors, attitudes, or beliefs that ultimately relate to the psychology of risk taking. I review a trader's performance in terms of helping him to overcome a wide range of obstacles that keep him from reaching his trading targets in line with the capital allocations he has been given by the firm.

My objective is to help traders get the highest return possible in a disciplined way, within the constraints of good risk management principles. As a trading coach interested in the behavioral and emotional dimensions of trading, I try to determine what keeps traders from doing those things.

Part of my job is encouraging traders to use more capital, take bigger initial positions, add to winning positions, and hold winning positions longer, all within the framework of maintaining their same risk-adjusted approach. In doing my job, I often rely on their statistics by way of impressing them with their batting average, as I noted in Chapter Five. The idea goes like this: If you are a .300 hitter, and you have more at bats while still maintaining the same batting average (or Sharpe ratio), you will likely continue to perform in the same way. Again, while your losses may be greater, your profits will be greater too. If you maintain consistency, you are likely to continue to do as well as you have when managing smaller amounts of money.

Statistics are useful for helping to identify how risk-controlled your trading has been so as to determine how much more risk you can comfortably take, how to effectively size your positions, and what steps are available to increase the amount of volatility in your portfolio through the increased use of options or futures markets. Statistics also can help you to establish the extent of hedging strategies needed to balance your portfolio and whether you are adequately using the capital allocated to you.

For example, the Sharpe ratio (one of the standard statistics easily calculated from a series of trading days), while frequently used for comparing trading performances among traders, can also act as your guidepost for calculating whether you are managing risk appropriately. I have found that the Sharpe ratio can bolster your confidence in your performance and to underscore psychological issues such as coping with anxiety and fear of losing.

Statistics help provide a mathematical underpinning for helping you to stretch. Looking at the numbers, you can tell more precisely how much risk you need to take in order to reach your targets. In my opinion, most traders, however, don't seem to rely on their statistics as much as they might, and have generally learned to trade quite independently of what the statistics show.

"I don't miss having statistics, because your risk statistic is really your P&L," said one trader. "I am interested in the losing, in the winning, and in the total number of trades I have made, to see if I am overriding and how long I am holding."

Although you can succeed without knowledge of these figures, most traders benefit from examining their statistics.

The key to success is to learn to play more than just defensively: Be willing to take the risk and to keep playing and measuring the risk/reward of your trades. If you know your goal and what you are producing on a daily basis, you will be able to figure out whether you can reach the goal and if not, how much you have to expand your size, capital, or risk. But remember, when you use more, you will lose more—as well as make more.

For example, say your average P&L swings are on the order of $100,000 a day, which equates to a risk fluctuation or variability of $1.6 million on an annualized basis.* With an assumed Sharpe ratio of 3:1, you are trading at a risk return of 3:1 (disregarding the risk-free rate). If you multiply the risk fluctuation of $1.6 million by 3, you get an expected annualized profit of $4.8 million, which in turn averages out to $400,000 in net profit per month. If you doubled the size of your positions, and your risk-adjusted performance (your Sharpe ratio) remained the same, you would get to an annual income of $9.6 million. However, to do this you would have to overcome the biggest hurdle, namely, the fact that you could expect perhaps a few negative $200,000 days a month. To increase your profitability by increasing the size of your positions, you have to build up enough

---

*When one puts profit swings in terms of standard deviation, time is not directly proportional but is scaled by the square root of time. With random movement, the variance, or dispersion, is directly proportional to time. Double the time and you double the variance. The standard deviation is the square root of the variance calculation; therefore time is scaled by its square root. There are 252 trading days in a year. So to annualize daily movement, you must multiply (scale) by the square root of 252, which is roughly 16.

confidence to ride out those kinds of losses. One way of doing this is to cut your risk when you are down. As you draw down, you get a little bit smaller so you don't give away too much.

Bear in mind, if a trader has consistent performance, he can usually get bigger and maintain that regularity as long as he is comfortable with greater losses. In effect, one of the means to trading mastery is learning to take greater risk so as to maximize profitability without triggering a variety of emotional reactions and defensive responses, which may interfere with your trading success. Another way to overcome the fears involved in trading larger size is to think of your P&L swings as a percentage of your capital base. If you are risking twice as much, presumably your pool of capital has doubled and percentage swings remain constant.

Practical Steps

Insofar as the best traders usually make 100 percent of their profit from 3–5 percent of their trades, they find it is useful to identify as soon as possible those trades that are likely to comprise this 3 percent of the most profitable trades—to focus their efforts on doing as much work on these trades to bolster their level of conviction in the size they are taking. An awareness of the significance of a select group of trades in the overall profitability of the portfolio leads traders to focus on maximizing their profits when the opportunity presents itself. This, more than any other assessment of trading performance, is likely to reinforce behaviors that are profitable and modify behaviors that are unprofitable. Try to establish the following in regard to your own portfolio:

- Know the volatility of your trading style.
- Size the volatility in terms of the amount of capital available.
- Discover how you can increase the potential profitability of your portfolio.

• Beware of excessive volatility that may cause you to blow all of your capital or paralyze you.

The chances are that, like most traders, you will be using less volatility than you are able to use in your portfolio. Seeing the stability of your performance should serve as an incentive to increase the amount of volatility you allow by holding positions longer, adding options, and doing more hedging. Ultimately your portfolio should be sized in terms of an effective level of P&L volatility, which will contribute to the preservation of capital and the maximization of profitability. Different levels of risk are ultimately associated with different degrees of return. Sizing your portfolio is also linked to the notion of adjusting levels of risk and trading styles after periods of strong profitability.

Case Study on Sizing Positions

Gavin, a successful trader with a high Sharpe ratio, has been working to get bigger. He is trying to use more of his capital and increase his absolute profitability even at the risk of lowering his very high Sharpe ratio and reducing his high win/loss ratio.

In the first two months of 2001 the Nasdaq was dropping and there were fears of recession in the economy. Gavin was expressing great concern about the months ahead. The markets were particularly difficult, and there was a huge disconnect between the fundamentals and the tape action. Stocks with good fundamentals were dropping, and those with bad fundamentals were dropping less than they should have been. It was difficult for Gavin and other traders to translate his fundamental work into profitable trades as he had done in previous years of the bull market.

Gavin expressed this concern one day in February in a very prescient way: "I am worried in the next month or two [March and April 2001] about our ability to make money. I think it will be very hard. You have to be in fewer positions and be nimble. The fundamentals stink. The analysis of the companies doesn't translate into good trades as they have in the past because the market seems to have its own momentum and direction and sentiment. This is making it hard for us to make money—it is like we are in a storm with low visibility and the usual things that work, don't work as well. It is requiring us to be more focused and more disciplined, but at the same time we have to make bets to make money. The fundamentals aren't getting any better.

"I have been trading pretty well, considering how badly the markets have been doing. We're up $25 million so far this year. That's not bad for two months. I have been doing a better job using more of my capital. I have been trading a lot of size. My win rate is way down. I don't have the conviction level that I would like. If I play bigger, I will have more swings and greater volatility. I have been putting on more positions with more capital. It is harder. It is a different game, but the only way we can get to the next level is to play that game. I actually had a day where I had $15 million in positions on. My goal for the year is to double my performance for last year. It is definitely a bigger game that I am playing.

"I do homework most nights. I go through my positions, listening to conference calls, working harder than I ever have. I want to take my game to another level. I am not at my peak performance. I am capable of more. But I am a little negative on my prospects. I am worried about my ability to make money in this market.

"I will make my money building a big position in something and then having it miss. It won't be on a day-to-day basis. I make most of my money in a handful of positions. Everything else is a wash. My biggest 20 trades probably account for the profitability. I need the other stuff to feel around for it. When I am right, I have to pile in."

Using Specialized Techniques

Once you have settled on the amount of risk that you need to take, there are a number of specific trading strategies to follow to adjust your risk. A trader can increase his risk by increasing the duration of his holding periods or by using derivative instruments like options to leverage his risk (by increasing the amount of risk he gets for a specified amount of risk that he is taking.) He can also learn to reduce market risk by hedging, diversifying, or increasing trading frequency in selected sectors. Moreover he can also learn to trade his P&L by expanding his risk profile after profitable periods and reducing exposure during drawdown.

Suffice it to say, any problems you have in handling risk will manifest themselves as well when using these more subtle and sophisticated techniques. However, to the extent that you have learned to trade in the zone and to manage the psychological issues of risk, you may be more flexible. At that point you are capable of adopting a wider variety of useful strategies that will make your risk even more manageable. To do this you must have learned to do some of the critical psychological things we have examined throughout this book.

Practical Steps

There is a range of risk to which every trader should adhere. In almost 70 to 80 percent of cases, traders are likely to be taking too little risk and need to be encouraged to be more aggressive. In the fewer cases, where a trader may be taking too much risk, he has to scale down the size of his risk within parameters established by good risk management principles.

When you commit to a stretch target and trade in a committed way, you raise the level of your game and begin to play in terms of reaching the objective. To ensure success you have to pace yourself. When trading you have to ask yourself:

- What will it take to reach my targets?
- How big do I have to get?
- How much volatility do I need?
- How careful do I have to be?

• How much more fundamental understanding of the companies I am trading can I get?

You have to keep adjusting to reach your target. You have to trade at the level. Your goal should not be a fantasy number, but one you are willing to pursue, taking into account liquidity constraints in the market, market volatility, and other factors that may influence the outcome.

Learn to live with the discrepancy that you create between where you are and what you have targeted. It's not a question of saying it and hoping to make it happen. It is about putting on the kind of risk consistent with the kind of targets you are shooting for and developing a willingness to tolerate the fluctuations in profit and loss that are likely to occur when you do that.

Writing out an analysis of your target and strategy, along with any big mistakes you have recently made, will force you to define what you have to do to realize your plans. Keep reviewing what you are doing. Track yourself—trying smaller increments if that makes it easier. Stay on target as much as you can.

How do you reconcile day-by-day trading with the 3 percent rule? You keep trolling. You avoid pitfalls, recognize opportunities, manage P&L volatility. The good traders pounce on the best opportunities and manage their day-to-day activities so that they can lever up their good opportunities and not have to force trades when they are down.

Your task is to increase the size of the bets as they prove to be profitable, to keep your losses down as much as possible, and, wherever possible, to try to take that amount of risk appropriate for reaching the levels of profitability you are seeking. Of course, most traders pay attention to their P&L ratio, but what is critical here is that you understand the importance of making more money in your winning trades than you lose in your losing trades. Just getting out of losers quickly is not enough. You also have to add to your winners. So, concentrate your efforts on maximizing your profits in the 3 percent of trades where things are going your way.

Case Studies on Obstacles to Increased Risk

Devon is a long-term trader who was trying to integrate the short-term, catalyst-driven approach into his trading style. Devon placed a lot of significance on weighing the risk/reward of his trades and balancing his portfolio with a number of good ideas. He handled risk by measuring the risk/reward of the trade, sizing his position in terms of his objectives, carefully defining entry and exit points, and finding short-term catalysts to increase the likelihood of success. Additionally he diversified his portfolio so that he was not dependent on four or fewer stocks, which could lose money in market downturns. Despite all these precautions he found he was taking too little risk, not using all of his capital, and being weighed down by a need to have perfect analyses.

In looking for psychological factors that might influence his risk taking, I explored with him whether there were any obstacles to taking on more risk:

- What is the cutting edge for him?
- What impedes the development of appropriate risk or of risk taking itself?
- What holds him back, if anything, regarding taking more risk?
- What is there that he has to tweak?
- Are there any concerns about how it feels or looks to make mistakes or anything of a subjective nature that may be a constraining force on his capacity to play as fully as he can?

Devon admitted: "I tighten up and try to be more perfect when I am trading. So, I have fewer ideas to which I am willing to commit more capital. It's only having 10 ideas, instead of doing 10 more. I want to be perfect. I am not afraid to lose money on bets I am taking for the right reasons. But I am afraid to make bets when I don't have good reasons to be there. I don't trust my gut, because I don't have a good enough game plan for what to do if I am wrong. I don't have confidence in the short-term when I don't know where the stock will go. I would rather have a longer-term position based on the fundamentals than to trade instinctively in response to the market movements and the intraday volatility."

"I don't mind trading short-term positions, having a core position and trading around it in terms of short-term catalysts. I am uncomfortable putting on a new position, just for a short-term trade. I need to do it for a reason."

The stopping point for Devon is that he is too wedded to the need to have more analytic data before he takes trades, especially short-term trades for the first time. Here the basic paradigmatic model of trading has become somewhat of a handicap, preventing him from stepping into the abyss and risking himself in the shorter-term trade. Obviously the place to begin is in long-term positions that he is already in and taking short-term trades around the long-term positions based on catalysts.

"It's the life experience imbedded in you that triggers what is important," he said. "It has to do with time periods relative to the analysis. If the data point is significant for six months, it is different than a data point for six hours.

"My experience in life has never been to develop data points for short-term events. So, it is difficult for me to do this, except where I already have a leg up in understanding the fundamentals of the companies I am in for the long term. You get good data on the big cap companies I trade, and if you know when the data is being released and you have a sense of the expectations going into it, there can be good trading opportunities. I am trying to get that data at regular time intervals. They are not daily opportunities, and you can't simply develop them because you want them.

"I can take more risk in my own strategies by trading around long-term ideas. My interpretation of taking more risk is to make sure my thesis is relevant, not necessarily just getting bigger. If I have 100,000 shares of something that trades 500,000 shares a day, it is difficult to get bigger on a daily basis. It will take hours to get out of it."

For Devon, increasing his risk involves staying in positions longer and noticing his tendency to get too critical of the fundamental analyses. He tends to undervalue the quality of his analyses and assume that others know things are out there when in fact they don't. In many instances he has been too impatient to act. He gets in and thinks it is not working and assumes incorrectly that the market knows it, rather than hanging on and riding out the trade a little bit longer until the information becomes relevant and impacts the stock. He doesn't recognize the edge that he has for getting in early. He doesn't lose money in the short-term trades, but he doesn't make money either because he gets out too quickly.

Here his thoroughness has worked to help him build good models of the companies he is trading. His inexperience leads him to second-guess the value of his data, particularly when he gets into trades too early and doesn't see the kind of confirmation from the market action that he would like to see. He is too critical, but there are times when he needs to put this critiquing on hold so that he can hang in on the trade, allowing it develop. He needs to learn to trust his instincts a bit more so that he can play the short-term game better.

Devon is very methodical and finds the short-term game too chaotic. He gets a lot of satisfaction from building models and therefore is more frustrated with short-term trades. He gets pleasure when his thesis is right, especially his short thesis when the company goes bust. He needs to work on sizing positions around catalysts and events and having reasons to be involved.

While having a daily target is difficult, it has value for the short- and longer-term trader in terms of helping Devon to decide which positions to get out of. The same is true for you. Use the target as a reminder that you need to do something to get to this number. It should be a prompt and motivating force so that you don't get to November and realize that you are way behind your targets. Develop the game you are already playing and become aware of where your instincts can be better supported and stay in trades longer.

When you are practicing tennis or golf and are not in a competition, there is an ease of stroke. You are relaxed. But when you raise the level of competition and add spectators, you become more tense and self-conscious in your strokes. As you get better, you can handle these difficult circumstances as you raise the competition and the pressure.

Adrian is the kind of systematic trader who is very confident and who is not afraid of the markets. He thinks: "If you are running $10 million and your objective is to make $5 million, you have to decide on some rules for establishing the size of your positions." Adrian sizes his positions in terms of his chosen targets and then reduces his risk by running a market neutral portfolio (to take the market risk out of the portfolio).

"I try to pick my best universe of stocks for my long positions and balance the portfolio with my worst universe of stocks for the short positions," he explained. "While I am trying to create a hedged or balanced portfolio for insurance purposes, at the same time I am trying to select the best possible shorts in terms of trying to maximize the profit potential of these trades. Sometimes I do paired trades, picking shorts and longs in the same sector with the expectation that they will move in the opposite direction and thereby protect my capital when a stock fails to move in the direction of my choice, that is, that a short may become profitable when a long is not working and is going down. I basically take the top 5 percent of securities and go long with them; I take the bottom 5 percent and short them. Say you start with 100 securities in the portfolio. Optimize the portfolio by having a certain percentage in different sectors neutral based on beta and subindustries."

While Adrian sizes his positions in terms of his targets or objectives and balances his portfolio to increase the risk-adjusted nature of his returns, many traders don't calculate how big they should be to produce a specific result. They take the view that they'll see what the market gives them and then measure their performance relative to an index, trying to beat the averages by a few percentage points. According to another trader, Jordan, the best traders do this process of sizing intuitively. They know what they can get out of a trade.

"The downfall of the traditional method is that you can't be sure of your correlations because the volatility of positions changes from day to day because of market conditions so that you cannot be certain of your forecasts. Market conditions keep changing and the validity of the estimates aren't very good. They are thinking as long as it goes up over the long term it is OK. They are not thinking about how much it moves down tomorrow. They aren't controlling that.

"That's what I like about the goal-oriented approach. You always have to think about the downside. I can estimate a number and eventually can do this on every stock. For example, if the average move has been three points on a bellwether stock, you can estimate whether to take profit tomorrow if it moves three points."

Practical Steps

By stretching and upping the ante on yourself, you will enhance your concentration by tapping a hidden dimension within yourself. Keep challenging yourself. Stop playing it safe to avoid failure. From an existentialist viewpoint, there is no failure. There is just engagement or nonengagement.

Increased consciousness means making continual small adjustments of the drift, consciously tracking what you are doing and bringing greater intensity to your efforts without trying too hard. Intention and intensity will heighten concentration on the task at hand. Continual monitoring of your trading is like keeping your hand on the rudder and not going to sleep. When you do constantly monitor, you reduce withdrawal, rationalization and all kinds of avoidance mechanisms that dilute concentration.

When you are totally focused on what you are doing and are giving 100 percent, you just commit to a result and relate to the events that occur in the context you have created. If you feel out of control, you keep going. One hundred percent is not about what you feel or even the results. It's about engagement.

One hundred percent means total involvement of your heart and soul. It's not about producing a specific result. The result only tells you whether you kept your commitment. To produce the result, you have to surrender to the action before you and stop trying to manipulate the outcome.

It's difficult to scrap what you've done and start over. It's difficult to let go of the past, even though the critical issue is what you can produce now, bringing all of your talents to bear on the task that is before you.

When I refer to total concentration, I'm talking about taking responsibility. It gives you clarity so that in a short space of time you can produce incredible results. Yet most of the time you only look like you are 100 percent engaged when in fact you extend more effort into appearances than actual commitment.

Giving less than 100 percent produces an excessive preoccupation about winning or losing. To sustain momentum, it is essential to keep moving forward into the realm of the unknown. This must be done with greater consciousness, because when you are dominated by an unconscious drive to be less than you can be, you unwittingly withdraw energy from your actions.

It is often best to learn to increase your risk progressively, alternating between increasing the complexity of the steps you take and increasing the size of your positions. When you increase the complexity of a task or increase the size of your positions, you increase the requirements for focusing attention on the task and must let go of even more of your past issues of ego, which are likely sources of distraction and reduced energy.

In effect, commitment to your vision means bringing more and more of yourself to the next moment by increasing the demand characteristics of the task, ultimately reaching a point where all there is of you is your involvement in the task at hand. Such total involvement requires a progressive increase in the amount of attention required to produce the result. Increasing your risk is in fact akin to increasing your commitment. As the complexity of the task increases, and you are able to let other concerns fall by the wayside and pay more attention to the task in front of you, you will begin to transform your trading.

CHAPTER NINE

HANDLING FAILURE . . .
AND SUCCESS

If you're a tennis player, you normally rely on a good first serve to keep you in a match. Inevitably, there comes a time when that serve goes off and you start to miss by just a bit. To maintain your game, you don't abandon your serving mechanism entirely and serve underhand. Instead, you adjust. You ease up on that first serve until you get back in the groove.

You need to keep the same kind of adjustment in mind in trading. Because a by-product of risk is loss, sooner or later you will stumble and lose. The object of trading, however, is not to avoid losses, but to learn how to handle them in such a manner that you come out a winner in the end.

It is worth repeating, successful traders make most of their profit from only 3 percent of their trades. They don't allow the downs of trading to take them out of the game. They learn to manage their wins appropriately.

You, too, may want to win, but you may be afraid of going all out because of your fear of failure. This ambivalence often results in inaction, avoidance, or in extreme shifts from minimal to maximum effort. You may think you are not good enough or smart enough to realize your vision. You may not be able to stand outside your negative self-concepts and commit yourself to your objectives, regardless of how you feel or what you think.

Perhaps you get distracted from your objectives by your emotional responses to wins and losses. That is why it becomes important to get a handle on the basic underlying fears that may be dominating your trading and casting a shadow across your vision.

That vision provides the standard against which to judge your performance. It may not be realized, but it sets up the target so that you can keep bringing more of yourself into action in the present moment. Choosing what you have is to appreciate the present reality and then to work with it—whether it be success or failure—to realize your vision.

Recognizing a Breakdown

Sustaining momentum involves handling breakdowns or failures and approaching them as opportunities for more intense involvement in the experience of your trading. If things have been moving along very well and then you suddenly slip from maximum performance, it may be due to a failure in concentration. You may have become bored, or you may have stopped following your strategy. Additionally, you may have failed to continue to take responsibility for your actions.

Failures in concentration may result from faltering in your commitment to your vision and slipping into automatic thinking, self-justification, or denial. You may veer away from following your plan, find yourself unwilling to trust or empower others, or refuse to assume responsibility for a trade that goes awry. If you don't produce specific results, there is often a tendency to deny the facts and to avoid looking for a way to get back on track.

When this happens, you can bolster your concentration by recommitting to your vision. Here it helps to think about what else is possible rather than function with preconceptions of immutable truths that box you in.

Be alert to slippage of commitment when you sabotage yourself by listening to the doubts of others or when you distract yourself with unnecessary trades. Be willing to recommit to your goals, and be ready to discuss what is necessary to make things happen. Don't blame others for your failures. When things aren't going well, don't give up or resign from your commitments if you fail to produce the result. Figure out what was missing in your trades, and try to establish a procedure that will make your trades work better.

‹ Failure is part and parcel of all trades. Recognize that when it happens it doesn't mean that there is something wrong with you. It simply means that you have not handled some of the specific issues vital to reaching your goal. In other words, failure simply means that you need to correct something.

The key is to notice that you are no longer aligned with your goals. Goals and vision erode because people do not want to face breakdowns. In order to move on, you must be able to declare a breakdown and recognize when you are compromising and faltering so that you can correct your actions in the present and bring them in line with your strategy.

Managing the Emotions of Breakdown

A certain psychology is associated with drawdowns. When a trader is down, it changes the way he trades. The scenario usually involves thoughts along the lines of, "How can I get back to even?" When a trader thinks that way, he tends to cut his profits a little shorter and to psychologically take himself out of the game. When you are down, your psychology often shifts from a winning one to a risk averse one.

"When you become risk averse, you become more like an accountant who bills for his time," says master trader Randy. "You say,

'I don't want to waste a whole day here. I want to make a little money, and if I do it for 30 days I am even.' The whole psychology that you follow for successful trading is different."

When you do something that isn't working, the tendency is to withdraw and become defensive. Instead of getting smaller and following the same strategy, you are more likely to change your style than your size. But the key is to stay with the winning psychology, minimize your losses, and continue implementing your strategy rather than playing defensively.

Of course, the emotional aspect of loss can be overwhelming. You may have characteristics of dysthymia or a chronic depressed mood when you are in a significant drawdown. You may be irritable, depressed, inclined to undereat or overeat. You may develop insomnia, a low energy level, or feel fatigued. You can suffer from low self-esteem, have trouble concentrating, and have difficulty making decisions. This state of mind often accompanies a series of losses and may lead to feelings of hopelessness and a sense of despair. You may then begin to believe that you cannot turn your trading around and may complain about being uninvolved in the markets or may express envy over a colleague's ability and enthusiasm.

Sometimes when you are going through these emotional difficulties, you may even begin to experience anxiety disorders that may range from generalized anxiety disorder to a panic attack to more subtle forms of anxiety disorder such as are seen in obsessive compulsive disorders. I am not talking about clinical phenomena, merely the range of symptoms of anxiety and mood disorder that often accompany high-risk activity and which, in turn, complicate the activity.

Once again, the important thing to remember is that breakdowns or failures are inevitable. When they are experienced as reflective of your personal worth, then they are likely to trigger anxiety, embarrassment, and guilt. Instead, you must learn to face the failure and ride out the emotions—seeing the experience not as something from which to run, but as an opportunity for breakthrough.

Case Study on Managing Drawdowns

The most dangerous time is when a trader is in a losing pattern and has nothing to lose by losing more and very little to gain, because he is now not earning any money and must fight his way back. This presents a big danger of further blowing up. Here is a conversation with a technology trader who was in a big drawdown in 2000 after great success in the previous few years of the bull market and who is starting to feel psychological pressure.

Kiev: You are in a tough situation. You are down. Your capital has been cut. You can't do what you were doing before. You have to play smaller. It is easy to choke under these circumstances.

Andrew: I used to do some good things. I feel like my whole game has been taken away by having my size restricted because I am in drawdown. It's as if I am expected to start over.

K: Everyone is judged in their own way.

A: Now more than ever, no one listens to my ideas. I have a hard time getting my ideas across. Status in this firm is based on P&L [profit and loss]. My credibility is down.

K: Can you get it back?

A: Hopefully by January I will be there.

K: It sounds like you are preoccupied with your losses and how bad things are relative to last year, all of which may be taking you out of your game.

A: Now I am thinking about making money. I don't want to bust my ass and make back the $5 million dollars I am down and then discover that my style doesn't fit into the firm.

K: You can't be playing that way.

A: I want to make it because I want to be paid.

K: How do you handle that?

A: You generate a lot of P&L, which gives you status and credibility. I am not talking about the money. The P&L equals credibility. That is the key. I have lost it. In order to get it back, I have to put up the number. I feel expendable.

K: As hard as it is, you have to try to let go of that notion, because it is ultimately self-defeating.

A: How do you do that?

K: You have to substitute some larger concept or metaconcept to govern your trading so that you are focused on the actions that you have to take consistent with the results. Every time you have these negative, self-defeating thoughts, you have to notice them, record them, and then shift into the positive thought framework.

A: It's not getting in the way of my trading. It is a set of feelings that I have quite separate from my trading. I feel expendable. Is that difficult to understand? I will get rid of that thought when my P&L is better.

K: I understand. The more you can let that thought go and focus on the game in front of you today, the better off you are going to be. Can you let that thought go? Can you focus on playing to win.

A: It is difficult to work for five years and to let go of it.

When you get into a state of drawdown, you must remember to maintain a proactive state of mind, which is critical to successful, goal-oriented trading of the kind I have been writing about. Confidence comes from knowing what to do in all situations. If you are in the state of mind associated with drawdown, where you are feeling the urge to shift off your strategy, then you are in big trouble. When you are under water, the most important thing to do is to stick to a strategy that avoids a rapid downside, but do not change your game plan to the point where you can't get back in to shore.

Once you commit to a goal, getting there involves handling a succession of errors and failures. If you learn to wait your emotions out, as discussed earlier in this book, in time you will become familiar with the feelings of failure. You will know how long they last, know that they eventually will diminish, and will learn not to give them much credence.

Practical Steps

One of the major problems associated with the creation of a meaningful personal objective is likely to be the belief that you don't deserve to have what you want. So, you are hesitant to create and commit to a new vision of yourself. This kind of belief is reflective of fear and anxiety in the form of self-critical perfectionism and self-doubt, which blocks the creative and positive effort needed for productive trading. In fact, the belief and expectation of losing (or that things will remain the same, i.e., resignation to your failure) often has more impact on the outcome of trading than the expectation of winning.

Here it is worth considering any way in which you can keep your expectations down to avoid the frustration of losing. Are you so certain of losing that you deny yourself even the ordinary desire to try to succeed in achieving your goals? A yes answer may reflect the fact that your standards are too high, that you are too self-critical, and that you cannot tolerate failure. You may not even try for fear of not measuring up to your standards. This withholding can produce a negative self-image and feelings of inadequacy. When you do try, you may become so racked with anxiety and tension that you end up quitting before you have given yourself a fair chance.

If you are afraid to fail, you may be a victim of fatalistic thinking and a self-fulfilling prophecy where you lose because you expect to lose. For example, if you are too concerned that you may feel guilty if you don't succeed, you may be unable to relax long enough to reach your goals.

What can you do? Develop better self-monitoring skills so that you can pace yourself and stay centered as you approach your goal.

Doing this will enable you to monitor your anxiety, stop restraining yourself, and help you sustain motivation in the face of fatigue.

In every area of life involving performance, the truly successful are those who have the patience to allow the action to be completed. They can wait before impulsively acting. Pacing involves knowing when to act and then acting with the confidence that you are going to be on target. When you are feeling confident of reaching your goal, when you are not hampered by thoughts of past failures or future disappointments, you can reach into yourself to find extra strength, drive, energy, and enthusiasm to achieve the impossible. At the bottom of what appears to be a motivational effort is the capacity to be able to stay focused long enough to complete the total action.

Believing you can succeed will give you that extra confidence to function so that you do succeed. Given that you expect a certain result to occur because you are committed to it, you will not hold back in your efforts because of doubt, uncertainty, or some imagined concerns about how others might react.

Nothing can guarantee that you will win or achieve your goal, but if you expect *not* to achieve your vision, you most certainly will give up long before you have had an opportunity to test your abilities. The sense of resignation to fate or failure (which is tantamount to an expectation of losing), must be overcome if you are going to succeed in achieving your vision.

Of course, there is a general tendency to react negatively to poor results, which further intensifies distress. A more appropriate response is to accept the results as reflective of what is—without becoming too attached to them or assigning too much meaning to them. This approach to your trading experiences is more personally empowering and will enable you to sustain momentum.

• Stop worrying about the outcome. Just keep working toward your goal. Don't get drawn into your own depressed, angry, or fatalistic attitudes. Keep active despite the anxiety that inevitably comes with losses. Anxiety doesn't mean anything. Don't get caught up with notions of "I can't do it." Just keep working.

When you fail, or veer from your game plan, be willing to acknowledge it so that you can begin to realign with your objectives. Recognizing breakdown frees up energy that might otherwise have been used to rationalize the breakdown or to cover up insufficient efforts resulting in the breakdown.

When you acknowledge a breakdown, you pierce the shell of appearances and get closer to the reality of actual events. To do this, you must be willing to see reality as reflective of itself, not as reflective of you and therefore not as a reason to feel guilty or a reason to justify withdrawing from your commitment. Reality is a measure of where you stand in relation to your vision as it is.

As you run into breakdowns, the task is to keep renewing the commitment to the objective and looking to see what you need to do to concentrate on the tasks before you. You can handle these breakdowns by looking to see what dropped out from your concentration, replacing it, and then doing what needs to be done to produce the result. Breakdowns immediately become opportunities for breakthroughs when you shift your stance and see what's missing in your strategy and what you need to do to take action in line with your objectives.

Turning Breakdowns into Breakthroughs

The first step in recovering from a loss is to deal with the emotions that follow failure, but the second, and equally important, step is to minimize the loss. This step reflects the simple concept that I have emphasized throughout this book—maximize your winners; minimize your losers. Again, much of this recovery involves not giving in to the temptation to make larger bets in losing trades in hopes of gaining back your losses.

When you are losing, go back to your goal. Consider what positions to downsize to reduce possible losses that may interfere with reaching that goal. If you look through the lens of the goal, what adjustments can you make to stay the course, reduce your losses, and achieve your specific results?

The losses from last year are "spilled milk." Although despondent, you have to recover from the process at the same time as you prepare for the future. What is your risk tolerance, your ability to invest capital, your ability to take those same risks again? If you are uncomfortable, then you should find less risky situations. You need to review some of the factors considered in this book and determine what went wrong and how to redesign your portfolio in terms of greater profitability and greater control over the risk process.

The worst thing to do in a speculative market is to try to get back the money you have lost. If you are comfortable with your long-term strategy, even though you have lost money, you may want to assess how much money to allocate to the strategy. Determine what your comfort level is.

Try to be rational. Cut your losses. Be resilient by attacking today. Consider today's plan rather than focusing on the past. Learn from what you did. Use the past to assess benchmarks and to review strategies that can be improved. But plan going forward.

It is important that all traders weigh their risk tolerance by assessing the upside and the downside of the trade and what the implications of the trade may be all the time and then trade accordingly. It is imperative that you learn to evaluate how you are handling the process and not become too discouraged by your failures.

If you do find yourself getting panicky, you are probably holding positions that are too big, and you might want to pare them down to the level where the panic goes away. This game is not about toughing it out but is about "keeping your powder dry" and staying nimble. If the positions reverse, you can always get back in.

When losing consistently, it is important to play smaller until you get back in the groove. If possible, look closely to see if there is any change in your pattern of stock selection or your decision making that may account for a losing streak. It may be necessary to go home lighter, with fewer overnight positions. You most definitely want to avoid a second or a third blowup, because this can have a very bad effect on your morale and lead to withdrawal and failure to recover.

For example, in the week of October 30, 2000, Brandon was beginning to recover from the previous week where his stocks had been killed and he had lost money trying to short things too early. The key for him was managing his risk by playing smaller, having more positions, and not getting shaken out of his basic game.

"I have started taking smaller positions," he said. "It is easier to handle them. If something isn't working, I just get rid of the positions. When I was holding larger positions and they weren't working I would sit there frozen. Now I just cut it out like a cancer. I am getting my feet back. I just have to grind it out every day."

The idea is to get to the goal. Use that idea to manage your risk. This approach allows traders to reach their goal in the long run, if not on a particular day. Sometimes you have to step back to move forward.

Case Study on Sizing Positions to Reduce Losses

Tad is a trader who seeks an adrenaline rush. He is easily bored and often unwilling to do the work. He is inexperienced and compulsively plays his P&L because he believes he is a big hitter. Therefore, he gets trapped by holding on to losing positions, holding long positions for no reason, hoping things will turn his way, and not taking his profits. His stopping points are greed, an inability to face reality, and an arrogance that leads him to believe he is better than he really is. He shows no consistency in handling risk very well. He makes some money and instead of taking his profits, he gets bigger and runs bigger risks and invariably blows up. He does not get big for good reasons. His lack of fundamental work makes it difficult for him to adequately size his positions, and he ends up losing the little profit that he has been able to make early in the day. He is a gambler, and he needs to develop the maturity to control his impulses.

Tad: I wish I were up 3 million and going to 7 million. Mentally I am in a hole.

Kiev: It is hard when you are in the hole to play smaller. You want to get out rapidly and want to hit a home run. This happened to one trader I know who blew up trying to hit a home run. The pressure on him became very great.

T: I feel that pressure.

K: It takes discipline. When you are in the hole, your confidence goes. They won't give you the money to get out. You have to get out systematically by doing $20,000 a day for a month, then $40,000 a day.

T: That's what I am doing. I am very disciplined.

K: You have an inflated view of your ability because you had some great successes. You are not consistent.

T: If I can make $20,000 every day, then I will hope to be able to get bigger.

K: Is it boring?

T: It is frustrating.

K: You think that if you make a lot of money it will validate you. Then you will be on top of the world.

T: You are right.

K: You have to learn the discipline and stop trying to get off on how much money you can make and how good you can feel. Having it all doesn't make anyone very happy.

T: I feel horrible sometimes.

K: You feel horrible because you think you made it?

T: It is about the errors that I have made. It is proving to myself that I have to become disciplined. I am a gambler. I am like an addict. I want to prove to myself that I can do it. I can make 30 grand just like that. I was beating this other trader at midyear. I said I am going for it. It cost me a lot of money. It didn't work.

K: Some of it is boredom, wanting the action. You need to use your intellect to dig in deeper to understand the companies.

Just like Tad, you may have difficulty seeing how you are causing conflict and dissatisfaction for yourself. It is not enough to make superficial changes in your trading behavior. To really understand what you must do to find satisfaction, you must identify how your own life principles create your conflicts and fears and activate the need to be self-protective.

Losses are inevitable, but your decision as to how you handle a loss determines whether you ultimately recover. If you learn how to deal with your emotions and minimize the drawdown, you will begin to see failure as a source of information. In failure, you will be able to find clues to the corrections to make or new actions to take to get you closer to your goal.

Recreating the Wins

Remember the old adage, "It's not whether you win or lose, it's how you play the game"? Despite the truth of Grantland Rice's statement, our culture still emphasizes winning, not merely 100 percent participation. In fact, winning is so highly valued that it has become an end in itself, which leads traders sometimes to avoid trading for fear of losing or of looking bad for not winning.

Although the problems associated with losing are pretty obvious, there are also problems associated with winning. Just as losing can lead to depression, winning can trigger periods of elation that also can hurt a trader's ability to continue focusing on the goal.

When a trader wins, he may develop an inflated sense of self that borders on grandiosity. He may experience a heightened sense of energy that may manifest itself in the lack of need for sleep, increased pressure of speech, and a subjective sensation that he is on a high. This often involves racing thoughts and increased activity, both in goal-directed and pleasurable activities that may have negative consequences. For instance, there are numerous stories of traders spending excessively on fancy cars and homes during periods of great success, which may put them in a bind later on when less prosperous periods occur.

As one trader expressed it, "Success is easy. The problem is if you become overzealous and think you can do no wrong. You feel overcompetent and make the same bets and think that things will keep happening the same way."

Success may also foster complacency and a failure to adhere to the winning strategy. And if you become complacent, you may get bored and lose your edge. Because success creates the appearance of commitment and competency, winning traders may also find themselves taking extra precautions not to lose. To this extent, they may avoid losing because it doesn't look good and marks them in terms of vulnerability and inadequacy. They may begin to feel that the risk challenges their coverup of competency and success.

Therefore, it is useful to note when your trading becomes routine, dull, and boring or leads to withdrawal and avoidance. When this happens, it is desirable to consider whether you are facing obstacles and are retreating behind your life principle of looking good or whether you have reached your objective and now need to raise the stakes in order to create a greater challenge for yourself.

Handling Failure... and Success

Listen to one trader's description of his problem with success: "I am good at cutting things down if I lose money," said Philip. "I also like to run things up when I do well and run the risk of losing money—losing everything and then shutting down. It has happened a couple of times. I have made $3 million to $4 million a few times and then lost it. I get complacent when I trade well. In the future, it will come down to focusing on profit potential versus loss potential and making sure in my head that I am trading the proper risk reward—not making my positions too big relative to my profit objectives. I think if I do well, I will increase my size and then get hurt and go back to zero."

. When a trader becomes excessively attached to the results, he can confuse success with his identity so that he loses his flexibility and freedom to create. If you are driven by winning or succeeding at all costs, you may create so much pressure for yourself that you get little satisfaction from your efforts and are dominated by concerns about your image and the opinions of others.

. An excessive preoccupation with winning may, in turn, lead you to focus too much attention on results. Fear of failure increases the chance of error by setting in motion a self-fulfilling prophecy, where your expectation of failure leads to failure either by reinforcing an inclination to quit before reaching your objective or by leading you to interpret cues as indicative of failure so that you tense up and do whatever you are doing less well than you would if you were relaxed.

Unfortunately, the fear of losing that winning often creates can actually cause traders to nose-dive into a losing cycle or prevent them from maximizing their wins. When a trader is afraid of being wrong, he is also more reluctant to put on size. But that is exactly what you should do when you are winning. Just as you need to minimize losers, part of the formula for reaching your goal involves taking full advantage of your winners. You need to increase your size in the winning bets—maximizing your profit potential.

· When a trade is going your way, you have to scale up and gradually demonstrate your ability to take risk. You thus build the confidence necessary to trade bigger without being afraid to take the larger losses you are likely to encounter. The biggest obstacle to overcome is fear of losing big, but naturally you are going to lose bigger as you get bigger and win bigger. Scaling up, which gradually inoculates you against your fears, is the way to go.

"When it is working, add aggressively," said Matt. "You have to learn to add to winners. You are moving all the time, constantly fighting emotions and the urge to stick with it and say that you are right [when you are losing]. Then you have to be able to say you are wrong and get out. All this takes a lot of mental effort."

Once again, this trading example underlines the necessity of staying conscious throughout the trading process. You want to make sure that you adhere to your risk limits, even after you have done well, because there is still the risk of losing focus.

The San Francisco former star quarterback John Brodie has formulated a sensible approach to winning that stands somewhere between Vince Lombardi's aphorism, "Winning isn't everything. It's the only thing," and Grantland Rice's phrase, "It's not whether you win or lose. It's how you play the game." In his autobiography, *Open Field* (Houghton Mifflin, 1974, p. 218), Brodie wrote:

> You play to win. There's no doubt about that. But if winning is your first and only aim, you stand a good chance of losing. You have the greatest chance of winning when your first commitment is to a total and enthusiastic involvement in the game itself. Enthusiasm is what matters most. If I was enthusiastic about the game, enjoying it and doing my absolute best, then I had the best chance of winning it. But then I could also handle losing, because I *had* done my best. If you can't handle losing, you'll never be a big winner. It's never easy to lose. But if I knew I had performed at the top of my ability, with total involvement, that would take care of the winning or the losing.

Case Study on Holding Winners

The subtleties involved in maintaining a winning attitude were illustrated by Stanley, a long-term fundamental portfolio manager who was learning to trade in terms of the shorter-term, catalyst-driven style of trading. First he concentrated on learning to get out of long positions that were dropping in order to keep his losses down. While this helped him to preserve capital, it influenced the way he was trading on the upside as he found himself becoming a bit gun-shy about holding his winning positions for longer periods of time when they were advancing in the right direction. By taking his positions off too soon he avoided the possibility of losing, which he had become concerned with, but he missed some of the upside profit potential of the trades. After he began to observe this pattern it became clear that he needed to divide different aspects of the trade and then practice learning how to do the different components.

"XYZ Corp. should be a 300,000 share position instead of a 60,000 share position," Stanley said. "It's $20\frac{1}{2}$. It was at 23. I got short before earnings because I believed they were going to be bad. The stock didn't go down much. So we covered. Looking at a longer time frame, it was 28 before earnings, and now it's 20. That's a 40 percent return on the short side. I shorted at 24, 25. I know it is a bad story. I am not as big as I should be, because I keep covering every time it goes down two points. That's not how I can make bigger profits. I am afraid it will go back up, and I will lose my profits. It didn't go down for three or four days. I started to think I wasn't right. I came this close to buying it back today. It was starting to go back up. Nothing has changed. The fundamentals are still terrible."

Here Stanley is talking about a critical issue. He knows the fundamentals are bad, but the market activity keeps driving certain stocks up because of short-term market sentiment or psychology, and he wants to play that but doesn't want to get hurt. The ultimate challenge of trading is to catch the right trend at the right time, even though the long-term story may be bad, as in the case of shorts, and good, in the case of longs. This challenge is a particular problem for the long-term, value-driven portfolio manager who likes to buy cheap and hold for a long time and does not feel as comfortable getting in and out in response to the intraday volatility, even though to do that will garner him the biggest returns.

Kiev: When it is back up, why not put it back out? You have already booked some profit. You went from 250,000 shares. Now you are at 60,000 shares. So when it goes up a little bit, why not hit it?

Stanley: I am waiting for it to play out instead of getting big again in the same idea.

K: Every trade has multiple opportunities.

S: I am still not thinking of the day as three days in one or as being compartmentalized into three time periods such as the opening, the middle, and the close and various distinctions in between, each of which represents a different trading opportunity. Whatever I did yesterday has now worked. So now I am preparing for tomorrow, as opposed to focusing on what is going on now. To me a stock at 49 and 47 is the same stock.

K: There are many trades along the trend.

S: The stock is going down. My instinct is to cover. Are you saying that now is the time to short more?

K: The master trader will do that. You have to be able to read the price action and the amount of activity in the stock. Is it liquid?

S: It trades 10 million a day. I am angry because I should be bigger here and that is taking me out of the game.

K: Let go of the anger. Stop focusing on your mind-set and start looking at the opportunity here. You are still invested in beating yourself. It is totally irrelevant to your profitability. What is the next move? Once you tell someone you are distressed or angry about your trading, there is an unconscious need to keep feeling that way, especially if they come back to you and ask you whether you are still distressed. It is better to notice those feelings and then let them pass. You don't want to let this demon become an entity. You want to disconnect it from your trading.

S: It is true. I don't hold things as long as I should. I am trying to figure out why I am not sticking with winning trades as long as I should. It hit 21 today. I could have gotten back into it.

K: You just have to take the swing. If you missed it, get back into it as a short every time it goes up. There may be more trades to make.

Handling Failure... and Success

S: I need to keep coming back and taking the swing. I think, erroneously, that I will only get one bite of the apple. You are saying I can come back many times. Now it is 20⅜. I was about to cover. Thank God I didn't get in at 21.

I have to stick with the winners longer. I am hunting rabbits. I need to get to the bigger game mentality. There are 13 million shares of pricing. I am surprised it is only down one-quarter this morning. The Nasdaq is up 1.5 percent. That's helping the short up. How much of this is the market? How much is stock specific?

K: How are you feeling? Are your feelings reflective of what others are feeling? If you think you have to take a profit, does that mean others feel the same way? Can you use your own response as an indicator of what other people are likely to do in these same circumstances and then take advantage of knowing what others are doing to figure out what to do? This is the ultimate counterintuitive indicator. ⋅

S: I think about this.

K: This is the value of a variety of traders of different levels of experience trading in the same room. The master trader can read the response of the marketplace by reading the responses of the people in his immediate environment. It's all information.

S: This is like analyzing noise.

K: Your own reaction is a signal to what others are doing. The shorts are being squeezed when the stock price moves up. This subtlety can be factored in. Now figure out the money flows. Who are the buyers and sellers?

S: I need to move beyond taking the trade. I was in the 'take the trade' mentality in order to get out of the hole. Now that is costing me something in terms of getting out of longer term trades too soon. I need to cut the losses but not cut the winners too soon. I don't want to lose more than 5 percent. But I am not taking more than 5 percent. Now I need to hold the trade longer. I need to let the winners run and cut the losses.

I am predisposed to a bull market. I cover my shorts 10 times faster than I cover a losing long. This stock is against me half a point. I don't even want it off the sheet. I can stay in longer in longs that aren't working.

I play the short game well enough to keep me flat in a down 6 percent market. That's a big improvement from last year when I would have been

223

destroyed. I can run $12 million net short. Now I want to not cover these shorts when they are working.

K: You have to time it. How long can you hold a short? Learn to handle the discomfort. Learn to handle bigger positions. It may not be right for the first 15 minutes. You can't psyche yourself out thinking about the commissions if you are getting out.

S: Now if it goes down a point or two, I get out of half down a point. Down two points I get out of all of it. If it goes up a point, I buy it back. If it keeps going, I haven't been good about buying more. I would rather buy big to begin with than add to it. That's a preference. I am learning all of this now.

K: This is all played against a background of fundamentals. If it is down for a rumor maybe you won't get out of it.

The opportunities for developing your potential are to be found within you, not in situations or factors external to you. The key to tapping these resources is not in acquiring something you don't have but in developing the natural and unique abilities that you possess that have not been developed fully or that may have been suppressed early in life. The key to tapping your resources involves awareness of the obstacles you have been putting in your own way so that you can transfer energy from wasteful activities designed to meet the expectations of the world to meaningful activities designed to express your creative self.

Remembering the Plan

Living by your commitment to a larger goal can produce energy, vitality, and renewal in the face of fatigue, boredom, and even failure. Commitment to a vision enables you to ride out any sense of frustration and anger that you might experience in the course of events when you are not able to produce the results you want. Commitment sets the stage for the development of self-mastery, looking within for the actions you must take to realize your vision.

But commitment does not come without problems. Commitment to a vision means living on the cutting edge and being willing to expose your vulnerability. Life will be full and enlivening and more interesting and action packed than if your principle focus is on avoiding pain and discomfort. But commitment will produce both failures and successes and will not always be comfortable.

Thinking creatively, you can accept the possibility that you cannot know what the future will bring nor what you can create in the future and that there is power in creating from the future rather than predicting from the past. With this view you can allow yourself to live with uncertainty and then begin to create the context—what is necessary to bring your vision to fruition. You relate to the events created by the commitment rather than live your life in terms of your preconceptions.

German mathematician, Carl Gauss, said: "I have had my solutions for a long time, but I do not yet know how I am to arrive at them." In other words, the steps to the solution or vision will unfold as you progress.

Declaring the truth about where you are and recommitting to your vision enables you to see what direction to put your energies into and activates creative energy to find solutions or new ways of approaching the situation. It means being willing to face the fact that your results aren't consistent with your stated objectives and considering what needs to be done to bring about the desired results.

Commitment is not an obligation but an opportunity, and there is no reason to get frustrated or elated with results. Committing to a vision is not about getting a result in order to be complete; rather it is about being complete because you have the vision.

Results are simply a measure of your commitment. If you don't produce a result, look to see what is missing from your actions so that you can start doing what it takes to express your vision and include all elements for creating the result rather than rely on chance factors, rationalizations, or the opinions of the people around you.

Do not become attached to the result either exulting in having reached it or feeling inadequate for not reaching it. The result is only feedback telling you how you are doing and what is missing.

Yes, it is easy to be distracted from your larger purpose by transient fluctuations in your results or to confuse your results with your identity, thinking that they mean something about you. But the master trader simply notices the results and considers what is missing from his strategy to ensure the realization of his vision. Most of all, he lets go of the inclination to keep discouraging himself by measuring where he is in relationship to the outcome.

True mastery doesn't entail the limitation of problems. Rather it entails the willingness to take on problems and live in the gap between where you are and where you have committed to be. Remember, creating a challenge produces results beyond expectations. The finest expression of creative ability often doesn't come to the surface until well near the end of a task. Many discoveries are made only after you come to a point of frustration and believe that you can go no further.

Trade in an effort to express yourself, not to get some other result. The result is only a marker to tell you whether you were committed to the result and whether you got past your resistance and expressed yourself. Don't think about the result as a measure of your worth. Don't invalidate yourself if you don't reach it.

CHAPTER TEN

DOING THE WORK

Adam was a trained professional who believed secretly from the start that he was not going to succeed as a trader. Despite all his training and prior success, he held back. Although he never let on, he just did not have faith in himself. His fear kept alive a kind of passivity in his trading. Implicit in this belief was the contradictory message that it was not in his power to make success happen. Because of this mixed message he was inclined to hold back, passively waiting for results, rather than taking the initiative to make good things happen. The lack of results then justified feelings of resentment, powerlessness, and a sense of being unappreciated, which further reinforced a passive approach to the world.

Ultimately, Adam self-destructed. Despite apparent efforts to get it right, Adam failed to succeed because he believed that he could not succeed.

Adam's story is an example of how passivity or a tendency to resign yourself to "fate" can lead to failure. By contrast, when you live out of a positive vision, you actively create the present, and each moment becomes a space of possibility. You respond more immediately and completely to events before you instead of simply reacting habitually. Vision allows you to make order out of the chaos of experience and provides you with guidelines for acting.

Committing to a vision means consciously deciding to take *responsibility* for your trades and then *acting* accordingly. The decision to act in terms of your vision is not based on past experience or existing knowledge. Rather than feel powerless, as Adam did, you count on your power to create from the hidden potential within you. Still, it requires conscious intention on your part to realize the result.

What follows is a review of some of the critical components of data analysis, which to my way of thinking constitutes an essential ingredient of increasing your risk taking. To prepare to size your trades you must understand the nature of the companies whose stocks you are trading to understand the trading implications of news events, product announcements, earnings reports, and other catalysts for putting on specific trades. While it is not specifically psychological in nature, this chapter underscores the kinds of analyses that traders must explore to maximize their chances of trading successfully.

Discerning the Importance of Data Analysis

Taking increased risk in the marketplace requires a combination of understanding the fundamentals and the market and having the courage to trade your conviction. To gain the confidence to trade bigger requires more data and processing that data in a trading-oriented way such that it produces results. Taking bigger risk requires these four elements:

1. Creating an information edge so that you are ahead of the curve.
2. Having a thesis that you can support with data.
3. Making an assessment of the sources of the data.
4. Trading on the basis of this data against other data in the marketplace.

The trader who understands risk pays attention to corporate numbers and guidance and tries to analyze the relevance of these numbers to where the company stands relative to its major competitors. He is able to differentiate between companies and does not simply trade noise or daily movement.

"I talk to companies all the time. That gives me confidence to hold," explained Brett. "I try not to be too reactive to the tape and play only for a point or two based on short-term money flows, which reflect more buyers or sellers on a given day. I don't want to be distracted by all the selling going on in the room in response to the market frenzy. I want to stick to my convictions based on my talks with companies, which give me a fundamental edge. I combine money flows, psychology, earnings reports—all these factors."

The best traders focus on the company balance sheet, on the earnings reports, and on an assessment of the growth prospects of a company. They also compare the company on a relative valuation basis to other companies in the same space. They consider the state of the economy and any significant macroeconomic variables such as Federal Reserve interest rate cuts, the cost of energy, and other costs of doing business, and try to assess the nature of the market at the time. Is it a market that is trading on fundamentals, or is it trading on macroeconomic variables and market sentiment? They try to get a handle on relevant short-term catalysts that may influence the market's perception of the value of a stock, and they try to make a calculated bet on the impact this data will have on the price of the stock. For example, good news expected at an upcoming conference can lead to a bounce in a stock for a few days.

They factor all these things against their past experience in trading the stock, and then they buy or sell some of the stock to get a feel as to how the stock is trading. They are also interested in the price action and what that tells them about the supply and demand characteristics of the stock—how it is trading based on an interest in buying or selling it among other investors and traders. With all this data analysis they then make some determination as to the risk/reward of a particular trade—the upside versus the downside of the trade.

Finally, to the extent that it fits within their parameters (say a 3:1 risk/reward ratio), they enter into the trade, all the time being careful to balance the trade in terms of their net long or short exposure. Often they are hedged and protected by having a bet going in the opposite direction with a comparable trade or with options that they use to leverage their bet and protect their downside risk.

Determining What Is Relevant

How much data do traders need to rely upon to take action? Too little analysis is obviously a problem. Too much data can also be stifling because it may take so much time to collect that the trader misses a trade. Or it may overwhelm him with choices and lead to decision paralysis. In effect, the opportunity may have passed while you are deciding the best action to take. There is an optimal amount of data and a time-frame for determining what action to take.

If you are trading in a short-term time-frame, you don't always need to dig as deeply into the fundamentals of the company, and you can make use of such short-term catalysts as conferences, road shows, earnings announcements, new product announcements, and the like to provide a rationale for a short-term trade. If you are a short-term, catalyst-driven trader, you have to pay attention to the daily fluctuations.

Long-term fundamentally driven "value" traders usually adopt a more relaxed, longer-term perspective to the daily fluctuations, even though over time there are far more variables that can influence the price of a stock and contribute to the long-term risk of owning the stock. For the longer-term trade, accounting issues, structural issues, and other fundamentals about the company are more critical. In either instance, it is critical to consider the underlying business and ask the right questions.

Doing the Work

According to Jay, a very bright portfolio manager: "Stock prices reflect the available data and change as the critical data change. It is important to figure out what the risk factors are that affect a particular stock at any given time: Is it earnings? Is it a breakdown in the vision of the company? Is it a competitive threat? The critical element will vary from company to company. Drill down to figure out what that variable is and then decide if you differ from the consensus.

"The hierarchy of what is most important depends on the central question of what is important to change people's opinions about the stock. That is what you look at.

"Most of the time it is earnings, but sometimes it is a vision question," Jay continued. "The essential question is what is important for the value of the stock. Secondly, consider what is important relative to what people think. Drill down to what will be important for revenue in the quarter or EPS [earnings per share]. As the data become clear, you make your trading decision. The key is increasing your gains and lowering the volatility of losses by using whatever analysis works for you.

"The more you understand what makes a company work, the nature of the business, the business plan and the relationship of the company to its competitors and to the business cycle, the inventories, catalysts, and other critical variables necessary to its ultimate valuation in the marketplace, the more successful you will be in your trading. But here you also have to make sure that your analysis is relevant to your thesis and to understanding what is really going on with the company.

"For example, in February 2001 the Federal Reserve was going to cut interest rates by another 50 basis points, which was anticipated but never happened. By understanding the company's relationship to the economy you could have known the implications for the companies you were trading. If you were trading food stocks, you would have anticipated that a 50-basis-point cut by the Fed chairman before the next meeting of the FMOC (Federal Open Market Committee) on March 23, 2001, would lead to a drop in the prices of these stocks, because foods are a defensive group and a drop in Fed rates would give a boost to technology and financial stocks and take money out of defensive stocks like foods. Such a drop might last a day or two and if you had been paying attention to the Fed data, you might have made a lot of money shorting these stocks in January when the Fed cut the interest rate by 50 points.

"Consider how the stocks have acted in the past. Think about what the charts tell you. Are the payment cycles lengthening? Are customers being more cautious in their decision making? Call around. Do the work. Talk to a technician who may have some levels on these stocks. Look at what else is going on in the sector. Are there significant numbers about to be announced? Is there more money coming into the market on the first day of the month? Be nimble. Keep moving."

Understanding the Business Model

Understanding the business model—where the revenues are coming from and how they are recorded and reported—can have implications for assessing the risk/reward of a trade. Learn as much as you can about:

- The nature of the business and the basic assumptions of the business.
- How the business intends to make money and finance growth.
- The competitive factors in the sector that make for a good or poor prognosis for growth and competitive power in the marketplace.

When your analysis suggests that a company has a faulty way of recording revenues or booking them, you may decide to short that company on an upswing in price. While the public may think that things are going well, the trader's closer inspection suggests that it is not so good. If it comes out that the firm is covering up a defective business model, the inflated valuations will fall.

Case Studies on Analyzing Business Models

Once you understand the business model and the profit potential of the company, it becomes useful to know a bit about the competition, the economic environment, and other factors that may influence the success of a company. This means you should know what decisions the companies are making today. Consider whether management understands the business, and understand any outside factors that may be affecting the stock.

In addition, consider such things as its relative position to other companies in the same industry. Does the company possess a long-term potential relative to its competitors? Is it the top dog and number one mover in an important and emerging industry? Recognize leaders that have discovered an opportunity and moved with speed and conviction in order to gain leadership before anyone else does.

One of the critical things a trader must do in assessing risk is to understand what are real businesses and what are merely companies whose stocks have been hyped by Wall Street, as happened in the online businesses in 2000. These businesses were prime examples of ones that were built around nonviable business models. According to Peter, an Internet observer:

"The dotcoms were numerous and successful on the economic landscape in 1999, but by 2000 these businesses proved to be no more than a speculative bubble. The outsized multiples at which they were trading were not based on any real valuation models but rather on speculative hype which generated enormous sums of capital and speculative excess could not be sustained by reality. The master trader may take advantage of this kind of hype, for a while, riding the wave of bullish sentiment, but he is not fooled by the hype and is fast out of these trades when these companies start demonstrating that they are not based on sound business models.

"Be willing to ask why a company's business model doesn't work. Do the critical work necessary for assessing whether to put on so much risk. Don't buy into the hyperbole and fail to assess the business model.

"Don't just buy a stock because it is down, without doing the work to understand why it is down and whether it will stay down given that the source of its business is drying up. Have the tenacity to question the business model."

Let's consider a trade put on by Jim, who really understands what value you get from talking to companies.

"In 2000 we made a lot of money shorting wireless stocks because companies were overpaying for the rollout of a new kind of data product called 3G. We realized that this was an issue that investors weren't focusing on and that they would overpay for companies that were going to use this product," he said.

The 3G product, which the wireless companies required, was very costly but didn't really add value to the companies. As investors bid up the price of the stock, Jim, recognizing that it wasn't going to add value to the companies, started shorting. In the end this small insight allowed Jim to capture a substantial profit when the values dropped. In effect, he was able to find a particular piece of data that gave him conviction to hold a view that differed from the market consensus.

This kind of detective work provides the edge that enables the trader to take on more risk and is the kind of analysis that helps traders to make critical distinctions between companies.

As one trader described it: "You have to understand the subtleties of the stocks you are trading. It's quite a bit like understanding wines. To the uninitiated there are red and white wines. Then French and American. These French can further be differentiated into Bordeaux and burgundies. Then different estates, different years. Each distinction becomes a critical component of understanding wines. The same holds for companies. I want to understand the company in all its complexity and do more than hear the story from the analyst. The longer you stay in a position, the more analysis you need and the more you need a good reason and understanding of the company."

While professional traders and analysts spend a lot of time making these kinds of distinctions, even ordinary investors can dig more deeply to find out about stocks they own. One amateur trader talks to hotel operators and people who own travel agencies because of her interest in cruise lines and hotel stocks. She looks things up on the Internet to determine how these companies are doing in the current economic climate to make reasoned bets in these kinds of stocks. Her edge is obtained from conventional sources that are not the exclusive province of sell-side analysts at brokerage houses where the analysts provide analysis to their best professional customers.

So, remember professional and even amateur traders can manage their risk in a controlled way by searching for relevant short-term events or catalysts that are likely to have an impact on the short-term movement of stocks. This is even more important than looking for hot tips.

Paying Attention to the Catalysts

A big factor in reducing trading risk is having a catalyst. Earnings announcements and reduced production are two catalysts that can change the market's perception of a stock's value and move the price. Such catalysts provide another type of data that the trader wants to have.

Listen to another trader's comments on this subject: "As much as possible, try to pay attention to the guidance where the company announces in advance that its earnings numbers won't be as good or bad as originally anticipated or as suggested by Wall Street analysts. Companies give such guidance to lower or raise expectations so that when they miss the expected numbers it won't have as much of a negative effect on the market's response as it might have had. Missing expected numbers can move a stock, so companies guide the numbers down so that they don't disappoint or so that expectations are lower, and they can surprise with better-than-expected earnings and boost the value of the stock. The smart trader should be aware of this."

Case Study on Understanding Catalysts

Auto stock prices rose prior to the auto show meetings with analysts in January 2001, but Noel believed these advances would decline in the weeks ahead. His analysis suggested that the fundamentals in the auto group were in a state of disarray and that plans for up to 20 percent production cuts would create financial stress greater than the profit of the units lost and that earnings would probably go down. In his view, the industry would be hard pressed to show profits in the first quarter. He also noted that few of the mutual funds in attendance at the auto show were enthusiastic about buying the group. He believed that as the consumer saw more notices of layoffs, consumer confidence would slow further and vehicle demand would continue to drop. Traditionally auto stocks don't usually draw real investor interest until industry sales begin to turn higher.

Noel also considered that there was a 10 percent chance that his dire assessments could be wrong. If vehicle demand were to hold around 15 million units in the first four months of 2001, he thought that investors would expect second quarter production schedules to rise and that the group would be bought for a second half economic recovery.

On the basis of this analysis, he recommended a few shorts such as one auto parts company which had gone up on a spike and had room to go down $5–$8. It was also a short because it was very exposed to another company, which would be the least able of the auto manufacturers to plan its cuts reliably. It was also exposed to higher resin prices in the first quarter of the year. He also recommended shorting another tire company that had also spiked but, because replacement tire demand was going down, would be hit by reduced production. The same short thesis applied to a company making fasteners for the auto business.

While the ordinary trader not working in an institution may not have access to all of this analysis, she can level the playing field to some degree by gleaning some of it from the Internet, by calling the customer relations person at companies, and by trading or investing in companies that she understands or works for.

In effect, catalysts are incremental news events or data points, which can move stock prices in the short term. If you are trying to take on more risk in a controlled fashion by reducing the amount of time you hold positions, you will do well to hone in on these things, thereby increasing your trading edge.

Interpreting the Silent Data

There is another level of analysis required beyond what is obtained from the Street. Trading in terms of the larger objective, you are looking for an incremental advantage from your analysis. You can obtain that edge if you are willing to play beyond the constraints of the numbers. While you are gathering as much data as you can about the company from company reports, conference calls, and the Internet, start listening carefully for subtleties from the reports of those close to the seat of power, many of whom can often be heard on national television or at shareholders' meetings.

Here too it becomes important to listen with the third ear and to read between the lines. Sometimes the most useful data is what is *not* being said. Body language and interpersonal demeanor may suggest discomfort or the fact that a company official is dissembling or hiding something. Traders need to be able to interpret and use this kind of hidden data when making trading assessments.

THE PSYCHOLOGY OF RISK

Case Study on Looking Beyond the Obvious

One trader began shorting Company X because a number of recent events had suggested that there was negative news coming. He reports the following:

"Company X completes its annual strategic review the week after Thanksgiving. The CEO [chief executive officer] presents at a Lehman Conference on December 1, 2000. We expect a press release giving guidance for fourth quarter of 2000 and fiscal year 2001. The IR [investor relations] rep, who is usually very responsive to my inquiries, has blown me off for two days. She also indicated to me that she is working on something for the CEO. The CFO [chief financial officer] acted 'strangely' and recently cut short a dinner with a sell-side analyst after half an hour. The company disseminated conflicting data the same day they reported their third-quarter results. They are orally indicating that their premier program would be certified by year end, then printed in the 10Q that it has been delayed.* The implementation of one of their major contracts is not going as well as planned, and there is a delay in foreign product orders at risk to next year's numbers. In addition, the used market for another of their major product lines is weak, and their 10Q stated that 'a downturn in demand for this specific product could have a material adverse effect on the company's financial position.' "

Notice all the indirect factors mentioned in this report such as the rep not providing typical information, the CFO's strange behavior, conflicting oral and written reports, and untimely delays, all of which supported the short recommendation. Good trading is based on probabilistic estimates of what will happen based on these kinds of incremental bits of data.

The successful trader is objective and levelheaded. He understands the context and the analysis. He thinks the unthinkable, questions all premises, and tries to understand which are valid and which

---

*The 10Q is the SEC's (Security and Exchange Commission) form 10 containing a company's financial information. It is submitted to the SEC quarterly. The 10K is filed annually.

are not. He does a probability analysis based on the risk and reward to increase his edge when entering a trade. The same analysis helps him decide when to pull out and take profits. The information helps him remain emotionally balanced so that he never approaches anything from weakness. He continually assesses what is real and what is not based on the facts and perceptions. If the data suggest that something is not real, the successful trader considers how long the world will perceive it as real.

Whether reading between the lines or evaluating the truth of a rumor, it is important to get as much data as you can to make an educated prediction about what is likely to happen and how you should act—buy into the rumor to make a quick hit or hold off and keep your powder dry for more likely opportunities. This kind of work will enhance your capacity to take measured risks.

Using Technical Analysis

An object in motion tends to stay in motion. It is hard to stay on a bicycle standing still, but when it has momentum it tends to keep moving and has more stability. This theory applies to markets as well. Once a market is in a trend, that trend has a lot of momentum and tends to continue further and longer in that same direction, regardless of whether it is warranted by the fundamentals in the stock.

Technical analysis is another tool in the trader's armory to help him reduce risk and increase profitability. It is based on the assumption that trends exist in the market and it involves the ability to anticipate critical moves in stocks such as price exhaustion before a stock turns upward so that you can buy it early. Technical analysis tells you about supply and demand in the marketplace and gives you good entry and exit points.

Because changes in stocks have already been factored into the price before news events occur, technical analysis may give you a leg up on the news. Whereas fundamental analysts scale back their expectations after a company shows sales have dropped off, technical analysis helps to do that earlier because price is ultimately a reflection of factors that have been discounted into the marketplace.

The master trader looks for changes in supply and demand before earnings announcements to anticipate how sell-side analysts might change their expectations and their statements after the announcements, which often cause changes in stock prices. For example, a road show by a company usually has an impact on the price of a stock. Technically, while things are trading off and a stock price is dropping, you may see this kind of information showing up in the price. If you know it, you can start buying the stock on the way down, before its price turns upward.

A lot of technical analysis involves looking for breakouts when it is the time to buy a stock. The bigger your portfolio, the harder it is to buy when things are up. One technical system developed by Tom DeMark looks for periods of price exhaustion so that when a stock price is going down the trader can keep on bidding because of a plentiful supply of stock. When the stock turns, there is less supply of it and you have to chase the price.

One student of this system told me: "When the price is coming down from 40 to 35, it is important to know we are stretched on the downside and that the selling has been exhausted. That is a good time to buy it, even though people are still selling it, since it is likely that the price is going to turn upward. Once it has turned, it is clear to others that it is going higher. The master trader wants to use such a technical system to know about price exhaustion so that he can start buying it before it turns.

"As the price is going down, and he lifts an offer (or his bid gets hit), the price may go lower. But when it is further down, it may move up and it may cost him more. There is a different elasticity on the way down than on the way up. As price goes down, the trader can still buy it. As the price goes up, it is harder to buy it in sufficient size. As your portfolio gets bigger and you are looking to accumulate more stock, you will find it harder to do on the way up for a three-day move. This system of assessing price exhaustion is especially good when there is a capitulation."

The $64,000 question in trading is to determine the difference between perceived and real risk. Technical analysis does this by analyzing prices, which factor in all information available before news events occur and can be used to anticipate reality. This is reflected in the concept that the market is a discounting mechanism. The market factors in everybody's knowledge of the world and anticipates changes six to nine months ahead of time.

Real risk is reflected in the actions of prices. The perceived risk, as expressed by the press, television, and sentiment of traders, is related to the mismatch between the real price and how people are responding to the markets.

· Technical analysis helps determine what people and prices are doing and given that particular view of reality, how to play it. In effect, technical analysis may help you to anticipate trend changes before they occur so that you can get into a trade early. It is another tool for getting a handle on data to increase your capacity to take risk.

Case Study on Using Data to Increase Your Edge

By combining the various methodologies in the foregoing discussion, you can increase your edge. The following dialogue is with a trader who specialized in Internet stocks during the boom Internet year 1999. It illustrates the attempt by the trader to develop some understanding of inefficiencies in the pricing of the companies he is trading and his effort to develop a methodology for assessing the meaning of news events and earnings reports. Most interesting is the imagery he presents of solving a puzzle, the pieces of which have a significance that keeps changing over time. The general approach to trading illustrates the thought process of a short-term, catalyst-driven approach to trading the markets.

Tony: I am looking at Internet software.

Kiev: Do you understand the drivers and the companies and what the dynamics are? Are you able to evaluate the bits of information from a trading point of view?

T: More and more of that comes with time. A typical Internet software company gets a big contract and then I see how it reacts. Then three months later when it gets another big contract, I will get a good idea of how it is going to react. To really get a feeling of when it is overdone, when it is priced on the stock, when it is buy on the room or sell on the news—to get that feeling it takes a while.

For example, there is one German company in this space. Most of the analysts on Wall Street said it was not going to make the quarter. But the stock just sat and sat at the same price. I thought that was a little odd, that it was not going down after everyone said it was going to miss the quarter. I believed that it was going to come out with a surprise and all of a sudden it was going to be up 10 bucks in your face. Sure enough, it beat numbers, and the stock went from 50 to 60 in 10 days.

K: Sounds like a complex analysis.

T: The key was figuring out where the quarter was to be versus what the expectations were versus what the rest of the software universe was doing and what the rest of technology was doing. Today I am in two stocks that reported great numbers yesterday. Two weeks ago if they had reported those numbers, they both would be up at least 10 percent. Today one is down a little and one is down a few percent. The reason is they had the big runs with all of the software over the last couple of weeks. All of technology is getting hit today. There are no set rules. It is all fluid.

K: It is understanding the story and understanding the market and being able to process all of that. The generic phenomenon is the same, but how events interact with stock prices varies from sectors.

T: The business model of a technology company versus nontechnology is just instantly improving because it is growing at faster rates. Say your

Doing the Work

growth rate is 30 percent. In a software company your stock might drop 50 percent as a result, but if you report that in a commodity company, your stock might go up. It is everything specific to the industry and then on top of that it becomes specific to your stock.

K: You have to understand the subtleties of each industry and their bearing on the stock price?

T: You have to understand the industry relative to the individual companies. The key is to see what is going on and then piece it together. It is critical to ask why an event is happening. When you get the answer, you know your next move.

K: Do you ask those kinds of questions?

T: I think I always asked those questions because I was more macro-oriented, because I came from that side of thought opposed to these guys who came from the side of thought of "Is there good news in my stock? Is there bad news in my stock?" I try to piece everything together, and if I get it figured out, then I am sure it will all change. That is all the market does.

K: It keeps changing.

T: Ultimately it is a derivative of human nature. Once humans figure out everything, figure out one puzzle, it creates a puzzle somewhere else.

K: What is the explanation for that? Once you figure out how these moving parts are working, then you start responding and then it starts changing again.

T: What you want to do as a trader is to capitalize on inefficiency—where you think the market is wrong versus the price. You think it is worth $100, but it is trading at $75. You want to close the inefficiency gap. You want to buy at 75, and you think it should go to 100. So, you think it is inefficient. So you found out a reason why you think you should buy this at 75 when it is worth 100. You came up with some methodology. Let's say another trader, Mr. Z, does the same thing. Then, all of a sudden, it is at 90. All of a sudden those same people are saying that it is worth 100, and everybody is buying it. Then, if everybody has figured that out, there is always another to fight. Investors have changed the dynamics of investing that they have been very slow to address.

K: So now what happens in the marketplace to create the next inefficiency?

T: It could be in some other stock. It could be in some other type of security.

K: You are not going to make money unless you can find inefficiencies?

T: Right, and there are different types of inefficiencies—in that people don't have data or miss the value. I think in the Internet sector there is a lot of inefficiency, and I think that is why you see a lot of these huge moves back and forth. With stock investing, and especially at the far-end technology and Internet investing, there is a lot of information that people don't know. You can capitalize on that.

This dialogue illustrates how valuable it is to assess a wide range of data from a trading perspective, paying attention to the market trends and macroeconomic events—all the time maintaining an openness and flexibility, recognizing that everything is subject to change.

Risk taking changes depending on the nature of the markets. Some markets are particularly volatile and fundamentals don't seem to make a difference in how stocks move. However, even in these markets, fundamentals are still important. For example, in January and February of 2001, the markets seemed to keep going down on both good and bad news, and traders had enormous difficulty in making money on the basis of their fundamental analysis. I talked to Peter about this on February 28, 2001. His comments add some perspective to the significance of weighing the nature of the markets under those circumstances—when your thesis about particular stocks can't be substantiated by market movements. The Nasdaq composite had dropped considerably, so when traders like Peter shorted select technology stocks there was little place for them to go.

"The shorts are sticky. There is bad news out there in one of my shorts, and it is only down one-half dollar. We are getting to the point where it is hard to believe. The fundamentals suck, and the stocks are still expensive. There is a tendency to become lethargic in response to bad news. They are going to go down, but maybe not this week. I am short based on fundamentals. You really need to know the fundamentals, the business cycle, and the way companies evolve over time so you know why things happen the way they do. There is a reality that causes stocks to move the way they do. If you stick to that and can separate the noise from the facts, then you can make money by pressing your bets when you are right. Stocks express things over time. You can't get instant gratification."

He continued: "The issue is to get bigger progressively and take more risk in an intelligent way, sizing the positions in terms of the risk and reward and knowing when to expand the size of the positions. I use fundamentals to give me an edge in my trading so that I can get bigger in situations where the stock is moving against me. If I have the conviction, I can even get bigger when things are going against me and when it is cheaper to buy the stock or sell the stock. In fact I tend to do more work when things are going against me. That is when I build up my positions and make the most money.

"The key to the success of this model is balancing shorts against specific longs. Either you balance competitors or you balance two companies, both of which may be doing well, but one may be cheaper relative to the other. You have to be able to differentiate between the quality of companies. It is an art—balancing the understanding of a company and how to trade it."

Admittedly, this balancing is not as easy today as it once was, given the realities of Reg FD (Fair Disclosure Regulation), but there are still resourceful ways of finding out about a company and how it is doing relative to its competitors and relative to its past.* What you

---

*New Fair Disclosure rules require companies to make information available to everyone at the same time.

find out may give you distinct clues as to how the business will do in the future.

To take on more risk, the experienced trader needs to dig deeper and deeper in understanding company fundamentals, technical indicators, and other information—separating market movement from basic fundamentals and taking measured bets based more on his understanding of the companies than on their market action alone.

Practical Steps

Momentum requires a blending of action and *intelligence* to produce specific incremental results, which ultimately become the seeds of further actions. Momentum refers to that level of interest and involvement that allows you to keep focusing without becoming overwhelmed by excessive stimuli or bored by insufficient challenge. It requires careful monitoring of the process to bring all of your resources to bear on the actions before you. You must monitor the way in which you are functioning, paying attention to whether you are becoming distracted, whether you are fully engaged in the action, and the extent to which you are bringing all your energy or are participating in the process with all your heart and soul.

To sustain momentum once you have established a goal, it is critical to keep focusing on what is happening and to consider the next step to take. Ask yourself:

- What is the design structure for your vision?
- What do you need to get going?
- What steps can you take now to begin the process?
- What resources already exist?
- How can you allow the process to unfold without stirring things up?

Answering these questions, you begin to see the extent to which you hold back or become distracted by other objectives or unnecessary comparisons with others. Involving yourself in the here and now of the process enables you to intensify the amount of effort and energy you give to a task without experiencing the fear and anxiety that comes from focusing too much on the long-range outcome. While a goal sets the direction and provides a motivating force, only involvement in the here and now enables you to bring all of your resources to bear on your performance.

"Analysis doesn't always help, but if you take the view that it doesn't matter, you will lose in the end. You can hear it and not factor it into your thinking, but at least in considering it you are adding it to your decision-making process," explained one trader.

When gathering data, it is easy to become overwhelmed with the choices. However, there are some practical ways of sorting through the myriad amounts of data you may encounter. Data are best considered relative to how they relate to specific trading decisions. Data either make a trade look promising or should discourage you from taking action. A rating system is one way to help you keep tabs on the information you are gathering and the trades that the information represents. Consider developing a system like the one described by a team of traders in *Trading in the Zone* (Wiley, 2000).

"Our rating system has developed over time," Cody explained. "Now, trades that are in the trading account have a catalyst behind them and a short-term time-frame allocated to allow them to work. Long-term ideas, if they can pass muster, can find a capital allocation in the long-term account. Anything in between will just have to be missed."

Cody developed a 1-2-3 system.

#1 Trades—Trades that looked as though they would move up or down in the next day or two. They were backed with a lot of conviction and a short-term horizon.

#2 Trades—Trades that had a catalyst on the horizon, but the time-frame remained unclear. Although the traders didn't want to wait to buy/sell until the idea was a #1, they also didn't want to get too big in a #2.

#3 Trades—Trades considered an educated bet. The traders didn't necessarily have a "shocking insight, but we like the bet on a risk-adjusted basis." Number 3 trades were often used as sources of funds for #1 or #2 ideas.

This system is not necessarily a model for everyone to follow. In fact, Cody later adjusted it to coincide with his own tendencies to "get stubborn on the #1s and keep buying them." The point is that such a system is of value as a general example for how you can devise data guidelines or rules that complement your style and help you organize and sort the vast amount of data you are processing so that you can use them most effectively.

You may want to consider the following list of questions and comments when reviewing data and determining their relevance on any given trade:

- How long will this information about a company (an earnings announcement, a change in the basic structure of the business, a significant conference or meeting) be relevant for trading this stock? Be able to state your case in a simple manner that anyone can understand.
- If you have doubts, look at it again. Has anything changed? Is further research required?
- Remember that stocks are volatile and may fluctuate in response to events in the company, in the sector, and in the marketplace for shorter or longer periods of time and then revert back to the mean. Do you want to trade the intraday volatility for short-term profits? Are you holding the stock for a bigger gain over a longer period? Is your information and assessment relevant irrespective of the short-term movement in the stock?

- Consider the facts. If the business is still healthy and a stock is declining in price, it may still be worth holding or buying more, depending on your risk profile and your targets. Always weigh the information against the risk/reward of your decision to buy or sell a stock. Filter the noise and keep on learning more about the company and the reasons why it may be trading the way it is. Know as much as you can about the companies you are trading and the factors influencing movements in the company so that you can ride out fluctuations in the stock price.
- Be realistic and judge your performance based on how well you are sticking to your strategy. Remember that it sometimes takes a while to create a successful trading strategy.

The more data you have, the more confident you can be about decisions, but that doesn't necessarily mean you are going to make better decisions. Commitment to the goal means acting from it without any guarantee of success, with the same kind of enthusiasm you'd feel if you believed there was no chance of failure. I am talking about focusing on *efforts*, not on results.

The key to all of this is to be able to live in the present, to see every situation as an opportunity to hit a home run, to give it your best shot, and to keep focusing on immediate targets relating to the broader objective.

› The importance of understanding the fundamentals to assess the real risk inherent in a trade is a critical aspect of managing risk. You need to increase the informational edge that you have about a company so that you can properly size your position and make a directional bet based on such issues as earnings expectations and the growth potential of the company. To do so requires understanding the space or sector in which the stock trades and something about the other companies in the space and the kinds of multiples that they are going for. Once you have made these assessments, you also need to understand your own psychology and how it factors into your trading. Differences in beliefs and attitudes play a significant role in how the individual trader perceives the opportunities before him.

A broad introspective orientation to concentration is likely to be useful for strategic planning where it will help you to grasp a lot of information, to preview events, to adjust to unexpected events, and to continually analyze the situation. But, it will not help you to readily adapt to new circumstances or environmental shifts. You may have difficulty tuning into the feelings of others, handling new situations, or following your strategy. Learning, after all, is not just about absorbing information from a book but learning how to expand your ability to create the results that you want. Keep distinguishing between the neutrality of events and the requirements of personal events, interpretations, and reactions.

· "The only difference among traders acting on the same information is how well they handle their emotions," said Calvin.

And that leads us to Chapter Eleven, where you learn to manage the emotional potholes you will encounter as you learn to take risk successfully.

COPING WITH RISK: COACHING, TEAMWORK, SYSTEMS

Much of this book has focused on efforts to help you to think outside the box of conventional thoughts, to do the impossible, to enter into the gap between where you are and where you wish to be. To do these things you need to function independently of your old attitudes, to be able to look at things in a way that allows you to create the future, quite independently of where you were in the past.

In this last chapter I present three tools that can help you: coaching, teamwork, and the use of systems. I firmly believe that with these tools, you can begin to break free of the preconceived notions you may have brought to the trading arena.

Consult a Coach

The psychology of trading as approached in this book is about taking psychological risks by stepping into the abyss—entering the unknown where you are guided by your commitments to a future vision of trading results. There is a natural tendency to resist the unknown, so I want to provide some mechanisms for helping you to stay in the realm of commitment in the face of the drift toward the habitual return of the self-doubts, which you have been brought up to expect would be the nature of experience. The purpose of coaching, therefore, is to provide you with some mechanism of objective review of your trading. The aim: to see what is missing and what more needs to be done to help you function in terms of the goals you have set for yourself.

Coaching, as I see it, is less about showing you how to trade than providing a way of helping you see what you need to do to remain on target and to trade in terms of your particular strengths and strategies. The task of the coach is to assist you to stay focused on your commitments despite the natural pressure to get off task and lose focus in the course of dealing with the complexities of trading. Coaching can be particularly useful in helping you to:

- Tap your hidden potential
- Stay on target
- Get past self-doubts
- Move into a centered state
- Assume responsibility
- Stay committed to the vision
- Give up control

Coaching can present a broader perspective from which to review trades and to link you to a larger trading mission or result so that you have a greater sense of control. Coaching provides a frame of reference, a metaconcept about trading that encourages you to stand back and examine certain repetitive actions associated with it that may be beneficial or detrimental to the trading result itself. It encourages the development of strategic templates designed to help you become more engaged in the trading process.

- You need to learn to balance greed and fear, the desire for better results and the fear of losing, all of which can overpower you and create confusion. The task of coaching is to raise your level of consciousness so that you can maintain control of these internal drives that interfere with the clarity of mind you need to trade successfully.

"Coaching helps you to change your mental framework and reduces emotionality or overreactivity to the markets," said Franz. "It also lets you raise the level of possibility by helping you to see internal or mental barriers to performance. This increased self-awareness is also useful in allowing you to ride out continuous negative or losing cycles."

How does a trading coach accomplish these objectives? My own approach is to meet with traders like yourself and regularly discusses issues such as:

- The size of your positions. Have you sized your positions commensurate with your profit targets or goals?
- Your profit and loss. Are you making more in your winning trades than you are losing in your losing trades and if not, what steps can you take (like holding winners longer and cutting losers sooner) to correct this imbalance?
- How you are limiting yourself. What are you doing that is interfering with success? Are you reluctant to add to winners? Are you doing insufficient work? Are you compulsively gambling?
- What more you can do to improve.
- What's missing from your trading, for example, what may have dropped out of your trading approach such that you are no longer trading as profitably as you may have in the past.

Sometimes a coaching session is very simple, getting the trader to think about some rather obvious things which in the heat of action he or she may not have considered. Such was the case with Anne, an outstanding young trader who was stymied by the opportunity to handle more capital after a series of major successes.

Anne was experiencing anxiety about using an increased amount of capital to trade larger positions. She was basically fearful about trading larger size but was very receptive to coaching and was quickly able to translate a little bit of encouragement into profitable trading. Basically, she had to see how much her concerns about handling larger amounts of money and having bigger losses would be balanced by having bigger wins, especially if she continued to trade the way she had been trading. She needed to know that her fears were just that—a bit of uncertainty about the future that was making her uptight. To the extent that she relaxed and handled the bigger size trades the same way, there was no reason to expect that she would produce anything but the same rate of return.

"I followed your advice and followed my instincts," she said. I did exactly what I wanted to do. If I felt like buying something, I bought it. If I felt I should sell it, I sold it. I did it no matter what the size. I bought things up to $65 million, and we had an awesome day. I was very prepared. I got in early. I had a complete idea of what I wanted to do for the day. I knew how big I was going to be. The trading confirmed what I had prepared. I planned to add to positions. I was prepared for the opportunities that occurred. I prepared to trade with more money. I just did it. It was wonderful. I have been so proud of myself the last couple of days."

Coaching provides an opportunity to reframe the trading task and to give you that added bit of perspective you need to move to the next level. A coach can encourage you to play the game as if you were in a practice session with him.

Some traders need coaching in the areas of trading bigger, pulling the trigger, cooperating with a trading partner, finding more and better information about catalytic events, getting out of positions, or just about any other subject covered in this book. As mentioned previously, in my weekly meetings I provide traders with a chance to review their plans and their concerns and to get a broader picture of their risk taking as it relates to their objectives. Because of the inherent resistance that traders face in making their trading decisions, I often use these discussions as an opportunity to push traders past their comfort zones.

A trading coach asks psychological and motivational questions that empower people to change their perceptions. He conducts complex conversations that are brought down to everyday performance. He encourages traders to find what is getting in the way of higher performance.

I would, for example, try to help a trader who is the butt of criticism to use the criticism as a guide to looking more closely at the kinds of things he might do to improve his performance. In the same way, I will focus a lot of attention on helping a trader discover what more can be done to improve his trading. I try to help the traders see new behaviors that can be adopted in order to change the game.

One trader made the comment, "I think we have done all that we can do." I would try to discover why this trader feels this way and try to motivate the trader to push further and pursue greater goals. Is he afraid to explore? Is he afraid to admit the truth? Maybe he hasn't gotten the help he needed in the past or wasn't open or receptive to help.

An important part of coaching is to recognize that traders are often overstimulated and encouraged by the coaching conversation. They may then radically change their behavior and find themselves in over their heads. Some traders get too rash and start taking bigger risks than desirable. Therefore, all coaching must be presented with the caveat that the trader, while stretching to expand his risk taking, must trade in terms of well-established risk management parameters and without making any radical changes in strategies that have consistently worked. All changes must be done carefully.

The coach has to be the regulator, notice patterns, and encourage traders not to build their positions too excessively. His communication skills must be honed because it is imperative that he not be misinterpreted. A coach has to encourage *incremental* shifts rather than *radical* shifts in the trading process.

Case Study: Coaching Traders on Handling Emotions

A coach needs to remember that coaching different people requires different strategies. Different people require different kinds of help. Ideally, a coach will want to find your stopping point, that dimension of your trading where you are fearful of taking action despite what your fundamental or technical analysis or feel for the market is telling you to do. Here the coach may be able to give you some kind of exercise, such as keeping a diary or timing your feelings, to help you gain mastery over the problem interfering with your trading success. Listen to my discussion with Hillel, an anxious trader who needed help in handling his emotions.

Hillel tended to get scared out of trades too soon. His trading decisions were emotional rather than rational. Early in April 2000, on a Wednesday morning, he decided that the market was going to collapse over the following week. So, he put on a big short position overnight in the Standard & Poor's (S&P). For him this was 150 percent of his capital and was as big as he ever got. On Thursday the market was up about half a percent and was very quiet, but Thursday afternoon he was feeling what he called "high anxiety." So, he got rid of the shorts. Twenty minutes later the market started going down, but he thought, "I can't put the shorts back on because I just got rid of them. They were causing me too much anxiety."

However, the S&Ps continued to go down on Thursday. Friday they went down some more at the opening. His shorts and longs were balanced, and he let them go down and then covered his shorts when the S&Ps were down about 50 points. He got out of a long position an hour later when it was clear it wasn't going to work. In discussing this trade he talked about losing a big bet because of failure to follow his strategy.

Hillel: I'm always more fearful than I am greedy. I never want to let anything get out of hand. I will write it on a piece of paper in front of me: 'Do not get out of this trade unless you lose 1 or 2 percent.' Then by 2 o'clock in the afternoon I'm feeling anxiety, and I say, 'To hell with it,' and I get out of the trade. I can often do something strategically, which is probably my strongest suit, but I then exit because of anxiety.

On Thursday I started feeling the anxiety around 10:30 in the morning, and I started saying 'Gee, the market could go up a percent and a half quickly, and maybe I shouldn't be there.' Then I looked at the piece of paper that said, 'Don't get out of this position,' and by 2 o'clock I continued to feel the anxiety. I said, 'It hasn't worked yet. Maybe it won't work.' And what I felt then wasn't anxiety. It was remorse or stupidity or something. The right thing obviously (if I had been a perfect computer) would have been to put the position back on. But then again, sometimes I make a mistake, and the right thing is just to walk away and do nothing.

I would be better off if I would just put down my strategy, put my trade on in the morning, and walk away, because the strategies tend to be right. That's where I make my money, either as an analyst in individual stocks or as a strategist. When I get into the trading aspects, that's where I start to trip over my toes. My problem is that I exit trades when I start losing and sort of walk around the block. If I'm trying to make 80 percent a year, then I have to risk losing 6 percent on a day. But emotionally if it doesn't fit, I either have to change the emotion or walk around the emotions.

Kiev: Just because the market doesn't go the way you want it to go doesn't mean you should be out of the game. You want to notice that you're anxious. What's the amount that you can tolerate trading, given that you're anxious, as opposed to taking yourself out of the game completely?

H: When I feel anxious I start to reduce my positions by removing 20 lots, and then I feel better, but 10 minutes later the anxiety is back, and I start to reduce it 10 or 20 at a time until there is nothing left of it. When I started I said I was going to go from 120 to 100, and I was going to stay there because I have written on this piece of paper, 'Stay with this position.' I stayed for a couple of days, but then I couldn't.

K: What's the amount of capital that you can risk, given your strategy so you can practice riding out the anxiety?

H: If I had stayed with it I would have made 12 percent. So you're saying I should try to feel the anxiety and don't get out of the trade then?

K: Own it. This is the big leagues, the World Series.

H: It's a natural reaction that when you feel anxious, you try to reduce the anxiety. It never occurred to me to just own the feeling. If I could ride out the feeling, I could do better financially. That's interesting.

THE PSYCHOLOGY OF RISK

K: Wilt Chamberlain used to throw up before every game. You want to notice your feelings and keep a diary to record how long they last. Actually, turning on a stopwatch and measuring the duration of the feelings is the best way to frame them. You will discover when these feelings reappear that they last shorter and shorter periods of time until eventually you have mastered the art of riding them out. Most traders trade in a way that allows them to feel comfortable, but supertraders are willing to allow themselves to be uncomfortable to make it. They're playing it as smart as they can play. For example, astronauts are trained to observe their own responses when they're in a rocket ship. They get all the information as part of take-off—not just speed and altitude, but also their own pulse and heart rate. They know what to expect. Then when they level off, they settle down. When they're about to land, they know to expect some apprehension again. It's monitoring your own anxiety so it becomes another measure of what the markets are doing. Maybe it's getting scary, but it's telling you that possibly everybody is scared. Use it as information. I'm not suggesting that you stop feeling the anxiety altogether, and I'm not suggesting that we give you Valium to get rid of it. I'm suggesting that you learn to use it.

H: I really have a risk aversion that's been shown up by experience. The issues for me are getting the emotions out of the way and riding a winner properly. On the big trades I'm almost never able to sit with it.

K: Can you throw with your left hand?

H: No. I've never tried.

K: You could probably learn. It's a skill thing. Can you learn the skill of holding a stock from 24 to 50 or holding a third of the stock from 24 to 50?

H: I understand what you are saying. I can learn to play tennis with my left hand without any emotional scarring, but holding a stock working to 50 requires me to react differently. It's a different type of learning.

K: But it's still learning a skill. It's learning to hold it even though you're feeling uncomfortable. It's a discomfort in doing something new. If you haven't done it, it feels awkward or weird to do something that in your mind (as an analyst) you know makes perfect sense. So you're not able to translate the thought process into the key motion. Identifying it and putting a circle around it will make it easier to see. That's part of the game. It will also give you more confidence to handle the S&P short positions.

This discussion underscores the value of coaching an experienced trader such as Hillel who lost track of his objectives because of anxiety. Clearly he was able to benefit from the perspective provided by someone who understands the trading process.

Coaching is particularly relevant in helping you to adhere to your targets in the face of the natural inclination to rationalize your failures. It is also important in helping you monitor your emotional responses to trades, in particular helping you to stay alert to the danger of euphoria and complacency (secondary to readily achieved successes) and despair and depression (secondary to losses). The coach is there to help keep you on task so that your natural emotional responses to the ups and downs of trading don't muddy your rational thoughts.

This is what coaching is all about. A coach is there to encourage and sometimes even prod, but he should not push you too hard or come on too strong. The critical thing is tuning in to your specific needs and gauging what it will take to help you to enhance your performance. Here is another dialogue in which I coached a new trader to monitor his emotional responses.

Case Study: Coaching Traders on Handling Emotions (continued)

Kenneth is the junior trader for a large, market-neutral portfolio and has just begun to trade his own pad. The following dialogue gives some idea of the kinds of issues that are usefully addressed in an initial coaching session. These issues can help you understand how your emotional responses can help or hinder the way you trade. The objective is not to eliminate feelings but to create a greater awareness of the emotional responses to your trading so that you can use your own response patterns as a tool for facilitating your ability to handle the markets.

Kiev: There are three critical issues to address when you start trading:

1. What are your goals?
2. How do you plan to achieve your goal (i.e., what is your strategy)?
3. What are the most likely obstacles to implementing your strategy? Specifically, what are you likely to do that may interfere with the trading process?

Kenneth: My goal is $25,000 per day. I've done that so far. To do that I am positioning myself with $500,000 to $1 million positions. Today I was in nine positions, and it's the first day where I got hit. I usually follow three to five positions. I can react more quickly with that. Given my other duties, I got distracted by running too many positions and overreacted on the opening. I probably should have bought a bit more on the big dip this morning. I was up $147,000 coming in today in five days of trading.

Kiev: Trade the number of positions with which you are most comfortable. Build up a string of successes. Then you can get bigger in terms of the number and size of positions. It is critical to identify what gets in the way, what gets you scared so that you start doing stupid things. You are always reacting to something, which colors the way you respond to the next opportunity. Besides fear, another problem is how you respond to success. If you didn't get out and the thing reversed and went up, you might have felt like a hero when you were really lucky. Then you may do some stupid things. You want to track your responses so you know how you respond and can correct for emotional responses, which are not good strategically. This area is where you have to learn more about yourself so that you can develop a trading style that builds on your strengths and minimizes your bad habits. You can't let your feelings interfere with how you are trading. The target forces you to increase your size commensurate with your goals and to watch your losses.

Kenneth: I let my emotions get in the way yesterday. I made $25,000 by noon, and I started looking for more trading ideas. That's when I decided to go home long. I made $47,000, and I had a little swagger in my step. I decided to make a bet for the following morning. I was pumped and got speculative. Today's loss was started by yesterday's success.

Coping with Risk: Coaching, Teamwork, Systems

Kiev: You want to make a trade based on something you know, not based on how you feel. Notice this streak in yourself, an inclination to get too confident coupled with an inclination to beat yourself when you are wrong. Watch that tendency, because that pattern can get you off your game.

Kenneth: I have some doubts. Am I good enough to be in this room, to trade, to make money? When I came out of the gates, I made a little money. I made $47,000 yesterday and started feeling cocky. My successes from the previous day are hurting me today. It is all part of learning this whole game.

Kiev: Your own observations of your own responses will be more critical for you in your ultimate success than how much money you make in the early days. What separates one trader from another is the extent to which he has developed self-awareness, discipline, and good habits early on in his trading career. Once you get control of your own responses to your trades and understand how to make money, you can multiply your results by getting bigger. You have to ask yourself whether you know something that gives you an edge. You want to learn how to track that, so that you can use self-awareness in the trading.

Coaching is a tool for facilitating out-of-the box thinking and helping keep you honest and aware of how your own beliefs and preconceptions interfere with risk taking. Coaching is to help you understand the distinctions between commitment and going through the motions, between commitment and resignation.

Interestingly, this first tool is also relevant to the second—teamwork—and the third—systems trading. Coaching helps facilitate teamwork because ego and territory and other personality issues often interfere with the process of creating teams where you can expand your capability by functioning as a unit and contributing your special elements to the team effort. It is also relevant to the subject of systems in helping you to stay focused on the task and to surrender fully to the discipline of the system.

In terms of teamwork, you need a coach who can zero in on the strengths that you, and all the other team members, bring to the game and foster synergies between you and the other traders so that as a team you can do far more than you could as individuals. The team is a mechanism of social inspiration, of getting traders outside their egos.

Take Advantage of Teamwork

Although trading has traditionally been more of a solitary profession, I am convinced that there is value in teamwork and in the sharing of knowledge. Teamwork is one way of overcoming personal obstacles that interfere with the attainment of your goal. In fact, learning to be a team player is the next step in managing your risk appropriately. While many traders simply don't see the benefit of the team process in a trading career, the masters know that teamwork is vital to trading in the zone.

Teamwork is especially useful in helping you to master the following components of the psychology of risk taking:

- Making small changes
- Overcoming fixed ways of doing things
- Focusing on the now
- Staying in motion
- Trading proactively
- Persevering

While each of these components has been discussed in detail throughout this book and can be addressed in terms of the individual, the value of teamwork as it relates here can best be summed up in the Biblical verse from Ecclesiastes (4:9–10) "Two are better than one; because they have a good reward for their labour. For if they fall, the one will lift up his fellow: but woe to him that is alone when he falleth; for he hath not another to help him up."

When you are a member of a team, you can rely on the support, encouragement, and assistance of your teammates to help you as you learn to take these steps, and you in turn can help them.

One astute trader observing a top trading team in action opined: "They are all completely different. If they were on their own, who knows what they could do, but together they create a tremendous dynamic. They prevent each other from making a lot of mistakes. When you are on your own, you don't have a system of checks and balances. There is a human component in working with others which I don't have in what I am doing. I have it in the virtual world—the guys I talk to—but it is not the same thing."

A trading partner can help you get bigger, take a profit, or increase a position. Even just a little bit of encouragement from a teammate, especially a senior or more experienced trader, can often be very helpful.

"Rich and I trade differently," said Bruce, "but there is an advantage to being together. We pay commissions jointly and so get better coverage from the Street. We get to look at more fundamental research from the big brokerage houses. He will watch the 40 stocks I watch and vice versa. We will be able to put more money to work and become more of a force in the market. If my ideas are good, I will be able to be bigger because we have more capital."

These are just a few of the benefits of teamwork. By working as a team, each member can make a contribution of his particular strengths. However, too many firms are built around the erroneous notion that each trader should get as big as he can rather than trading in terms of teamwork, and many traders have difficulty adjusting to working with a partner.

"My partner and I get along very well," said one trader, "but we are not helping each other. I am not helping him. He is not helping me. There's something wrong. He is a talented guy as an analyst and finding out what is good about companies. I feel I am not using him at all. There is no synergy. The two of us get along together, but he is too busy. When we joined forces, we had the idea that he was going to visit the companies not sit in front of a screen."

Practical Steps

Most of us stop somewhere in our efforts to establish a result in the future. We are reluctant to commit to our visions and reluctant to enlist the support of others in the face of resistance. We withdraw from the negative responses of others instead of enrolling them in our activities. In this regard it is not only necessary to commit to your objective, it is also important to share the objective with others and get others to agree to participate or help you by making requests of them as it relates to your objectives.

To the extent that your trading involves other people, you must ensure that you communicate with them about your objectives and that you get their commitment to the results. At the outset of your trading day, assess what is needed to produce the results you want by considering what is missing in the way of time, space, personnel, or someone to take responsibility for making the trades work. Establish channels of communication with those involved to ensure that there is a structure for handling events. It is also useful to establish a timeline for the pursuit and completion of any analytic projects related to your efforts.

It is not always easy to clarify objectives, tasks, and designated duties as they relate to trading projects, and there is often a failure of communication at the outset to ascertain the willingness of others to participate. I have often seen this communication failure between portfolio managers (PMs) and their teams of analysts who have not been made accountable for their efforts or had their efforts aligned with the needs of the PMs.

Coping with Risk: Coaching, Teamwork, Systems

It is essential to establish the trust of others and to ensure that they understand what you want them to do. This holds true even if the people helping you are experts at what they do. You have to specify what you want. Otherwise, you can anticipate breakdowns and failure in getting things done. It is also important to establish a systematic way of checking on what is done so that you can be certain that everyone is participating in accord with your plan and there is a system of checks and balances in place so that you can periodically review their efforts.

Even when you enlist others to help you, you must ensure that things are done according to what you want, which means to be clear about what you want and certain that others understand what you want. Making sure the plan is followed requires periodic review. It also takes some skill in managing others by selecting people with the requisite talents for specific tasks, giving them a sense of purpose and sufficient space to express themselves fully. It does not mean trying to fit square pegs into round holes, which often results from the erroneous belief that "if they try hard enough, anyone can do the job."

Teamwork does not come naturally. Very often an attitude of envy or negativity toward what others are doing can adversely influence the way in which you move toward your goals.

When you feel envy toward others, ask yourself what others are doing that you would like to do. The critical step here is finding something within yourself to expand yourself by participating in the competition. Commitment means living by your word to overcome the tendency to hold back or withdraw in the process of moving toward your goals.

Working as a team involves the assumption of certain principles of leadership, which are not necessarily familiar or comfortable for most people. My concept of teamwork involves openness and participation of all the members of the team who should feel comfortable about expressing their views without fear of being dominated or ridiculed. Teamwork flourishes best in an atmosphere of trust. Teamwork involves banishing the notion that one person dominates others. There should ideally be group objectives where everyone is willing to take the stand or commit to the result so that the objective in the future becomes the lens through which the markets are approached by everyone on the team.

If you are the leader then your task is to challenge others to join you. From a willingness to state objectives and do whatever it takes to produce the results, you will be able to produce extraordinary results.

Case Study on the Struggle to Develop a Team

Teams are essential for expanding the amount of risk you can take, but it takes compromise on the part of the individual—compromise without so much sacrifice that it leads to frustration and depression. With conversation and inquiry it becomes possible to tweak the participation and the roles on a team to improve the efficiency and the morale of the team. Listen as one trader discusses his feelings about working on a team. I include this dialogue because it is almost a generic one that I have had with many traders who (to the extent that they have adjusted their trading to meet the needs of the team) often lack certainty about whether they are really making a meaningful contribution.

John: I am not as helpful to the firm now that I am part of a team. I went from pitching in the majors to the minors. I have regressed. I can't put on a large position without seeking reassurance that I am doing the right thing. I need to be able to live and die by my own sword. I don't do well being part of a team. I am too scared of losing money and letting the group down. Usually I am an animal. I drop millions and then come back. I am not allowing myself to be who I am. My ability to see something and react to it in a minute has been somehow curtailed.

Kiev: What's changed?

Coping with Risk: Coaching, Teamwork, Systems

J: I am off my game. I want to be accountable to myself, not to a group of guys. If I trade on my own, I would start winding them up.

K: Consider what you need to do, where you are, which will allow you to play as you might if you were trading on your own. You may not have given yourself a chance to overcome this obstacle. The team needs you.

J: It does?

K: It seems to me that everyone on the team contributes something to the process, and as a group you are able to handle bigger size and achieve synergies that you couldn't do alone.

J: What if I sit near the team, but trade my own account? Maybe I can be more helpful that way. I can be a team player without being on the team. The way I like to trade is to let it go—not to care if I lose money. I can't stand turning to the other guys and admitting to them that I messed up a trade. There's something in me—guilt or whatever. If it's my own trade, I don't care.

K: Wouldn't it be great if you could have that attitude while trading for the team?

J: I can't. I feel like I have to answer to everyone else on every trade. If I want to short ABC today and it goes up in my face, I want to be able to do that without having to explain myself. I don't know how to discuss this with everyone. For some reason, I am not willing to take the risks that I have always taken. I've been successful in the past when I traded on my own. What will it take to make it work?

K: One step might be to talk to some of the guys, and let them know what you are thinking and get some feedback. I suspect they think you are contributing a lot more than you are aware of and that once this is out in the open, there will be more space and freedom to 'do your thing' within the context of the team.

Later we brought in one of the team members to discuss his views on what John was contributing to the team. This was his response:

"Don't sell yourself short. You add value to the team. You add energy. I listen to what you have to say. You catalyze me a lot of times. You notice things before I do. I think you are going to have to recognize that this is a team effort and that it is a bit different than trading on your own. By giving up your own sense of ego, what you call living and dying by your own sword, you can gain a greater sense of participating in the game. But we are all role players, and in time you will come to see that you can get a great deal of satisfaction from being a role player and joining in the benefits that come from playing a bigger game, because there are more of us and we can really concentrate on what we each do best."

This dialogue, brief as it was, reassured James and helped him to refocus on the tasks at hand. Most important, it set the stage for an ongoing dialogue between Gino and him and between other members of the team and him, as they all began to realize the importance of sharing their self-doubts about their contribution to the team and the importance of clarifying their roles and the sacrifices that they needed to make to raise the level of their game.

This kind of discussion is critical to help traders get to the next level of trading. But it is not an easy one for macho and self-reliant traders to have. It requires a willingness on the part of everyone to recognize the value of sharing uncertainties and getting past the need to save face. In fact, having the dialogue and putting a value on openness is more important than the specific issues discussed, because it removes one of the major sources of tension and distraction, which is the need to keep one's own counsel regarding matters of feelings.

As you can see, an essential feature of teamwork is to ensure that all members of the team are committed to the team's objectives, are willing to do what it takes to realize those objectives, and feel useful and needed in the process. Of course, this is easier said than done, because traders often have their own personal styles and unspoken agendas that keep them from aligning with the team's objectives.

Therefore, it is critical that the team leader make every effort to clarify the willingness of each member of the team to commit to the team objectives. He can not assume that simply because a trader is on the team that he will automatically align himself with the team objectives.

People succeed because of their strengths as well as their weaknesses. Coaching and teamwork, as I understand it, are critical in this activity where the support of the delicate fabric of the person's psyche is critical for maximizing performance, where you must come back each day after losses and face the uncertainty of the market. The most critical variable of teamwork, then, is being supportive of the creative efforts of others. Being supportive is not easy to do when there are capital and risk management constraints on everyone that may intrude into your creative space and turn off the openness to take risk that is so much a part and parcel of trading success. So the wise coach has to be aware of the fragility of this process and encourage his team to do what is necessary within the boundaries of the discipline but without interfering with the individual creative process that is inherent in trading.

Working with others and recognizing the value that can be obtained from others helps you get past your ego and past your individual concerns so that you can do what it will take to produce outsized results. Again teamwork, as well as coaching, is designed to function within certain parameters while encouraging a willingness to take risk.

A successful manager focuses on targets and allows you to reach your targets in terms of your own methodologies and talents. He first breaks all the rules about managing people by setting the goals, and then he allows you to pursue your goals in your own ways, developing your unique talents.

Understanding the Limits

Of course, some traders will try to use teamwork as a crutch, and then it can become a limitation. Because you are a part of a team, don't assume things will be taken care of for you. Remember, you must produce the results. You must be clear with those who are assisting you about what you want and must review this with them. Don't assume things will go the way you want them to go unless you outline your needs and procedures and establish a structure to ensure the outcome to which you are committed.

A corollary of this admonition is not to assume that someone else will "do it for you." While it is critical to commit to the results to break through your complacency and fixed way of doing things, commitment is about being fully engaged in your trading, not about achieving the results.

• You play to win, but the game is less about winning than about playing wholeheartedly to tap all of your energy and potential. The objective is ultimately to tap a deeper creative dimension of yourself. If someone can produce the result for you without any effort on your part, you will not have experienced the value of being engaged or committed to your objectives. Teamwork involves acting in line with your strategy and enrolling others and empowering them to get past their resistance to act as well.

• Also, avoid the pitfall of comparison. Don't compare yourself to others, especially when the going gets rough and you are discouraged and it appears that others have gained their objectives effortlessly or that they have what you want. This trap is easy to get into if you are caught up in results rather than in the risk taking itself.

When you become envious of others, stop to see how engaged you are in your trading. The chances are that you are off-center and are not as engaged as you could be. Again, you are not your thoughts, fears, or feelings, nor are you your achievements. You are defined by the actions you take. This important point is worth noting every time you withdraw from action and retreat into your thinking and into erroneous concepts about yourself.

Stop waiting for approval. Stop waiting until your ideas or suggestions are unique. To be a valuable part of the team, you need to speak out and offer your opinions based on your work. If you get shot down, improve the quality of your ideas and keep offering them. Only by doing this will you be listened to. If others disagree, don't hesitate. Stand up for your opinions, and don't second-guess yourself. Present your ideas, but don't stop doing the work.

Don't use the team as an excuse. Don't blame others for your mistakes or use others as an excuse for why you aren't playing the game as fully as you could. Make declarative statements. Give your opinion. Play to your fullest. In fact, teamwork within the trading arena is not unlike teamwork in any other facet of life.

While teams seem like a natural solution to the need to expand, there is often insufficient time, effort, and thought given to how best to develop a team. People assume their interests will be aligned and their division of labor will unfold naturally. Not so. If traders do not put effort into making it work, it won't work. It cannot succeed without some effort.

The value of teamwork is setting the bar higher. It is motivating people and helping traders to take greater risks in line with an expanded vision of their trading.

The better you get at trading, the more you will realize how interdependent you are and then the more willing you will be to move toward a team approach to trading. If you get into trouble, you are going to need somebody to prop you up. If you become scared or angry, you are going to need somebody on your team to help straighten you out.

Working in a team can help you to develop new solutions and new ways of handling problems and to reach newer heights, individually and as a firm. To have a successful team, however, you must see the value in teamwork, understand the problems that can occur, and be truly ready to share information. Although these factors may not come naturally for you, the benefits can outweigh any discomfort if you understand how teamwork can help achieve individual and group goals.

THE PSYCHOLOGY OF RISK

See About a System

Developing a system is another way in which you can harness your emotional responses and build predictability and rigor in your trading approach, albeit at the expense of flexibility and the ability to process new information that the system has not been designed to handle. A system approach is another attempt to deal with the creation of order out of chaos which, on the surface, would appear to present a resolution of the psychological and emotional problems that traders ordinarily encounter. However, here too there is always the danger that the ego will take over and limit the willingness to surrender to the methodology of the system.

There are various systems ranging from simple rule-based discretionary systems to complex computerized systems or black boxes. I am not interested in discussing the differences among them but rather addressing some of the psychological issues associated with the use of any kind of system as it pertains to the issue of risk taking. Computerized trading systems provide a number of different benefits for increasing risk including the ability to handle more data and use more complex mathematical algorithms. But most interesting for our discussion is the system model's ability to help bypass many of the stopping points that are built into the personalities of traders.

The system, to the extent that it is adhered to, can offer freedom from reactions such as fear of losing control or increased sensitivity to noise and distractions and a further loss of concentration. The model ignores the emotional response to a loss, which often leads traders to start thinking about failure.

The systems model also circumvents emotional responses to winning trades. By not reacting emotionally to successful trades, it is not prone to losing after profitable days, an occurrence for many discretionary traders who interpret profitable days as a sign of natural ability, leading them to relax their discipline.

Coping with Risk: Coaching, Teamwork, Systems

Systems trading is meant to propel you past any personal tendency to play below your potential or to hold back out of fear of success. As a systems trader, you don't have to overcome your reluctance to play as big as you can or your inclination to lose after a streak of winning or to play not to win.

Case Study on the Advantages of Systems Trading

Trevor is a currency trader who has been paralyzed by his perfectionism and inability to execute more than a handful of his trades. His boss, George, thinks his ideas and analysis are excellent and that the firm can make a lot of money using his analysis by developing a trend-following system that is programmed to identify specific entry signals for taking low-risk trades that have consistently worked for him in the past. Since Trevor had problems making decisions, I wondered how the system would help him. In the past he was always very mechanical and would wait until things set up, and if he didn't have to risk too much he would put the trade on. Because of his hesitation, he missed a lot of trades.

It was his expectation that the system would correct for his risk aversion. Having put his criteria into the system (which made 4,000 trades over the previous five years), he believed "that the numbers were accurate and that it was a valid system." Trevor believed that he could trade his system in a risk-controlled way. "It will tell me when to get in and out. I won't have to worry about the profit and loss. The system will trigger the decision."

When I asked him about the risk of overriding the system, he did not answer my question but instead responded as follows: "The system is supposed to overcome our weaknesses as human beings—fear, greed, being afraid to pull the trigger. If you believe in the system, then that will take care of emotions. You have to follow the system if you are going to do it right. Everyone's system will be built around his own weaknesses and strengths. If I don't like a 50-point drawdown, but my system has a 200-point drawdown, then I would be uncomfortable."

It was Trevor's view that the system would overcome his failings as a discretionary trader. But to the extent that he still had the capacity to choose whether to use the system, I wondered whether the same constraints would apply.

"That defeats the purpose of having a system," he said. "You have to trade the system. The back testing will give me the confidence to make the trade when I use the system. I can look at five years of trading results and know that 60 percent of the time the system will make money. The system is built around my psychology. I don't like to risk much. I don't like to sit with a position. It is either a winner, or I am out quickly.

"The benefits of the system are that it is generic and can be run on different currencies. It can be run with a set of rules in any market over any time period. Some markets will do better than others. Instead of overoptimizing or curve-fitting the system, the real benefit comes from having portfolio growth. You smooth out the P&L [profit and loss] curve."

Trevor is right. There are a lot of advantages to systems trading. Traders do have more data on which to base a trade, and systems trading is perfectly designed for proactive trading. You can establish specific trading objectives and criteria. You can keep measuring your performance to ensure that all of the relevant data is taken into account in a scientifically measurable way. If your simulations make money but your actual trading does not, you can look at your model for clues about what has dropped out of your trading. You can also keep testing. You can ask easily answered questions and control the process in an emotion-free environment.

· The discipline of the system enables you to follow goal-directed strategies. You can be more fluid as you scale up, and the concrete feedback lets you keep transaction costs down as volume goes up. Systems trading is especially good for trading on target with rationale and logic, providing some kind of wall between you and your emotions. It can render a comforting sense of control. Deciding in advance the principles to follow and knowing the assumptions of the system, you may find that it is easier to make decisions based on your system's computations.

Coping with Risk: Coaching, Teamwork, Systems

A discretionary trader named Dana uses a systems program that measures volume as a percentage of price, sorting data by highs and lows, positives and negatives. "It's useful for confirming the value of a trade in a stock with a good story," Dana said. "It's also useful for confirming perspectives and generating new ideas. It is particularly useful at times when a good stock is trading poorly, and I'm unable to find an explanation for this. The systems program enables me to analyze more data than I can by myself. It watches all 3,000 stocks at once and sometimes comes up with recommendations on stocks I haven't followed for years."

· Systems can even help a discretionary trader by giving a more precise picture of the market than you might get ordinarily, especially in pressure-laden situations where you might be inclined to misread the trend of the market. If the market opens strongly and seems as if it will go straight up, a systems program might pick up more subtle cues that the market is weak and that certain key sector stocks are down, thereby correcting the trader's emotional misperception.

In this sense, systems can give the discretionary trader greater confidence about what is happening and what he or she ought to do. A systems program keeps you in the right type of market for days and weeks when your inclination might be to get out. Conversely, if the market is trading at an all-time high, where the market is becoming resistant and starting to turn around and catching traders flat-footed, a program helps you get out when you might be inclined to wish, hope, and pray . . . and then wait too long before selling off.

Another advantage to using a trading system is speed. At some point, the market is going to start moving so fast that most human traders will not be able to react to them quickly enough. The system sees and does things ahead of what the traders are capable of seeing and doing.

If the global financial market moved to 24-hour, electronic trading, it would speed up the dissemination of information. Some traders believe that in five years systems trading will be the only way to trade. Therefore, traders who are using systems now will have an advantage in knowing how to make them work.

One of the big advantages of a systems program is the ability to both maintain attention to the marketplace and establish a consistent degree of flexibility not subject to fluctuations brought on by fears and emotions. It is always able to assess incoming data with the dispassionate perspective that was built into it, and it does not freak out when things go contrary to plans. If you are using such a system, you only need to be able to make decisions about the information and analysis gathered and presented by it. Such a program suffers neither depleted energy, fatigue, nor depression. It doesn't lose its focus on events by being preoccupied with its own internal psychological state. Its data acquisition and reasoning capabilities keep errors to a minimum.

Unlike you, a systems program cannot develop anticipatory anxiety. It does not look ahead to repeated failure that intensifies the anxiety and throws off performance. Indeed, the great virtue of computerized programs is their steadfastness under dramatically changing, unpredictable market conditions.

It's Method, Not Magic

Whereas theoretically a system reacts unemotionally to the parameters built into it and can thus be an asset to your risk taking, a system cannot eliminate the urge to override and violate the discipline. Systems do not take the psychology out of the game.

Even though it defeats the purpose of a system to trade against it, there is still the temptation. And when traders are facing an emotionally difficult trade, it may be easier to override the system because of their own beliefs or gut reactions than to face the emotional turmoil.

For example, you may experience periods of loss where you feel helpless and feel the impulse to ignore the system. To justify this, you may point to particular exceptions that saved money—times when the computer was wrong and you changed course. Unfortunately, you may also forget that these exceptions are rare, and if you continue to override the system, it then becomes useless.

"Most traders do not want to stay with their decisions," said Carl, a trader who uses a trend-following system to track commodities and currencies. "They see the market trending and decide to trade with it or get out of other positions. They tend to react emotionally to events and don't stay with their system's decisions."

So, systems do not entirely insulate you from your own emotions. Moreover, as with discretionary trading, it is often just as difficult to determine the optimal strategy for ramping up—whether to go from $1,000 to $10,000 or $1,000 to $100,000. If you grow too fast, you can get excessive volatility. Or your investors may get nervous and pull out their capital. With systems trading you also are more dependent on technology.

In addition, systems traders lack the flexibility of discretionary traders in their day-to-day execution of orders. One systems trader said it was as if he were in a "foxhole with no time to relax." With some systems, depending on the frequency of the signals, you are trading in a narrow range and must pay close attention to the system's signals or run the risk of missing a trade. Your opportunities are limited, and you must keep trying to execute well by paying attention and trying to minimize your costs by getting good prices and reducing slippage. You can't take a day off or change the instruments you are using if you are having a bad day. You have less control over the implementation of your prescribed strategy. The ability to keep sticking to your strategy is thus both a strength and, at times, a weakness of the systems trader.

"I have to keep at it to make statistics work out," he explained. "I cannot miss a trade that may make my whole day by taking time off to take a break."

There are other stresses as well—technical failures, insufficient testing of the simulation model, and lack of congruence between the simulation model and real trading. Another problem is the potential for obsolescence of a particular system (which in some cases may be seen in as little as six months). The system trader is concerned about cost-effectiveness and the development of new products to be more competitive in a setting where there are concerns about security, theft, sabotage, and the problems of breaking up teams and having to redesign the program. All these factors contribute to stress.

The evolution of systems programs means making more effective programs and also the capacity for making quantum leaps. You can expand incrementally, then plateau, then suddenly jump from plateau to plateau. The systems designer must evolve over time. The system trader has fewer problems in the course of the day trading, but simply staying alert all day long in order not to miss any signals can be tension producing.

Therefore, many of the principles of stress management are certainly relevant to the systems trader even though they are not as critical for mastering emotion in making the kinds of moment-by-moment decisions needed by the discretionary trader. As a systems trader you can get much-needed support from learning how to turn off self-doubt, manage stress, and stay focused while pursuing the testing and implementation of a system.

The same issues would hold regarding ramping up and making decisions about when to extend oneself and when to exploit a system fully, judging when enough data has been developed and then dealing with the pain of discovering that what worked in the laboratory does not always immediately apply to the real world. These issues, too, can be sources of stress and withdrawal where, again, recommitment to the larger objective becomes a critical step.

Remember, while systems can collect and analyze large quantities of data, they cannot make your decisions. You have to call the markets, decide when to place your order, and choose whether to buy on the bid or on the offer. You're still responsible for missing a trade or for the slippage in executing a trade. In fact, you are never free of the responsibility—system or no system. Many of the same problems that haunt discretionary traders also vex systems traders.

Again, it is axiomatic that you do the trade based on the system's signal rather than override it and follow hunches. But even if you are committed to the system, there may be times that you have to make extraordinarily stressful counterintuitive maneuvers, especially when you believe the system could be just plain wrong. It is extremely hard to decipher when you are wanting to act out of emotion and when there is a valid reason to trade against the system.

The ramp-up period is a case in point. Until you know that what you created on paper really works, you are at risk of experiencing extreme stress. Can you tolerate the uncertainty of your particular system? While your system may relieve your sense of uncertainty, it creates another sense of uncertainty if you lack the patience required to ride out the normal distribution of profits on a probability basis. Can you deal with being unnerved by executive stress—a common phenomenon in watching your model operate?

While a system should help correct for a trader's faults, it should not do so in such an extreme manner as to unknowingly generate the very emotions that the trader is trying to avoid. If traders are not aware of this problem, they will find themselves increasingly overriding their system.

Through a simulation, the system showed one trader that by following its guidance, the trader could do 70 percent for the year. His performance for that year was 67.5 percent.

"I know how to trust the system," he said. "As time goes on, I learn how to trade the system more efficiently. It will do better than the simulation. When I intervene with the system, there is always a reason, such as a takeover, an industry conference, a road show, a preannouncement, or a new product announcement. The flaw is not in intervening, but in the follow-up of the intervening. We are never going to be done with any system. Over time there will be improvements at which point you will need a human being to watch. The system does not know if there is a takeover rumor and to get out of the stock."

If you are a discretionary trader with sufficient time, energy, and inclination, you may be able to develop a systems model that will give you signals that will fit your style. When you build your own, you know its assumptions and can build in the parameters you wish to consider. If you are a master trader, you can build a valuable program around some of your trading perspectives. You can build a program to alert you to more opportunities and give you more information while multiplying the extent to which it is gathering and analyzing information about more stocks along the lines of your most successful criteria.

In general, though, it would probably be close to impossible to model all of the rules of the expert trader. No system can model your intuition or your capacity to do the innovative, uncomfortable things you do when you are in the zone. Beyond that, unknown variables operate for master traders when they are trading their best that result from combinations of skill, experience, and some x factor that empowers them to push the envelope and play outside the box in entirely new ways.

As we've noted before, past experiences tend to persist in human beings in the form of beliefs so deeply imprinted that they can be modified only by considerable psychological work. Unlike the human trader, the computer is not constricted by negative or repetitive thoughts from the past and is able to treat each trade independently. Systems programs are inherently capable of doing this. The caution to remember is: There are limits to all computers just as there are to that most advanced computer of all—the human brain.

CONCLUSION

The market is like a blank canvas on which you can create your vision. If you can take risks in the present moment without regard to your history and without regard to your limiting thoughts about how things are supposed to be, you can begin to trade successfully in line with that vision today—in this present reality.

Today—this present moment—is your ally. It only becomes an enemy when you distort the present with limiting thoughts, life principles, and habits from the past. As I have emphasized throughout this book, correcting such distortions is an initial step in the realization of your visions.

Mastery can, in fact, be boiled down to two basic premises: (1) defining a goal and a strategy by which to reach that goal and (2) trading in terms of what is keeping you from the realization of that goal. When you trade through the lens of your vision, you will see reality more clearly and will be able to take risks more consciously with definite intentions to produce specific results in a specific way.

By committing to a specific financial goal within a defined time period, you will gain confidence and develop a focus for your efforts. A goal will help you to stop spending time thinking about maintaining an image or focusing on your past negative experiences or thinking about what you cannot accomplish. A goal will fortify you against the distractions that come from judging yourself in terms of standards of the past and the expectations of others. A realistic goal can be exhilarating. It will help you to give up unrealistic objectives and enable you to concentrate on the critical steps that you need to take to maximize your results. A goal will help you to overcome any inclination for indecision and procrastination and will give you a sense of direction and excitement. Having a goal will make it easier to assume responsibility for your actions and to master fear and anxiety.

• The goal draws you to it and creates the moment-by-moment experience of your trading. The more you take action toward your goal, the more you will learn to flow with events rather than create fear and complications in response to them.

• Your ability to handle risk will be enhanced by the success you experience in abandoning certain expectations and internal controls from the past. As you take responsibility for your trades, you will become better capable of facing the risk of trading in an uncertain environment.

But to change what you've got, you must be willing to recognize that you have chosen what you have, even if you have done so unconsciously. You have to be willing to give up the security, familiarity, and comfort of the status quo and your complaints about it. To pursue your dream means to trade courageously without certainty. You must become aware of the basic assumptions and expectations of the world that color your perspective and which ought to be the essential focus of change. The key to change is not so much in effort but in the development of increased awareness or attention to the way in which you think and how it interferes with your trading.

While your customary way of thinking creates stress for you and makes it difficult for you to trade in a purposeful way, it is my contention that the market is neutral and that you can learn to separate your reactions and responses to market events from the events themselves and create a new interpretation of the markets based on a new and consciously designed purpose or vision.

Conclusion

You can begin by first considering what you are doing now that you don't want to do. Consider how much time and energy you are diverting away from trading by expending energy in tasks that you are doing unwittingly or out of a sense of obligation to do what you believe you are "supposed to do" or to meet the expectations of others. With the time and energy saved from these activities, you can focus on building your strengths rather than trying to work on your weaknesses. It makes sense to focus on pursuing things that you do naturally and that you may have taken for granted until now. This is more difficult to do than it seems, since you are probably inclined to be thinking in terms of talents that you do not have, rather than focusing on undeveloped abilities that you do have. Imagine, if most of what you have accomplished has resulted from using only a portion of your abilities, just think how satisfactory things will be once you begin to use all of your talents.

The problem is that we live in a culture that teaches that life begins some time in the future when we become somebody else or when we acquire the much sought-after symbols of success, fame or material goods. We keep thinking that something in the future is necessary for our peace of mind or fulfillment and have not learned how to live in the present moment.

The lesson then is to commit to a vision of the future in terms of your trading activities and then each day begin to take the risks necessary to express that vision in the moments before you. As you succeed in doing this, you will find it valuable to raise the stakes by taking on more risk to increase the level of the challenge and bring more of your hidden potential into play.

Of course, trading through the lens of a vision of the future does not occur simply because you verbally commit to it, nor will it be a matter of more effort. To trade in terms of your vision requires a radical decision to produce specific results consistent with the vision and then take on the result like your life depended on it, all the

283

while recognizing how difficult it is to make this kind of contextual change.

In fact, when you try to take risks in terms of a specific result, you begin to realize that you are already taking risks at a level consistent with an unconscious level of psychological security that may be holding you back. With a goal, you can handle the pain of loss, because it is balanced with a strategy that provides an ongoing focus and guideline for action. Without a goal to provide this sense of direction, losses can cause you to lapse into negativity.

As Abraham Maslow, the famed psychologist, discovered, psychological health is not merely the absence of illness. As he puts it, to be psychologically well, you must also have the capacity for "peak experiences"—being able to immerse yourself in the pursuit of a goal and delight in the achievement of it.

Initially, effort directed toward a goal may prove frustrating and even fatiguing. But, as in long distance running, at some point, as you keep going beyond the fatigue, you will experience what effectively is a second wind, what psychologists have come to call *flow*, where you begin to engage in the activity in an effortless way and where time seems to slow down and you are totally absorbed in the activity, being energized by it. This state of mastery happens often to those who stay focused and disciplined.

One erroneous notion that keeps you from being engaged in this realm of high momentum is the idea that you have forever, that "this isn't it," that you don't need to act in the next moments of your life, but can delay acting. Unfortunately, this notion isn't so. In the realm of commitment, action is all there is. So, stay focused on the actions you need to take rather than retreating into your thoughts about the meaning of what you're doing or how it looks to anyone else or how long it will take.

If you experience fear and are reluctant to act, review your past experiences to see what may have happened in the past—whether in your personal life or in your trading experience—that has become a

Conclusion

generic source of inhibition for you. From this review, you will see how much past fears influence your interpretation of the present and how much you are stopped by the past and perhaps aren't even relating to the present. In fact, the act of commitment may help you to get in touch with critical events in the past that have permeated and blocked self-expression in many areas of your life, but especially as it pertains to trading. If you can see these events, you can begin to make critical distinctions between reality and your early learned preconceptions in order to be able to see how much they color events and thereby be able to change how you relate to reality.

The capacity to take risks can be enhanced simply by becoming aware of what you are doing, not simply doing more of something or even doing something new. This consciousness will give you choice in controlling your automatic responses and enable you to use your energy in new ways in your trading. This consciousness can have profound effects on your confidence and ability to take meaningful risks in line with your stated objectives.

Small shifts in your trading can generate challenge, excitement, and confidence that you can have an impact on your capacity to take risks. By making such changes you will discover the power to change and learn how to harness the power released in this process. Moreover, these efforts in modifying your thoughts and behavior will help you to get involved in trading at an experiential rather than an abstract or conceptual level.

Don't wait for perfection. Don't be burdened by details, self-doubt, or the need to look good. Action is a principle source of information and experience that will help you to learn to live outside the vicious circle of concept-dominated experience. Action will dispel fear and allow you to enter into a world of discovery where you can begin to discover things that you didn't even know existed.

In part you must let go of a dualistic thinking characterized by judgments of yourself and others and efforts to change yourself and others. When you can stop trying to make it or to succeed and can become at one with your vision by acting consistently, as if you were already complete and sufficient as you are, you will be able to succeed by simply focusing on the action to take in front of you, by choosing what you have, and investing yourself in the process fully. When you can do this, you will not be trapped by comparisons with the past, nor will you be focused on the next event or the future or something in the distance. You will be empowered to become fully engaged in the next moment in front of you.

Take action in the next moment. Listen for opportunities, which will appear before you in line with your commitment, and be willing to surrender to them. Your commitment will enhance your capacity to see opportunities and ways to empower yourself and others in pursuit of your vision.

While a realistic set of goals related to your natural trading abilities will enable you to avoid distractions and negative thoughts that may lead to disaster, it is not an end itself. Achieving a goal is exciting and may enhance your confidence, but if you are too afraid of not achieving your goal, you will not be able to relax as you approach the goal and may become overwhelmed. Excessive concerns about the outcome will produce the very failures you wish to avoid.

So, once you achieve a goal you must move on toward new goals if you are to maintain your ability to keep taking new risks at the cutting edge of your trading efforts. Otherwise the goal becomes part of your identity or concept of yourself and once again you are subject to the stresses and strains that develop when you are trying to trade in a self-protective way.

Commitment to your vision means to do all that is necessary to produce it, while at the same time not becoming overly attached to the result or putting special meaning on the result so that you are distressed when you don't produce it or too filled with an exaggerated sense of your own abilities when you do. The purpose of commitment to a future vision of trading results is to tap more of your resources and enable you to be psychologically free to take risk.

Conclusion

Selecting a goal will temporarily free you from your automatic thinking and propel you into the future, but there is a natural tendency to slip back into such thinking once you are moving toward the future. Therefore, it is important to be aware of this tendency so as to consciously choose to remain in the goal-directed domain of risk taking, which admittedly may be more uncomfortable and uncertain.

As anxiety and uncertainty mount and you are inclined to retreat into your self-doubts and rationalizations, it is important to notice any patterns of withdrawal that take you out of the action. When this happens, keep visualizing the results and taking appropriate risks consistent with the result, noticing where you stop and what gets in the way of committed action. Slowly but surely this visual imagery rehearsal will help you to do what is necessary so that you can bring reality into alignment with your vision.

Again, while this exercise will produce a certain amount of structural tension and eventually help you to create the result, it is important not to become attached to the result or to put too much meaning on the result. The result is not a commentary on you. It merely tells you how committed you were, what's missing, and what you need to do to produce the result you want, especially one that requires that you change some repetitive patterns of behavior.

To stay on course, keep tracking your efforts and have the courage to face up to "failures," so you can keep recommitting to your vision. Keep focusing on what is necessary to accomplish the task. Don't give too much consideration to your own doubts about what can be done or what you already have done.

If you put most of your energy into planning and preparation rather than actually engaging in the event, you will not work out the solutions in the midst of the action. As a result, you will tend more often to remain in place and keep doing more of what you have already been doing rather than creating something new by engaging in the activity itself. You may get good at preparation and planning but will not develop the kind of knowledge that comes only from actually taking risks and trading. It is possible to learn to respond to events as they occur as though you were already who you wished to be, developing mastery by repeated contact and interaction with the experience itself.

You can handle as much risk as you are willing to commit yourself to taking. By this statement I don't mean that you should use magical or positive thinking. I mean committing to reasonable risk objectives well within the parameters of success. I mean committing yourself to a specific amount of risk without certainty or guarantees, which means acting decisively in the face of internal thoughts of "I can't do it" or "shouldn't do it." Define a concrete objective and take committed action to bring about the result. In each instance, you will begin to trade more actively in the here and now as if the goal had already been accomplished.

Recognize that the early stages of a trade usually involve more effort and fewer results, and be willing to put the initial effort in without seeing too many results, knowing that down the line there will be greater results. This is a matter of faith. Too many people give up in the early stages when they don't see results, without realizing that it takes considerable effort to create the structure necessary for ensuring positive outcomes. In the initial stages the task is to create the strategy to ensure that the trade will be successful.

Don't just think about the things that you have read here. Put them into practice, and then keep going. The more you keep going, the more likely it is that you will not only accomplish your goal but that you will also discover the hidden potential within you and ultimately enhance your capacity and appetite for risk.

INDEX

Index

Index

Index